The Bondage
of the Will

The Bondage
of the Will

Martin Luther

𝕭
Baker Academic
a division of Baker Publishing Group
Grand Rapids, Michigan

Published by Baker Academic
a division of Baker Publishing Group
P.O. Box 6287, Grand Rapids, MI 49516-6287
www.bakeracademic.com

Baker Academic edition published 2012
ISBN 978-0-8010-4893-7

Previously published by Revell

Printed in the United States of America

Library of Congress Control Number: 58008660

18 19 20 21 22 23 24   33 32 31 30 29 28 27

TABLE OF CONTENTS

TRANSLATORS' NOTE

'WHAT is the good of giving . . . a stiff and strict rendering, when the reader can make nothing of it?' asked Luther. He was speaking specifically of translating the Bible, but the principle applies equally to all translation work. This edition of Luther's own *magnum opus*, *De Servo Arbitrio* (literally, *On the Enslaved Will*) was originally to have been a revision of Henry Cole's translation of 1823, reprinted in a slightly revised form by Henry Atherton in 1931. It became evident, however, that the tortuous, 'stiff and strict' style of this translation so obscured the meaning and force of the original that it was better to attempt a completely new translation, which might more adequately convey to modern readers the impetuous flow and dialectical strength of Luther's powerful Latin. Such a translation we have accordingly sought to produce.

The text used is that edited by Otto Clemen in *Luthers Werke in Auswahl*, III. 94ff. (Berlin, 1929), collated with that edited by A. Freitag in the Weimar edition of Luther's works (cited as *W.A.* [=*Weimarer Ausgabe*]), XVIII.597ff. The translation has been compared throughout with Bruno Jordahn's modern German version in the Munich edition of Luther's works, *Vom unfreien Willen* (1954) which contains a critical discussion of the main points of the treatise in full notes. The Diatribe of Erasmus, to which Luther is here making reply, may be conveniently studied in the modern French translation by Pierre Mesnard, *Erasme de Rotterdam. Essai sur le libre arbitre* (Algiers, 1945), though Mesnard's Introduction is not entirely reliable. The book's argument is summarised in R. A. Meissinger, *Erasmus von Rotterdam* (Vienna, 1942). We cite Erasmus' letters from the Oxford edition of P. S. Allen, *Erasmi Epistolae* (*Ep.*), the number of the volume being followed by the number of the letter.

The division of Luther's treatise into its eight main parts, and then into further sections according to subject-matter, is a new feature in this edition. It is hoped that the table of contents, together with the index of Biblical references, will make the work easy for study and reference. All Biblical references in brackets, and all verse numbers have been added by us. Luther refers only to chapters and sometimes wrongly, as will be seen. In Biblical quotations we have kept as close to the Authorized Version as Luther's Latin allowed. The statements which Luther extracts from the Diatribe for discussion are italicised in the text; those which he quotes verbatim are enclosed in quotation marks also. Where further extracts from the Diatribe seemed to be needed in order to make clear the point of Luther's remarks, they have been added in italics in the notes.

Our thanks are due to the Rev. S. M. Houghton and Mr. A. E. Grant for help with the proofs and the index.

J. I. PACKER
O. R. JOHNSTON

HISTORICAL AND THEOLOGICAL INTRODUCTION

I. ERASMUS TO 1517

DESIDERIUS ERASMUS was born in Rotterdam between 1466 and 1469. From 1474 to 1484 he attended the famous school at Deventer directed by the Brethren of the Common Life, a peaceful mystical brotherhood renowned for their simple piety and for the high standard of education which their schools offered. At the end of his school years he became a monk, much against his will, it seems. Though monastic life offered access to books and time for study, in the Augustinian monastery at Steyn Erasmus felt keenly the lack of congenial company, and the poor food and the daily routine were harmful to his delicate health. In 1493, however, after seven years at Steyn, he obtained a dispensation of temporary leave from this religious community, for he had been disappointed in his hope of finding time and opportunity to pursue the humanistic studies which had attracted him since his earliest reading. In 1495 he reached Paris—the great University city, with its libraries, lectures, learned men, and everlasting discussion. His order was never able to reclaim him.

Yet even Paris was disappointing. The official curriculum—if we may use such a term for the teaching of the day—was dry, academic, and suspicious of all new approaches in matters of divinity. The only theological differences allowed were quibbling and unreal; the great creative epoch of the twelfth- and thirteenth-century renaissance, the age of Albertus Magnus and Aquinas, was but a distant echo. Tradition reigned, and Erasmus was already tired of traditional theology.

In 1499 he made his first visit to England and met the English humanists. At Oxford he heard Colet lecture on St. Paul's Epistles, expounding them from the Greek in a direct and personal way without allegorical interpretation. The influence of men like Grocyn and Linacre and the friendship of Colet and Thomas More showed Erasmus that there were other humanists who valued Greek as highly as he himself was coming to do, and this made him all the more eager to apply himself to the task of mastering the other great classical tongue. Further, he found that they too were ready to castigate in merciless sermon and epigram the corrupt state of contemporary religion, especially the laziness and vice concealed in the monasteries and the empty subtleties of the scholastic theologians, so far removed from the pure simplicity which, to Erasmus, was always the distinguishing feature of the religion of Christ. He now conceived the plan, no doubt under the influence of Colet and More, of turning humanistic learning to the service of religion by purifying theology and practical piety of false teaching, obscurity and superstition. This he hoped to bring about by a scientific study of sacred literature, i.e. the writings of the early Fathers and the Biblical texts themselves. He was further spurred on by his discovery of a forgotten work on the text of the Vulgate, the *Annotationes* of Lorenzo Valla (1405-1457), the scholarly secretary of Pope Nicholas V. In this book the Italian humanist had criticised numerous renderings of the Vulgate New Testament on the basis of the original Greek. At the instigation of Erasmus, the Parisian printer Badius reprinted Valla in 1505, and an important step had been taken towards Erasmus' greatest work—the production of a critical text of the Greek New Testament.

After his return to France in 1500, Erasmus continued his study of Greek, annotating and translating and preparing himself for large-scale work on Greek texts. To this period belongs the first edition of the *Adagia*, a collection of Latin sayings from classical authors with comments. This work laid the foundation of his European reputation as a scholar. He was dogged by poverty and ill-health, and seems to have lived by teaching and lecturing. But his friends in England were always an attraction, and in 1504 he wrote to Colet announcing that he would like to return to England, that he now knew Greek and that he had already worked on Origen. On this visit, 1505-1506, he was welcomed in all learned circles as a gifted humanist, and came to know Prince Henry (later Henry VIII), William Warham, Archbishop of Canterbury, and John Fisher, Bishop of Rochester. He visited Cambridge and perhaps lectured on Greek there. In 1506 he visited Italy as a kind of guardian-tutor to two young Italian gentlemen and received his doctorate at Turin. At Venice he met the greatest of all the Renaissance printers, Aldus Manutius, and compiled the second, much enlarged edition of his *Adagia*, this time including Greek as well as Latin material. He also did some work on the Aldine Press editions of Plautus, Terence and the tragedies of Seneca, which were then in preparation. A visit to Rome brought with it the great temptation to accept an attractive ecclesiastical post there. Italy had priceless manuscripts in abundance, enlightened printers, congenial scholars, a friendly climate and a way of life which suited Erasmus. But he valued his intellectual freedom above all things, and the reigning Pontiff was especially repugnant to him.

Then in May, 1509, he received news of the death of Henry VII, and England became at once a land of promise. The invitation to return suggested that real reward would now accompany scholarly labours under the Prince who had grown up among the brightest stars of English humanism. So Erasmus came back to England almost at once, and there wrote his *Encomium Moriae (In Praise of Folly)*, an original and biting satire on the stupidity and self-contradiction of human nature in every age and estate. In private readings the work was well received by Thomas More and his English friends, who greeted it as a brilliant and amusing piece of writing. It contained serious and damaging criticism of the Church. Scholasticism, Bishops and mendicant friars all suffer under the pen of Erasmus, and even the Curia itself is castigated. Apart from the identification of the Papacy with Antichrist, much of the scorn which Luther was to pour out on reigning abuses can be found in this early work of Erasmus. Erasmus was, of course, by no means the only humanist to attack pride, greed and obscurantism in the Church. The affair of the brilliant scholar Reuchlin is another example; it was the *cause célèbre* of the world of scholarship until the Reformation overshadowed it by raising a greater issue still. Reuchlin, the most learned Hebraist of his day, found his career ruined by the anti-Semitic feeling encouraged by many in high places, the jealous ignorance of Dominican monks and the almost incredible prejudice of decadent scholastic theologians. The humanists were at one in deploring the efforts of a converted Jew named Pfefferkorn to have all Jewish writings, apart from the Old Testament, confiscated and destroyed. When the question was examined, Reuchlin alone of the authorities consulted had stood for preserving most, if not all the Hebrew writings. In consequence, he became the butt of constant attack, especially from the Dominicans, over a period of several years. A group of humanists, Ulrich von Hutten, Crotus Rubeanus and others, came to Reuchlin's aid with a scurrilous best-seller, the anonymous *Epistolae Obscurorum Virorum* (1515-1517). In these letters, the obscurantists are belaboured with every weapon in the satirist's armoury. The coarseness of tone which disfigures the German humanists' work is in marked contrast to the delicate mockery of Erasmus' wit. The *Praise of Folly* was first printed in Paris in 1511, and almost at once became the favourite reading of the day. It ran through many editions, Aldus produced one in 1515 with illustrations by the great Holbein, which must have increased its circulation still further. During the latter part of this, the last stay of any length he was to have in England (1509-1514), Erasmus lectured in Greek at Cambridge for about three years, working also in Queens' College at the letters of Jerome and his Greek text of the New Testament whenever he had the opportunity. But Cambridge did not agree with him. He seems to have had little interest in the other teachers and scholars of the town or in his lecturing work, for he was not there long enough to have a hand in radically reshaping the curriculum. The food, the wine and the climate disgusted him, and brought on renewed attacks of the stone, to which he had been susceptible for some years previously. Had it not been for the plague in London and the politically troubled state of the Continent, he would have left sooner. He began to long for Italy and finally left England in July, 1514, in spite of efforts from the highest quarters to induce him to remain. An attempt was made at about this time to reclaim him for the monastery which he had entered as a youth. But the warlike Julius II had been replaced as Pope by Leo X, a good friend of Erasmus. From him he procured not only official release from the vows he made when he first joined the Augustinian order, but also official blessing on his great enterprise now in hand—the production of a new Latin translation of the New Testament, based on a critical study of all the Greek texts available.

After leaving England, Erasmus found that his journey across Europe was something like a triumphal progress. Scholars and dignitaries welcomed him as he went from Hammes (near Calais) through Ghent, Antwerp, Louvain, Liege, Mainz and Strasburg to Basel. This was to be the headquarters of all his future activities. Here was a congenial climate, a liberally minded University and a very great printer—Johann Froben, with whom the name of the great Dutch humanist will always be associated.

Erasmus was now a man of unsurpassed learning. No man in Europe could rival him in reading and writing the classical tongues. No man had such mastery of the treasures of ancient literature, both secular and patristic. No man commanded the ear of Pope, cardinal and king as did Erasmus. To the thoughtful Christian, troubled over the state of Christendom, no one seemed more suited to lead the work of reforming the corrupt and worldly spirit of the Roman Church and of purifying its debased religious practice. And when the *Novum Instrumentum* began to come from Froben's presses in 1516, it must have seemed to many as if the reforming work was beginning indeed.

The New Testament of Erasmus was the first and perhaps the greatest step in the story of Biblical textual criticism. But besides the Greek and Latin texts, there were outspoken annotations and paraphrases, which did not fail to point out the contemporary relevance of the sacred word. As edition followed edition, these notes became fuller and even more pointed.[1] The results could not but be far-reaching and profound. As Froude put it in his forceful way: 'The living facts of Christianity, the persons of Christ and the Apostles, their history, their lives, their teaching were revealed to an astonished world. For the first time the laity were able to see, side by side, the Christianity which converted the world, and the Christianity of a Church with a Borgia Pope, cardinal princes,

[1] Succeeding editions appeared in 1519, 1522, 1527 and 1535.

ecclesiastical courts and a mythology of lies. The effect was to be a spiritual earthquake.'[1]

It was to be expected that the *Praise of Folly* and the *Novum Testamentum* (as the *Novum Instrumentum* was later called) would make enemies for Erasmus. The worldly wisdom of Folly, with the delicate rapier of her wit, pointed in precisely the same direction as the scholarly and serious notes on the New Testament. The clergy were more or less antagonised *en bloc*. Monks and friars protested in all quarters and began plotting the downfall of Erasmus. Universities, including Oxford and Cambridge, proscribed all his writings. Many attributed all the trouble to Humanistic scholarship itself, and were further confirmed in the obscurantist views which had been so pitifully displayed in the Reuchlin affair. Sir Thomas More defended Erasmus, and he was not alone. But at that time Erasmus needed no protection. His reputation was high in learned circles, the Pope (to whom the *Novum Instrumentum* was dedicated) was on his side, and the political powers of the Empire, France and England were favourable to him. Erasmus was not moved and continued to call for reform. The Pope, thought Erasmus, should lead the Bishops in a new peaceful crusade to correct abuses, to encourage preaching, reading of the Scriptures and holy living in accordance with the simple teachings of Christ, and to put down superstition and corruption by banishing ignorance.

But it was not to be. Vested interests—or, to put it more bluntly, as Luther did, lust for money, pleasure and power—had too great a hold on and in the system for an Erasmian reform to be even attempted. Nor could Erasmus see that the abuses in the Church were supported and buttressed by a whole theology, and unless a return to the New Testament teaching on grace, faith and salvation could be obtained, no really effective reform of the corrupt life of Christendom could be accomplished. Indulgences would go only when the power of the keys at Rome went, and the power of Rome would go only when the New Testament doctrine of grace was re-established.

---

[1] J. A. Froude, *Life and Letters of Erasmus*, p. 127. 'Borgia' is a slip for 'Medici' if the ruling Pontiff (Leo X) is meant. The last Borgia Pope was the profligate Alexander VI, who died in 1503.

Erasmus was no theologian. Theology did not interest him—he had been sickened of Aquinas and Scotus, for he had seen the barren intellectualism and spiritual poverty to which scholasticism led, and he knew of no alternative. Furthermore he was a man of peace, a scholar above all—and scholarship can only be fruitfully pursued if peace and order are preserved. Human nature and practical matters he analysed with penetrating acumen—from his desk. He had a conservative turn of mind, for all his clear-sightedness, and to him the revolutionary was more to be feared than the ignorant devotee of an old but corrupt system. His reforming ideals were based on an undogmatic Christianity, an eviscerated Christianity precisely because it was a Christianity without Christ at the deepest level. The epigram is irresistible—Erasmus was shrewd but shallow, a man of cool calculation rather than of burning conviction. He could never stand *contra mundum*.

The first edition of the Greek New Testament appeared in 1516. The next year an Augustinian monk nailed ninety-five propositions for discussion to the door of the church of Wittenberg in Saxony. And the nails in the door of the cathedral church were like nails in the coffin of an Erasmian reform.

II. LUTHER TO 1517

Martin Luther was born in Saxony in 1483, and was thus at least fourteen years younger than Erasmus. When he was one year old, the family moved from Eisleben (Thuringia) to Mansfeld; he was at school there, then at Magdeburg for one year (at a Brethren school) and then at Eisenach. He was an intelligent boy, he studied and learned well, his health was good and his disposition cheery. At the famous University of Erfurt, where he matriculated in 1501, he was soon renowned for his ability in debate and philosophical studies. He worked hard, played the lute and sang in his spare time, and passed his examinations quickly and easily, becoming a Bachelor of Arts in 1502 and a Master in 1505. But Martin Luther was not always cheerful company. He was troubled over the state of his soul, and unsure of his standing before God. The insecurity of human life was strikingly brought home to him by the death of a special friend during the examination for the M.A. degree, and by a narrow escape only a few months later when Luther himself was nearly killed by lightning during a storm. 'Like everyone else in the Middle Ages he knew what to do about his plight. The Church taught that no sensible person would wait until his deathbed to make an act of contrition and plead for grace. From beginning to end the only secure course was to lay hold of every help the Church had to offer: sacraments, pilgrimages, indulgences, the intercession of the saints. Yet foolish was the man who relied solely on the good offices of the heavenly intercessors if he had done nothing to ensure their favour! And what better could he do than take the cowl? . . . Monasticism was the way *par excellence* to heaven.'[1] Thus, to save his soul, Martin Luther, the promising young law student, became a monk. His father was furious, but on July 17th, 1505, Martin was accepted as a novice at the monastery of the Erfurt Augustinians. Here, in spite of fasting, scourging, the minutest self-examination and every form of self-discipline known to the strict order he had joined, he failed to find peace. The awful consciousness of the majesty and holiness of God which almost crushed him as he celebrated his first mass (in May, 1507) never completely left him. He was tormented by the recognition of his own sin, and by the question, 'Have I fasted, watched, prayed, confessed *enough*?'

His theological studies were no help to him in this predicament, for the Nominalist scholastic teaching—a more recent synthesis than that of Aquinas, founded on the work of Occam —served rather to increase his despair. Occam and his disciple Gabriel Biel taught that man could, of his own free will unaided by grace, choose to do what was morally good and avoid what was morally evil, follow and enjoy the Divine commands and 'of his own natural powers love God above all things.'[2] This Luther knew to be contrary to the state of affairs in his own heart and mind. A journey to Rome in 1510 brought no relief. At Rome, Erasmus had found learning and culture, and though he could not but be conscious of the mercenary motives, lax

[1] R. Bainton, *Here I Stand*, pp. 30-33.
[2] See E. G. Rupp, *The Righteousness of God*, pp. 87-95, 104 for refs.

morality and superstition around him, he had enjoyed himself. At Rome, Luther was blind to all the treasures of man's art; he saw only the monstrous organisation steeped in worldliness and corruption, purporting nevertheless to be the religion of Christ on earth. He did all that a pious pilgrim should do. But his bewilderment and dissatisfaction increased, and nothing could give him lasting comfort when he thought of God as his Judge. He knew he deserved condemnation and hell. The Vicar-General of the Order in Germany, Johann von Staupitz, spent much time with Luther in his spiritual torment. He could not fully understand the young monk's difficulties, but he gave him some wise advice. He seems to have shifted the emphasis from sins to sin, from acts to the very nature of man, and at the same time to have suggested to Luther that *poenitentiam agere* in Matt. 4.17 meant 'to be repentent in the heart' rather than 'to do the prescribed acts of penance,' which was the standard interpretation. Staupitz was a man of real faith with a strong leaning towards mystical religion, and Lindsay affirms that he spoke to Luther concerning personal trust in God, the righteousness of Christ which is accessible to faith, and similar topics.[1] Be that as it may, Luther found no lasting peace, though he began to see certain things more clearly. But by far the most valuable thing that Staupitz did was to tell Luther that he should study for his Doctor's degree, undertake preaching and Bible study and finally assume the chair of Theology at the new University of Wittenberg. In 1508, the young monk had begun to lecture there in Aristotelian logic and ethics; after his journey to Rome, however, he transferred to Wittenberg and began to study Augustine and Bernard, as well as continuing his Biblical studies. In 1512 he graduated as Doctor of the Holy Scripture and three weeks later succeeded Staupitz as Professor of Theology.

On August 16th, 1513, the young Professor began his first series of lectures. The subject was the Psalms. When he began his exposition he was still not clear as to how a sinner could be received by a Holy God; "When I became a Doctor, I did not yet know that we cannot expiate our sins," he said later.[2] But

---

[1] T. M. Lindsay, *History of the Reformation*, Vol. I, pp. 202-203.
[2] *W.A.* 45.86.18.

during these lectures (the exact date will probably never be known[1]) the light broke through the mists of doubt and despair caused by scholastic theology, ignorance and personal soul-anguish. Martin Luther discovered that the *justitia Dei* of which the Bible speaks is not exclusively retributive justice, the righteous wrath which is all that sinful man deserves at the hand of his Creator. The righteousness of God is also a gift, springing from His mercy and made ours by faith in Christ. This is a 'passive justice' which we cannot attain by striving or merit. It is offered to us freely in the Gospel of Christ. This is the doctrine of justification by faith, the heart of Luther's theology. When he finished his lectures on the Psalms in 1515, his heart and mind were assured on this vital issue. And in his lectures on the Epistle to the Romans (1515-1516) the teaching is clear. He knew now the meaning of Rom. 1.17. Luther had grasped the essentials of the character of God, the mediatorial work of Christ and the nature of faith as revealed in the New Testament. He was to develop these great Biblical insights, but never to change them, and they form the basis of all his controversy, exposition, preaching and piety. But, like Erasmus, he could not but compare what he had found in the New Testament with contemporary Christendom. Thus, it could not be long before he collided with the official doctrine and practice of the Church.

Significantly enough, it was a practical issue which marked the beginning of the break. As well as being a professor and a theologian, Luther was a pastor and a preacher ministering to a congregation—that of the Castle Church at Wittenberg. His people knew that there was never a man farther removed from the dry academic than Dr. Martin. His teaching was vital, personal and compelling. The light he had gained from the Scriptures forced him to live by and preach the truth which he had found. The same was true when he applied his doctrine to his congregation. He knew eternity was in the balance every time he preached to his sturdy Saxon audience. To safeguard them he might have to protest, to say unpopular and even objectionable things. But he could do no other in all honesty, for immortal souls were under his care, and he was responsible

---

[1] See Rupp, *Luther's Progress to the Diet of Worms*, p. 38.

to God for their welfare. Thus in 1516 he felt constrained to preach three times against indulgences.

Indulgences had been a permanent part of the Roman system for at least 400 years before Luther's time, though there had never been complete agreement as to what exactly they effected. The great mediaeval schoolmen Bonaventura and Aquinas had supported indulgences and integrated them into their theological systems. The Council of Trent was further to confirm their use after the Reformation.[1] Though not originally a Papal prerogative, the power of granting indulgences had gradually come to be regarded as confined to the Pope, and anyone to whom he might delegate it. Strictly (though this was far from being clearly understood in Luther's time) an indulgence is a remission of all or part of the *temporal* punishments due to the sinner for his sin. Confession to, and absolution by a priest secure the removal of the *guilt* and *eternal* punishment of the baptized sinner. But temporal punishments still remain. These are in part imposed by the priest as penances to be executed in this life, and in part the sufferings in Purgatory after death, more or less according to the extent and nature of the sins committed in earthly life. But in the popular mind there was naturally no distinction between the guilt and the penalty of sin, or between the temporal and the eternal nature of the punishments due. "Indulgences save you" was the universal conviction of mediaeval Europe. Generally speaking, the more you paid, the greater were the punishments remitted. The abuses were obvious. Indulgences were granted to raise armies for Papal wars, to build churches and cathedrals, and to attract new members for religious orders. They were granted to those who visited shrines where holy relics were preserved. By visiting the Wittenberg collection of Luther's own prince, Frederick the Wise, and making the stipulated contributions to the Church there on All Saints' Day, a man might receive from the pope "indulgences for the reduction of purgatory, either for themselves or for others, to the extent of 1,902,202 years and 270 days."[2] Luther was certain of one thing—forgiveness depends on true interior contrition; the God-man relationship is determined

[1] *Conc. Trid.*, sess. xxv, 2nd day, art. 1.
[2] Bainton, *op. cit.*, p. 71. Rupp, quoting Scheel, gives the figures as 127,799 years and 116 days (*Luther's Progress*, p. 52).

by the state of man's soul towards God himself, whatever else may be true of his relation to the Church and to earthly penalties.

In 1517, as a result of a bargain struck between Pope Leo X, who needed money for the completion of the new St. Peter's at Rome, and Albert of Brandenburg, the young German prince-bishop who wanted to add the Archbishopric of Mainz to his other titles, a plenary indulgence was proclaimed in Brandenburg by an experienced salesman, the Dominican friar Tetzel. Part of the money raised was to be used to repay the moneylenders from whom Albert had borrowed in order to pay the Pope for his appointment to the empty see, and part would go towards the building of St. Peter's directly. The indulgence proclaimed that all who contributed would enjoy perfect remission of all sins and reconciliation with God, and would be completely out of danger from purgatory. Luther's own parishioners were marching across the border from Wittenberg and buying these indulgences. On October 31st, Luther decided that the matter should be publicly aired. The following day, Frederick would be selling his own indulgence in Wittenberg itself. On the eve of All Saints' Luther preached a sermon on indulgences and the grace of God. The same day he nailed to the door of the Castle Church 95 propositions in Latin for debate. They are crisp, clearly reasoned, easily grasped and forthright in their denial of any Papal power to remit spiritual punishment. Luther writes now in righteous anger, now with the gentlest irony. Indulgences are positively harmful, according to the *Ninety-Five Theses*, since they induce a false assurance of peace, and cause the recipients to neglect true repentance. The Gospel, not the accumulated merits of the saints, is the true glory and treasure of the Church. The money given for indulgences would be far better spent on the poor at home than on a splendid church in Rome. Luther was only asking for theological disputation, official definition and the correction of abuses. But students copied the theses, translated them and took them to printers. Within two weeks they were known all over Germany, and throughout Europe in as many months.[1]

[1] Erasmus casually sent a copy to Thomas More from Louvain on March 5th, 1518. See *Ep.* 3.785.

III. LUTHER AND ERASMUS FROM 1517

From 1517 onwards, the relationship between Erasmus and Luther was a matter of great interest and speculation to men of letters, theologians, bishops and princes. As early as 1502 in his *Enchiridion* Erasmus had declared his distaste for dogmatic theology, and Luther was above all a theologian. Yet the older man was noted for his mocking attacks on the corruption of many parts of the ecclesiastical system, his rather loose connection with the Church and his reputation as a leading critic and proposer of reforms. Many anticipated that the outspoken young Saxon and the cool clear-thinking Lowlander would join forces. For three years after the *Ninety-Five Theses* it was by no means obvious that the two ideals of reform before the Church —the ways of peaceful (albeit undoctrinal) humanism and of revolutionary Augustinian evangelicalism—were utterly incompatible. As an example of this we may note the position of the Lutheran élite (as Mesnard has called them), men like Spalatin, Melanchthon and Justus Jonas, who were all close friends and admirers of Erasmus. The fact that the break eventually came clearly revealed the primacy of theology in Luther's thought and activity. Erasmus regarded theology as the bugbear of the Church's life.

Writing to Spalatin in October, 1516,[1] Luther had remarked that he considered Augustine the greatest exegetical writer and Jerome a poor second. Erasmus would have reversed the order. Erasmus followed Jerome in interpreting the justification by works against which Paul writes as merely justification by outward ceremonial observance. Luther, believing that any kind of effort or contribution man may attempt to make towards his own salvation is works-righteousness, and therefore under condemnation, preferred the thorough-going exegesis of Augustine, who magnifies the grace of God. If the person is changed, then—and only then—will the good works follow. Such was Luther's position. We find outlined in this letter the foundations of the cleavage which was to become explicit and irreparable with *The Bondage of the Will*. In March, 1517, he

---

[1] *W.A.* Br. 1.27, p. 70. The substance of this objection was courteously passed on to Erasmus by Spalatin in December, *Ep.* 2.501.

wrote to the Augustinian Johann Lang[1] that he found himself liking Erasmus less and less, since the latter tended to value human opinions above divine things and failed to make much of Christ and of grace. Perhaps to anticipate and answer the charge of presumption in criticising so great a figure, Luther added that a man is not made a truly wise Christian because he is a good Greek and Hebrew scholar. But he had by no means given up hope of what Erasmus might become, for he concludes the letter by saying that he is keeping his opinion of Erasmus secret, so as not to lend strength to his enemies, and he trusts that God will enlighten Erasmus in His own good time. Writing again to Spalatin early in November,[2] Luther again shows how deeply he felt the difference of attitude. He describes a dialogue of Erasmus he has just read thus: 'It is so agreeably, learnedly and wittily put together, that is, so thoroughly Erasmian in fact, that it compels one to smile and jest on the subject of the faults and misfortunes of the church of Christ, which, however it is every Christian's duty to deplore before God in deepest grief.'

In the summer of 1518 Philip Melanchthon, a gentle young scholar of immense learning, arrived in Wittenberg to teach Greek. He had been—and was to remain—a respected friend of Erasmus, and many must have hoped that he would bring Luther to a milder opinion of Erasmus. In 1518 Luther's name first begins to appear in the voluminous correspondence of Erasmus. In general he affirms that Luther has done and said much that is good, but that his rough manner will lose him many friends. If nothing else, it seems that the German reformer has at least turned people back to examine the fathers for themselves. Concerning particular doctrines maintained by Luther, Erasmus is discreetly vague. About the same time, however, he seems to have cautioned his printer Froben of Basel against bringing out works by Luther.[3] Erasmus also corresponded with Johann Lang, a respected friend in German humanist circles. Writing to Lang on October 17th, 1518,[4] he states that Luther's views were approved by the best men and

---

[1] *W.A.* Br. 1.35, p. 90.   [2] *W.A.* Br. 1.50, p. 118.
[3] See *Ep.* 3.904. l. 19n.
[4] *Ep.* 3.872. See also his comments to Lang some months later in *Ep.* 3.983.

mentions the universal welcome that the *Ninety-Five Theses* had found. "As the chair of Roman Pontiff stands to-day," he goes on, "it is the plague of Christendom."

In the following year, 1519, the rapprochement between Erasmus and Luther was probably as close as it could ever be. In January, Melanchthon wrote to Erasmus:[1] 'Martin Luther is your convinced admirer and would like your approval.' But those who hated Erasmus were also at work. His inveterate enemies were the Dominican and Carmelite monks at Louvain, and one of them now struck a shrewd blow. In a lecture on St. Paul, a certain Egmond bracketed Luther with Erasmus as two men who both needed converting, after which they might both become warriors of the true faith. It was not long before the foes of humanism—and they were many—were maintaining that Erasmus was the father of Luther's heresy, that he had helped Luther with his writings and that the German movement with all its revolutionary and anarchical possibilities was the result of too much Greek and Hebrew. By using Luther as a stick to beat Erasmus, the opposition hoped to discredit him if he remained silent, or to drive him into the Reformer's camp, where he could clearly be seen as a heretic. Nor was it only his enemies who sought to align him with Luther. A letter dated March 28th[2] arrived from Luther himself, asking for support in friendly and respectful terms. The request was a difficult one. Luther was acclaimed by his order, as the chapter meeting at Heidelberg in April, 1518, had shown, and hailed by his fellow countrymen as a deliverer from Italian tyranny. He had many followers among the ranks of the humanists. He had the respect and the protection of Frederick, one of the most powerful of the Electors. Cajetan, the Papal legate in Germany, had opposed Luther in Augsburg in October of the previous year, ordering him to recant and to be silent, but was generally held to have acted in a high-minded and peremptory manner. The printed account of the discussion only served further to alienate support for the Papal cause. Erasmus could see things developing into a clash which would certainly involve passionate disputation, and probably heresy trials and all the persecution

[1] *Ep.* 3.910.
[2] *W.A.* Br. 1.163, p. 361; *Ep.* 3.933.

and hatred which he so much deplored. For Erasmus, to side openly with Luther would certainly be to antagonise the Pope, and the Pope's friendship and protection were of inestimable value to him. Largely as a result of Papal favour, he enjoyed a unique position in Europe, able to say and write what he liked and as he liked. Erasmus did not reply to Luther at once. But when on April 14th he had occasion to write to Frederick of Saxony, Luther's prince, he spoke generously.[1] He did not know Luther and he had not read his works, so he was not concerned to praise or blame any particular doctrines or opinions. But everyone knows, continued Erasmus, that Luther's life is pure, free from ambition and covetousness; so where is the Christian mercy of those who shout for his blood? Luther is willing to discuss and be proved wrong if his opponents can produce satisfactory evidence to refute his views. It is the prince's duty to protect the pious, and not to allow an innocent man to fall into the hands of the ungodly under the pretext of religion. And I notice, he concluded, that those who read Luther's books most avidly here are the best men. This letter was soon published in Leipzig, where a ready sale was assured in view of the forthcoming disputation. This guarded siding with Luther must have had a considerable effect, in spite of the fact that it was not to be a lasting alliance. Nevertheless, Erasmus was always careful to leave a way of escape open, and on the 22nd of the same month he wrote to Melanchthon that he had not read any of Luther's works.[2] And in a letter to Wolsey of May 18th he is careful to say that he has read only an odd page or two (*unam aut alteram pagellam*) of Luther, and has not had time to read more.[3] Then on May 30th he replied to Luther directly.[4] It was a friendly letter, advising caution and restraint. Luther should not attack the Pope or princes, but rather abuses of power, for ancient institutions cannot be uprooted in a moment. Paul did away with Jewish law by turning it all into an allegory! He admits to having glanced at Luther's Commentary on the Psalms and found it good. Luther should persevere, but take care not to start a faction. Above all he counsels coolness, courtesy and moderation. The

---

[1] *Ep.* 3.939. Mesnard's dating is incorrect.   [2] *Ep.* 3.947.
[3] *Ep.* 3.967.   [4] *Ep.* 3.980.

letter does Erasmus credit in many ways, but it shows that he had not yet fully grasped the issues at stake. Luther's friends immediately published this letter,[1] hoping to force Erasmus to identify himself completely with them. But this was not to be.

In June and July, 1519, Luther, with others of the Wittenberg faculty, disputed with the controversialist Eck at Leipzig. The first debate was between Carlstadt and Eck on the freedom of the will, the second between Luther and Eck on the primacy of the Pope. Luther was now sure that this doctrine was absent from Scripture, unknown to the Fathers and based on fraudulent decretals. Eck cunningly sought to involve Luther in arguments which would lead to his ranging himself with opinions already pronounced heretical by the Church—the teachings of Wycliffe, the Waldensians and in particular John Hus (c. 1370-1415), the Bohemian reformer burned at Constance. When Luther hesitatingly admitted, after a little reflection and research into the opinions condemned at Constance, that some of Hus' views were scriptural and blameless, there was sufficient evidence to have him safely declared a heretic. A Papal Bull would certainly follow to this effect. Luther had been forced to see that his blow against indulgences and his teachings on grace involved a fundamental opposition to the Roman system. In September his Exposition of the Epistle to the Galatians appeared at Leipzig, and showed that Luther was both a scholarly exegete and an accurate and unashamed opponent of Rome. In the following month, in a letter to Albert, Cardinal Archbishop of Mainz,[2] Erasmus again states his carefully chosen position in the Luther affair: I do not know him; I have only had time to glance at his books; I have advised him to be moderate; I am neither his patron nor his accuser; all the world knows him to be a person of good character; certain theologians can only shriek heretic and never indicate where Luther is wrong. In view of the publication of his private letter of May 30th to Luther this disclaimer is by no means ungenerous. But Erasmus makes a further point which seems to

[1] Though not at Luther's instigation, apparently, see *Ep.* 4.1041. Luther seems to have written to Erasmus again in the autumn of 1519.

[2] *Ep.* 4.1033.

indicate that he has taken particular interest in certain aspects of Luther's case. There are things which Luther maintains and which are decried as heresy which can be found in the writings of Augustine and Bernard. The bloodthirsty, avaricious mendicant friars have taken on more than they realised. Luther should be given a fair hearing. In this letter to the most powerful prelate in all Germany Erasmus makes an outspoken and fair-minded protest against injustice to Luther which cannot but command our admiration.

The year 1520 was decisive. During its course came Luther's final breach with Rome, both in person and in print, while at the same time Erasmus began to see how deep was the gulf which separated his own position from that of the German reformer. Luther recognised the value of printed propaganda, and sermons, expositions, pamphlets and open letters began to pour from his fluent pen. The more sure he became of his position, the more outspoken were his tracts. In May appeared a *Sermon on Good Works*. The following month Erasmus wrote to Melanchthon[1] admitting that perhaps offences had to come, but that he (Erasmus) would not be one of those who caused them. Erasmus reports that most people wish that Luther had written with more courtesy and moderation, but none the less he is able to inform Melanchthon that he has advised Wolsey against the burning of Luther's books,[2] and sends friendly greetings to the Reformer and his friends. In July, writing to Spalatin,[3] Erasmus affirms it to be his prayer that Christ will moderate Luther's style and spirit. Truth may not always be spoken; much depends on how it is proclaimed. But on June 15th, the Bull for which Eck had laboured had been issued at Rome—*Exsurge Domine*. In August appeared Luther's *Address to the German Nobility*—a work which was distributed and sold at a phenomenal rate. It was an appeal to the new Emperor and the princes—a vigorous, far-sighted and comprehensive scheme of reform. It attacked Papal supremacy in the matters of temporal power and Biblical interpretation, asserted the priesthood of all believers and the right of any Christian to summon a General Council, and spoke strongly against the corruption of the Curia. As well as advocating a national German Church

---

[1] *Ep.* 4.1113.   [2] See *Ep.* 4.1102.13n.   [3] *Ep.* 4.1119.

and a German ecclesiastical council, Luther pressed for a reduction of the mendicant orders, of pilgrimages and of holy days, and for a married priesthood to put an end to the disgraceful concubinage so general among the clergy of the day. Sadly apprehensive, Erasmus wrote to Gerard Geldenhauer on September 9th:[1] 'If only Luther had followed my advice. . . . I shall not become mixed up in this tragic affair.' A few days later he felt it necessary to write to the Pope himself.[2] Gracefully, and without stating a blunt refusal, he declines the offer of a bishopric if he will write against Luther. He disclaims any connection with Luther in most submissive terms. He had not written against Luther because he was ignorant of his theology and had not been able to find the time for the task. All he had done was to advise moderation, and his friendly letter had been written two years earlier, before the quarrel had become embittered. He had never defended Luther's opinions. Then in October the most decisive of all Luther's writings to date appeared: *On the Babylonian Captivity of the Church*. In this work he attacks the elaborate system of the seven sacraments and reduces them to three—the Lord's Supper, Baptism and Penance. He denies the doctrine of transubstantiation with its teachings that the priest "makes God" and "offers God." The cup of communion should be given to the laity, who receive Christ by faith, not *ex opere operato*. The book also contains an important and controversial discussion of marriage and divorce which shows Luther grappling courageously with the thornier problems of Christian ethics. The heart of the Roman system had been attacked. The reaction throughout Germany was almost instantaneous. It was a fateful step which cost Luther innumerable supporters,[3] and gave the opposing front a real solidarity, as Meissinger has pointed out.[4] But it was at least clear now what Luther's objective was. Thus, when the Bull *Exsurge* was brought across the Alps by Aleander and Eck late in October, Luther had burned his boats behind him. A few

---

[1] *Ep.* 4.114.

[2] For a summary of this letter, see Froude, *op. cit.*, pp. 271-272. For the letter itself, see *Ep.* 4.1143.

[3] See, e.g., Erasmus' remarks in *Ep.* 4.1186.

[4] K. A. Meissinger, *Erasmus von Rotterdam*, p. 265.

weeks later, however, there appeared a little work remarkably free from the bitterness and controversy of this fateful year— *The Freedom of a Christian Man*—in which Luther shows the centrality of faith in Christian experience and in the right use of sacrament and ceremonial. The work restates the priesthood of all believers and the possessions of the Christian man through faith in such impressive terms that it made a most useful manual of private devotion, and as such it enjoyed considerable popularity.

But Erasmus found himself involved in the dispute once more before the year 1520 was out. In October Luther's prince, Frederick the Wise, had set out for Aix to attend the crowning of the new Emperor, the young Charles V, but had been delayed at Cologne until November by an attack of gout. The Papal nuncio Aleander arrived, bearing the Bull and a Papal brief demanding the burning of Luther's writings and the handing over of Luther in person as a captive. Frederick asked for time to consider the matter, and sent for Erasmus, who was also in Cologne at the time. When asked what Luther's real offence was, Erasmus is reported to have said: "He has sinned greatly; he has attacked the monks in their belly and the Pope in his crown." The account, presumably due to Spalatin who was present, also reports the comment of the nonplussed Elector on Erasmus, 'An amazing fellow! You never know what to expect of him.'[1] Back in his lodgings, Erasmus complied with Frederick's request for a confidential written memorandum on the matter. He handed to Spalatin a sheet on which twenty pregnant sentences were written.[2] The burden of these 'Axioms' is as follows. The affair is more serious than many believe. Luther is honest and well-intentioned; his enemies are actuated by evil motives. The cruelty of the Bull is unworthy of a representative of Christ; the Pope should not allow himself to be imposed upon, but prefer the honour of Christ to his own, and the winning of souls to any other gain. It would be better to strive for caution and restraint, to avoid rash haste and to put the matter before a court of enquiry made up of honest and unbiased scholars. Frederick's answer to Aleander was based

1 *W.A.* Tischr. 1.55.
2 See Meissinger, *op. cit.*, pp. 268-269 for this document in full.

on this advice. Before this confidential document was returned to Erasmus at his own urgent request, a copy was made of it, which found its way to the University of Wittenberg. Soon afterwards it was mysteriously printed in Leipzig, and Erasmus found himself further compromised. On December 10th, Luther burned the Papal bull in public at Wittenberg, together with the Decretals on which the doctrine of Papal authority was founded.

On January 22nd, 1521, the new Emperor Charles V opened his first Imperial Diet at Worms. As King of Spain, he had had domestic matters to attend to between the time of his election (June, 1519) and his coronation (October), but now the Lutheran heresy was to come before him at Worms. The Papal envoy, Aleander, armed with the Bull of excommunication, simply aimed at having Luther condemned unheard by the secular power and handed over. The Emperor's Spanish education and the historic mediaeval pomp of his position all tended to make him side with the Papal cause. Furthermore, war with Francis I of France was threatening, and he must not alienate Italy, where there would doubtless be fighting, and the Pope's support was vital. Yet in his vast German territories pro-Luther feeling ran high, and the Estates—or the majority of them—asserted that there would be bloodshed if Luther were condemned without a hearing. The Germans in the Diet maintained that no man should be placed under the Imperial ban without being heard in his own defence. Under an Imperial safe-conduct Luther came, arriving on April 16th after what seemed like a royal progress through the German villages. The next day he was shown his books, asked whether they were his, and ordered to recant them all. He asked for time and the sitting was postponed until the following day, when on his re-appearance he attempted to maintain a distinction between his various works, and to secure a debate from Scripture on them. This was refused and he was peremptorily ordered to recant. Already he had spoken at greater length than the Emperor and Aleander had intended. Luther answered that unless convinced by Scripture or plain reason he could not recant, for Popes and Councils were fallible and had contradictory voices, while his own conscience was captive to the

Word of God alone. The main hearing was over, and private conference in the succeeding days could effect no solution or even a compromise. Luther left Worms, for his safe-conduct was to expire in 21 days, after which he would be liable to seizure and the death penalty. On the return journey to Wittenberg he disappeared. Rumour ran throughout Germany that he was dead, and that the unscrupulous Aleander had poisoned him. In fact he had been secretly taken to the Wartburg, one of Frederick's castles, there to spend several months in disguise, thinking, studying and above all beginning his German translation of the Bible. Meanwhile the Imperial edict against Luther's writings was openly flouted throughout Germany and the Lowlands. Alike in Imperial free cities and peasant villages the new doctrines were preached and received, the pamphlets—many of them with vigorous woodcut cartoons —sold in vast numbers, and the hatred of Roman doctrine increased.

Aleander was a sworn enemy of Erasmus, and always hoped to involve the Dutchman in Luther's condemnation. (In a dispatch to Rome dated February 8th, 1521, he called Erasmus 'the great cornerstone of the Lutheran heresy.') Further pressure was exerted on Erasmus by popular sentiment at the time of the Diet, Albrecht Dürer being among those who hoped to see Erasmus champion Luther. But Erasmus was too moderate to be able to affect the Emperor one way or another, even had he attempted it. On May 14th he confessed that the evil now seemed to him to be incurable.[1] On the 24th, writing to William Warham,[2] Archbishop of Canterbury, he comments, 'It's all up with that spark of gospel love, that tiny star of gospel light' (*Actum est de scintilla caritatis evangelicae, actum est de stellula lucis evangelicae*)—showing apparently genuine regret at what seemed to him to be imminent—the burning of Luther. Again to Warham on August 23rd[3] he mentions that certain people are urging him to write something against Luther. It would be useful, and he seems to be looking forward to the task. Meanwhile, in the Wartburg, away from the moderating influence of Melanchthon and free to re-think the whole of his theology according to the Word of God, Luther realised that

[1] *Ep.* 4.1203.   [2] *Ep.* 4.1205.   [3] *Ep.* 4.1228.

he would ultimately be drawn into conflict with Erasmus. In a letter to Spalatin dated September 9th[1] he remarked that Erasmus does not aim at the Cross, but only strives for peace. Which was true, as Erasmus himself testified in other letters of the same year. To Louvain he wrote,[2] 'I have opposed the pamphlets of Luther more than any other man (sic), not because he does not give good advice, but because I realise it is better to keep a respectable silence than to attempt a remedy by questionable means (sinistre),' and to Mountjoy,[3] 'Even if Luther had written all things truly, his disruptive lack of restraint (seditiosa libertas) would displease me greatly. I for my part would prefer to be deceived in a good many things rather than to fight for the truth in so great a universal tumult.' Not that Erasmus was ignorant of the awful dilemma posed by Luther. Almost any solution seemed to be a bad one. In the humanist's letters of 1520 and 1521 a constantly recurring expression is that of Scylla and Charybdis. In silencing Luther, Erasmus was certain that the authorities would go to the opposite extreme. Intransigence, bitterness and oppression would rule in the church.

Towards the end of 1521 Erasmus moved to Basel to escape the plotting and denunciation of the theologians at Louvain, and on December 1st Pope Leo X died. The new Pope, Adrian VI, was an old school friend of Erasmus, and the latter on hearing of the appointment wrote to assure him of his fidelity. Early in 1522 he dedicated his paraphrase of St. Matthew to the Emperor and it was received favourably. In December, 1522, he received a letter from Adrian[4] saying that he had never attached much importance to the insinuations against Erasmus, and inviting him to come to Rome where he would have leisure to write against Luther. Courteously Erasmus refused both requests.[5] He was busy with his writing and the preparation of his editions for the press. But he counsels moderation and urges Adrian to attempt real reform at Rome. In March, however, it had become known that Luther, long suspected to be in hiding, had returned to Wittenberg to quell the disturbances caused by the Zwickau prophets and the irresponsible

---

[1] W.A. Br. 2.429, p. 387.   [2] Ep. 4.1217.   [3] Ep. 4.1219.
[4] Ep. 5.1324, esp. ll. 90-97.   [5] Ep. 5.1329 and 1352.

behaviour of Carlstadt. Erasmus still maintained throughout 1522 that there should be an amnesty; burning of books should cease, heated and insulting polemical writings should be banned, and a council of serious, generous, dispassionate and independent scholars should be set up to decide what to do. But in 1523 it became obvious that he would soon have to take sides. No less a person than the King of England urged him to write against Luther,[1] and all Europe knew that he would soon have to enter the lists in earnest. In September the new Pope was elected, and he wrote to Erasmus beseeching his help. In July the first martyrs of the Reformation had died at Brussels and events were taking an ugly turn. Erasmus never approved of this method of repression, if only because it made more Lutherans.[2] He never ceased to deplore the situation. In a letter to Peter Barbirius in the April of this same year, he had written, 'What Luther wrote of the tyranny, avarice and iniquity of the Roman curia—would that it were false!'[3] Nevertheless, writing to Zwingli at the end of August[4] he complains of Luther's 'riddles' and 'paradoxes', listing among them the view that 'free-will' is an 'empty word' (nomen inane). Meanwhile, perhaps in anticipation of the entry of Erasmus into the fray, Luther had begun to mention him more freely and less sympathetically. He wrote thus to Oecolampadius, the Swiss Reformer, on the 20th June,[5] 'Erasmus has done that which he was destined to do. He has introduced the languages. Perhaps he will be like Moses in the land of Moab, for he does not move on into the better studies of the things which concern godliness.' Luther goes on to explain that Erasmus had shown the world the evil of the Roman system, but was not able to show the good and lead on into the land of promise. The early Swiss Reformers had all been humanist scholars before they accepted Reformation. teaching, or found it for themselves, but though they strove to avert an open clash between Luther and Erasmus, their efforts were in vain. Writing to Henry VIII on September 4th, Erasmus announces, 'I intend to write something against the new teaching,' and adds with grim humour, 'but I daren't publish it before I've

---

[1] See *Ep.* 5.1408.   [2] *Ep.* 5.1496, 11.197-199.   [3] *Ep.* 5.1358.
[4] *Ep.* 5.1384.   [5] *W.A.* Br. 3.626, p. 96.

left Germany.'[1] We first hear of the subject in a letter to Faber of November 21st; it is 'the little book on free-will.'[2]

In the April of the next year, 1524, Luther wrote to Erasmus[3] in a rather patronising tone, suggesting a truce. He almost certainly knew that Erasmus was writing against him; and so he suggested an agreement that neither of them should write against the other. He counsels Erasmus to remain a spectator of the tragedy. Luther's language is direct, and even threatening. He thanks the humanist scholar for the pure Scriptures (his critical text of the Greek New Testament) but comments that the Reformation cause is a matter which Erasmus would do well to leave alone if he wishes to enjoy a peaceful old age. The matter is beyond his capacity now. Erasmus answered bluntness with bitterness. He replied on May 8th[4] that he was greatly afraid that Satan might delude Luther's mind by some device. All around him he saw broken friendships and the threat of bloody insurrection. 'At least *I* cannot be accused of abandoning the Gospel to the passions of men,' he commented. And on September 1st, 1524, his *Diatribe seu collatio de libero arbitrio* (*Discussion, or Collation, concerning Free-Will*) appeared, probably printed by Froben at Basel. Conscious of the magnitude of the step he had taken, he wrote to Henry VIII five days later:[5] 'The die is cast. The little book on free-will has seen the light of day.'

It is beyond all reasonable doubt that the *Diatribe* was produced as a result of the constant pressure brought to bear on Erasmus from both friends and enemies.[6] His attempt to play the part of Gamaliel had failed.[7] The Pope claimed his support for the old faith, princes expected it, and friends urged him to clear himself of suspicion. His enemies increased the difficulty of his position month by month by classing him as a secret Lutheran. The evidence for this is given at length by Freitag in his fine introduction to the Weimar edition of Luther's

[1] *Ep.* 5.1385.   [2] *Ep.* 5.1397.   [3] *Ep.* 5.1443. *W.A.* Br. 3.729, p. 270.
[4] *Ep.* 5.1445.   [5] *Ep.* 5.1493.
[6] Freitag in *W.A.* 18, p. 567, says, with perhaps unconscious humour; '*Es lassen sich eine Menge weiterer Stellen aufweisen, die zeigen, dass auch nicht die mindeste Freiwilligkeit seinerseits dabei im Spiele war*' (a host of further passages can be quoted to show that from his [Erasmus'] side not even the smallest amount of free will entered into the matter).
[7] See his remarks to Melanchthon in *Ep.* 5.1496.

reply). The *Diatribe* appeared without a dedication, for the public might imagine that Erasmus was writing merely for princely or papal favour, and suspect his sincerity. The subject of the work was probably also a result of outward prompting rather than inner conviction. In an important letter of February 1st, 1523,[1] we learn that he had been accused by the Lutheran party of attributing 'just a little bit' (*minimum quiddam*) to free will in his paraphrase of the Epistle to the Romans when dealing with ch. 9. Then Cuthbert Tunstall, writing to Erasmus on June 5th of the same year,[2] had urged him to come to grips with Luther. Anticipating an objection of Erasmus, he had raised a particular issue: 'But, you say, I have a bad reputation with Luther and the Lutherans. But no worse than God Himself, whom that fellow [i.e. Luther] makes the author of all wickedness, inasmuch as he takes away free-will from men, and roundly maintains that all things come to pass by fixed laws of necessity, so that there is no freedom for anyone if he wishes to do well.'

The work of Erasmus was well received by the Pope and the Emperor, and was praised by Henry VIII, who had himself written against Luther in 1521 and to whom Erasmus had sent a first draft before its publication.[3] On September 30th Melanchthon wrote from Wittenberg[4] that the work had been received there *aequissimis animis,* and there were still many points of agreement between Erasmus and Luther, though he hinted at a possibility that the quarrel might become a violent one. In fact this letter was far too optimistic and was probably a piece of wishful thinking as far as the state of affairs at Wittenberg was concerned. The general reading public—and we must not forget that the Lutheran Reformation was the first historical movement to have nation-wide printed publicity— was disappointed. The issue did not seem to be as clear cut and practical as the other matters Luther had brought up. Luther's reply did not come at once. There was writing and action against the 'heavenly prophets'—the fanatical extremists—to be undertaken. Then there was an outbreak of agrarian unrest such as had been common for the previous 100 years, and

---

[1] to Marcus Laurinus, *Ep.* 5.1342.
[2] *Ep.* 5.1367.   [3] *Ep.* 5.1500.   [4] See *Ep.* 1430.

Luther had to make his position *vis-à-vis* the Peasants' Rising clear, and bring what influence he could to bear in the interests of order and peace. Marriage too had brought increased responsibility and further calls on his time. In December, 1524, two letters of Erasmus show his attitude clearly. Writing to George of Saxony, who was opposed to the Reformation, Erasmus explains that he sees Luther as one of the long line of those used by God—like Pharaoh, the Philistines, Nebuchadnezzar and the Romans—to chastise the chosen people for their own good, a necessary scourge.[1] To Henry Stromer (Auerbach) on the 10th he writes,[2] 'Whatever Luther's opinion of me may be, when it comes to a question of faith I obviously consider him of little worth.' Erasmus is willing to grant that his opponent is an honest man, worthy of respect as far as his personal life is concerned. The qualifying clause is no small admission, in view of the way Erasmus treated most of his enemies. In December 1525, Luther's answer finally appeared—*De Servo Arbitrio* (*On the Enslaved Will*). It was four times the length of the *Diatribe*[3] and strongly controversial in tone, considerably blunter than Erasmus had been. Luther wrote to Erasmus, apparently to explain his forceful language and to mitigate the effect he expected his work to have. Erasmus replied in a terse bitter letter of April 11th, 1526.[4]

Yet in a letter to Johann Henckel dated March 7th, 1526,[5] while still smarting under the sting of Luther's answer, Erasmus could partially excuse Luther's outspokenness in his writings in view of current abuses, and even confess to having enjoyed reading some of his earlier works. Nevertheless he answered Luther in two lengthy volumes—the *Hyperaspistes* (1526 and 1527), a work bitter in tone and involved in argument. It is a personal apologia and an accusation in which Luther is depicted as the destroyer of civil, religious and cultural harmony and order. Erasmus' resentment seems to have cooled in later years, however. Writing on Church unity in 1533 he said: 'The

---

[1] *Ep.* 5.1526.
[2] *Ep.* 5.1522.
[3] Erasmus called it *ingens volumen* (a huge book) in *Ep.* 6.1686.
[4] *Ep.* 6.1688.
[5] *Ep.* 6.1672.

freedom of the will is a thorny question which it profits little
to debate; let us leave it to professed theologians. But we can
agree that man of his own power can do nothing and is wholly
dependent on the mercy of God; that faith is of great value, a
gift of the Holy Spirit, though we may have differences of
opinion as to the precise mode of its operation.'[1] Basically, this
shows little change from the attitude of the *Diatribe*—except
perhaps the initial warning from a man 'once bitten.' The
last part of the statement leaves plenty of room for the widest
interpretation of the earlier part of the sentence. Luther did
not trouble to reply to the *Hyperaspistes*. He did not speak of
Erasmus favourably again, and there are thirty or more harsh
judgments on the writer of the *Diatribe* for those who care to
seek for them in Luther's Table-talk. He saw Erasmus as an
enemy of God and the Christian religion, an Epicurean and
a serpent, and he was not afraid to say so.[2] Though we may be
saddened by the intrigue and the invective which disfigure the
relationship of these two men, yet their literary duel deals
directly and uncompromisingly with the basic principles of
religion—the nature of God and the nature of men—and as
such led to the production of one of the enduring monuments of
evangelical doctrine, a masterpiece in the realm of polemics,
dogmatics and exegesis—Martin Luther's *De Servo Arbitrio*.

IV. THEOLOGICAL ISSUES

The Bondage of the Will is the greatest piece of theological
writing that ever came from Luther's pen. This was his own
opinion. Writing to Capito on July 9th, 1537, with reference
to a suggested complete edition of his works, he roundly
affirmed that none of them deserved preservation save the
little children's Catechism and *The Bondage of the Will*; for only
they, in their different departments, were 'right' (*justum*).[3]
Others have agreed with Luther in giving this treatise pride of
place among his theological productions. B. B. Warfield, for
instance, endorsing the description of it as 'a dialectic and

---

[1] Quoted in Allen, *Erasmus* (Oxford, 1934), p. 90.
[2] See, for example, *Ep.* 5.1522, ll. 40-42, 6.1688, ll. 14-15.
[3] *W.A.* Br. 8.3162, p. 99.

polemic masterpiece,' styles it 'the embodiment of Luther's reformation conceptions, the nearest thing to a systematic statement of them that he ever made . . . it is . . . in a true sense the manifesto of the Reformation.'[1] And Professor Rupp quotes with approval the description of the book as 'the finest and most powerful Soli Deo Gloria to be sung in the whole period of the Reformation.'[2] In its fertility of thought, its vigour of language, its profound theological grasp, its sustained strength of argument and the grand sweep of its exposition, it stands unsurpassed among Luther's writings. It is the worthiest representative of his mature thought that he has left us, and is a far finer memorial of his theological prowess than are the smaller tracts of the preceding years, which are so much better known.

Its character stands out in relief when we compare it with the booklet to which it is a reply. Erasmus' Diatribe is elegant and gracefully written, but for all that it is by no means a significant production. There is ample evidence, as we have seen, that Erasmus had no desire to write it and no particular interest in its subject. His book suggests as much. It exhibits much learning but little insight. It makes plain what its author would not have been concerned to deny—that Erasmus of Rotterdam, the learned Biblical scholar, was no theologian. It is brief and superficial. Erasmus is deliberately noncommittal on the question which he discusses. He writes on the 'free-will' debate, so he tells us, as a commentator and critic rather than as a contributor to it. His chief point is that it is not a very significant issue, one way or the other; and his main complaint against Luther is simply that the latter shows a defective sense of proportion in laying so much stress on an opinion which is extreme and improbable in itself and relates to a subject which is both obscure and unimportant. *The Bondage of the Will*, on the other hand, is a major treatment of what Luther saw as the very heart of the gospel. It was no mere pot-boiler, written to order; Luther welcomed the opportunity which the appearance of the Diatribe afforded for a full written discussion of those parts of his teaching which to his mind really mattered, and

[1] 'The Theology of the Reformation' in *Studies in Theology*, p. 471.
[2] *The Righteousness of God.* p. 283.

plunged into his subject with zest. 'You alone,' he tells Erasmus, 'have attacked the real thing, that is, the essential issue. You have not worried me with those extraneous issues about the Papacy, purgatory, indulgences and such like—trifles, rather than issues—in respect of which almost all to date have sought my blood . . . you, and you alone, have seen the hinge on which all turns, and aimed for the vital spot. For that I heartily thank you; for it is more gratifying to me to deal with this issue . . .' (p. 318). 'Free-will' was no academic question to Luther; the whole gospel of the grace of God, he held, was bound up with it, and stood or fell according to the way one decided it. In *The Bondage of the Will*, therefore, Luther believes himself to be fighting for the truth of God, the only hope of man; and his earnestness and energy in prosecuting the argument bear witness to the strength of his conviction that the faith once delivered to the saints, and in consequence the salvation of precious souls, is here at stake. 'As to my having argued somewhat vigorously,' he writes, 'I acknowledge my fault, if it is a fault—but no; I have wondrous joy that this witness is borne in the world of my conduct in the cause of God. May God Himself confirm this witness in the last day!' (p. 271). It is not the part of a true theologian, Luther holds, to be unconcerned, or to pretend to be unconcerned, when the gospel is in danger. This is the explanation of what Warfield calls 'the amazing vigour' of Luther's language.[1] The gospel of God is in jeopardy; the springs of Luther's religion are touched; the man is moved; the volcano erupts; argument pours out of him white-hot. Nowhere does Luther come closer, either in spirit or in substance, to the Paul of Romans and Galatians than in *The Bondage of the Will*.

Why did Erasmus and Luther approach the discussion of 'free-will' in such contrasting attitudes of mind? The answer is not far to seek. Their divergent attitudes sprang from two divergent conceptions of Christianity. Erasmus held that matters of doctrine were all comparatively unimportant, and that the issue as to whether a man's will was or was not free was more unimportant than most. Luther, on the other hand, held that doctrines were essential to, and constitutive of, the Christian

[1] *op. cit.*, pp. 470f. "Its words have hands and feet."

religion, and that the doctrine of the bondage of the will in particular was the corner-stone of the gospel and the very foundation of faith. Here we are confronted with the deepest difference that there was, or could have been, between the two men; and we must say a little more about it.

Christianity, to Erasmus, was essentially morality, with a minimum of doctrinal statement loosely appended. What Erasmus professed that he desired to see in Christendom was a return to an apostolic 'simplicity' of life and doctrine, and this he thought could be brought about simply by eliminating the superstitions and abuses which had crept into the Church's life over the centuries. The Reformation that Erasmus advocated was like a course of slimming; its aim was confined to the removing of unhealthy surplus fat. But what Erasmus actually advocated under the name of 'the philosophy of Christ' as the true, slimmed, 'simple' version of Christianity, turns out on inspection to be no more than a barren moralism. Erasmus recognises no organic dependence of practice upon faith. That the life which pleases God springs only from living trust in Christ as the Word of God sets Him forth—that is something that the great humanist never saw. That is why he could profess to find so little pleasure in theological dogmatizing that he would gladly side with the Sceptics whenever Scripture and the Church allowed him to do so—although, as he hastened to explain, he uniformly submitted his judgment to these authorities, whether he understood the reasons for what they ordained or not. Luther takes him severely to task for this remark, and not without justice. Erasmus cannot be acquitted of the charge of doctrinal indifferentism. His attitude was that what one believes about the mysteries of the faith does not much matter; what the Church lays down may safely be accepted, whether right or wrong; for the details of a churchman's doctrine will not affect his living as a Christian in this world, nor his eventual destiny in the world to come. Therefore, however sure one might be that the Church was at some point wrong, one was never justified in disrupting Christendom about it (as Luther was doing); peace in the Church was of more value than any doctrine. The churchman would be wise not to bother his head about problems of doctrinal definition, but to concern himself simply with guiding his life by the moral law of Christ. In particular, the question as to whether or not man's will is free, to Erasmus' mind, can be ignored with perfect safety; it can have no possible bearing on a man's endeavour to keep the law of Christ, except perhaps to distract and discourage him. Wisdom and humility alike dissuade us from prying too deeply into such an abstruse subject; and it is a sign of pride and folly when a man lays much stress upon it. The Christian church is better off without rash ventures of that sort.

Luther's attitude was very different. To him, Christianity was a matter of doctrine first and foremost, because true religion was first and foremost a matter of faith; and faith is correlative to truth. Faith is trust in God through Jesus Christ as He stands revealed in the gospel. Accordingly, 'assertions'— doctrinal statements embodying the contents of the gospel— are fundamental to the Christian religion. Christianity was to Luther a dogmatic religion, or it was nothing. 'Take away assertions, and you take away Christianity,' he writes. 'That would be denying all religion and piety in one breath' (p. 67). As Principal Watson emphasises, Luther's first concern, as theologian and reformer, was with doctrine. 'I am not concerned with the life, but with doctrines,' he declared. This, he held, was what distinguished him from reforming spirits of earlier days. 'Others, who have lived before me have attacked the Pope's evil and scandalous life, but I have attacked his doctrine.'[1] Accordingly, Luther will have no truck with Erasmus' conception of an undogmatic Christianity, and the humanist's airy indifference to matters of doctrine seemed to him as essentially un-Christian as anything well could be. For the Christian 'assertions' were no mere hit-or-miss rationalisations of religious experience; what they contained was the revealed truth of God, recorded in Scripture for the Church's instruction and sealed upon the believer's heart by the saving enlightenment of the Holy Spirit. 'The Holy Spirit is no Sceptic, and the things He has written in our hearts are not doubts or opinions, but assertions—surer and more certain than sense of life itself' (p. 70). In particular, the denial of 'free-will' was to Luther the foundation of the Biblical doctrine of grace, and

[1] Quoted by P. S. Watson, *Let God be God!*, p. 29.

a hearty endorsement of that denial was the first step for anyone who would understand the gospel and come to faith in God. The man who has not yet practically and experimentally learned the bondage of his will in sin has not yet comprehended any part of the gospel; for this is 'the hinge on which all turns,' the ground on which the gospel rests, as Luther shows in detail in the final section of his book. Accordingly, he finds Erasmus' lack of interest in this subject of all subjects, his cool dismissal of it as a theoretical matter of no importance, and the shallow confusions of thought which he reveals in his arguments against the will's bondage, simply incomprehensible in a Christian man. He constantly reproaches Erasmus for not taking the debate seriously enough, and calls attention to the muddy inconsistency of his statements as proof of the charge. And this is not a case of the professional theologian throwing his weight about. What Luther voices in these passages is not the pique of the Doctor of Holy Scripture at the temerity of the Master of Good Letters in venturing on to his own private stamping ground. Luther finds Erasmus' attitude genuinely distressing, and is deeply and unfeignedly concerned for the great humanist's spiritual welfare. Such bored detachment from the issue 'free-will', such a muddled and wrong-headed approach to it, were to his mind fundamentally irreligious and in a theologian irresponsible, and could mean only one thing: that Erasmus, the oracle and monitor of Christendom, was a stranger to grace himself. Luther feels quite justified in dropping broad hints to this effect in the course of the treatise.

It will be clear from what we have said so far that the Luther whom we meet in *The Bondage of the Will* is not Luther the pamphleteer, nor Luther the (largely extempore) preacher, but Dr. Luther, the systematic theologian—and one of a high order. That Luther was a thoroughly systematic thinker is not always appreciated. His fondness for paradoxical and hyperbolic forms of statement, the hasty, uneven character of so many of his occasional writings, and the very size and variety of his total output, have tended to obscure this fact; but fact it is. Again, his unflagging polemic against the abuse of reason has often been construed as an assault on the very idea of rational coherence in theology, whereas in fact it is aimed only at the ideal of rational autonomy and self-sufficiency in theology—the ideal of philosophers and Scholastic theologians, to find out and know God by the use of their own unaided reason. It was in her capacity as the prompter and agent of 'natural' theology that Mistress Reason was in Luther's eyes the Devil's whore; for natural theology is, he held, blasphemous in principle, and bankrupt in practice. It is blasphemous in principle, because it seeks to snatch from God a knowledge of Himself which is not His gift, but man's achievement—a triumph of human brain-power; thus it would feed man's pride, and exalt him above his Creator, as one who could know God at pleasure, whether or not God willed to be known by him. Thus natural theology appears as one more attempt on man's part to implement the programme which he espoused in his original sin—to deny his creaturehood, and deify himself, and deal with God henceforth on an independent footing. But natural theology is bankrupt in practice; for it never brings its devotees to God; instead it leaves them stranded in a quaking morass of insubstantial speculation. Natural theology leads men away from the Divine Christ, and from Scripture, the cradle in which He lies, and from the *theologia crucis*, the gospel doctrine which sets Christ forth. But it is only through Christ that God wills to be known, and gives saving knowledge of Himself. He who would know God, therefore, must seek Him through the Biblical gospel. We must not expect to understand all that the gospel tells us, for the fact of Christ (that is, the achievement of our salvation by the death of the incarnate Son of God) is beyond man's rational comprehension. That is why the gospel has always seemed foolishness to the wise men of this world. But we are not entitled to make rational comprehension the condition of credence, nor to edit and reduce God's Word (as Luther accuses Erasmus of doing) so as to make it square with our own preconceived ideas. That, again, is to try and make man into God, for to understand all things perfectly is the prerogative of the Creator alone. And it is also to exclude faith; for the very distinguishing mark of faith is that it takes God's word just because it is God's word, whether or not it can at present understand it. Man's part, therefore, is to humble his proud mind, to renounce the sinful self-sufficiency which prompts him to treat himself as the measure of all things, to confess the blindness of his corrupt heart, and thankfully to receive the enlightening Word of God. Man is by nature as completely unable to know God as to please God; let him face the fact and admit it! Let God be God! let man be man! let ruined sinners cease pretending to be something other than ruined sinners! let them realise that they lie helpless in the hand of an angry Creator; let them seek Christ, and cry for mercy. This is the point of Luther's polemic against reason. It takes its place as a part of his all-embracing prophetic onslaught against the proud vainglory of helpless sinners who deny their own helplessness. But it has nothing to do with his conception of the theologian's business. Luther was no foe to the ideal of systematic consistency in formulating and organising the contents of the *theologia crucis*; how could he be, when he found that ideal so clearly exemplified in Scripture itself, in the great dogmatic epistles of St. Paul? 'Reason in the sense of logic he employed to the uttermost limits,' says Dr. Bainton.[1] He does so here; and we find him telling Erasmus again and again how discreditable to a theologian is such illogicality and inconsistency as that of the Diatribe. It is common to picture Luther as an incoherent and one-sided thinker whose stock-in-trade consisted of a handful of key ideas, very robust but very rough, and to contrast him with Erasmus as the cool, shrewd, balanced rationalist, who could see things steadily and whole. This was Erasmus' own view of the matter, as the Diatribe makes plain; but a study of the debate reveals that all the incoherence was on Erasmus' side, and that it was Luther who saw things whole, opposing Erasmus' woolly notions with a clear, well-organised system of Biblical truth.

This, then, is the Luther whom we meet in *The Bondage of the Will*: a great-hearted Christian warrior; a thorough exegete (he wins the battle of the texts hands down); a profound systematic theologian; and above all, an unflinching defender of the grace of a sovereign God. For this was the real matter under debate. Luther and Erasmus were not arguing about, and did not disagree about, the reality or the psychology of human choice; though Erasmus did not altogether see this, and sometimes speaks as if Luther's determinism involved a doctrine

[1] Bainton, *op. cit.*, p. 172.

of psychological compulsion. But Luther's denial of 'free-will' has nothing to do with the psychology of action. That human choices are spontaneous and not forced he knows and affirms; it is, indeed, fundamental to his position to do so. It was man's total inability to save himself, and the sovereignty of Divine grace in his salvation, that Luther was affirming when he denied 'free-will', and it was the contrary that Erasmus was affirming when he maintained 'free-will'. The 'free-will' in question was 'free-will' in relation to God and the things of God. Erasmus defined it as 'a power of the human will by which man may apply himself to those things that lead to eternal salvation, or turn away from the same' (p. 137). It is this that Luther denies. He does not say that man through sin has ceased to be *man* (which was Erasmus' persistent misconception of his meaning), but that man through sin has ceased to be *good*. He has now no power to please God. He is unable to do anything but continue in sin. His salvation, therefore, must be wholly of Divine grace, for he himself can contribute nothing to it; and any formulation of the gospel which amounts to saying that God shows grace, not in saving man, but in making it possible for man to save himself, is to be rejected as a lie. The whole work of man's salvation, first to last, is God's; and all the glory for it must be God's also.

This was just what Erasmus would not say. Standing in the semi-Pelagian Scholastic tradition, he champions the view that, though sin has weakened man, it has not made him utterly incapable of meritorious action; in fact, says, Erasmus, the salvation of those who are saved is actually determined by a particular meritorious act which they perform in their own strength, without Divine assistance. There is, he affirms, a power in the human will (though, admittedly, a very little power only) 'by which man may apply himself to those things that lead to eternal salvation,' and thereby gain merit (though, admittedly, a very little merit only). It is by this meritorious application to spiritual concerns that salvation is secured. In expounding this opinion, Erasmus echoes the Scholastic theory of a distinction between *congruent* merit (*meritum de congruo*) and *condign* merit (*meritum de condigno*). The first of these, according to the theory, was that which a man attained by what he did in his own strength (*ex puris naturalibus*) in applying himself to spiritual concerns. Its effect was to make him a fit subject for the gift of internal grace. It did not positively oblige God to give internal grace (from this point of view, it was meritorious only in a loose and improper sense); it merely removed the barrier which had hitherto stood in the way of God's giving it, i.e. man's unworthiness of it and his unpreparedness for it; however, it was held to be a certain fact that God in mercy gives internal grace to all who have made themselves fit subjects for it. Grace (i.e. supernatural spiritual energy) having thus been given, its recipient could use it to do works of a quality of goodness previously out of his reach, works which God was necessarily bound, as a matter of justice, to reward with further supplies of grace and, ultimately, with heavenly glory. The merit which these works secured (*condign* merit) was meritorious in the strict sense, and put the Creator under a real obligation. The purpose of the whole theory was to hold together, on the one hand, the reality of God's freedom in giving salvation and, on the other, the reality of man's merit in earning it: to show that God really becomes man's debtor (because He is under obligation to reward man's merit) while yet at the same time remaining sovereign in salvation (because He gives the grace which creates the merit freely and without obligation).

The distinction, of course, is purely verbal, and Luther sweeps it away. All ideas of merit, he insists, whatever names you give them and whatever distinctions you draw between them, come to the same thing—man performs some action independently of God which does in fact elicit a reward from God. On this basis salvation comes to man through God's response to what man has done. Man earns his passage; man, in the last analysis, saves himself. And this is in principle Pelagianism. Erasmus had supposed that by stressing the smallness of the power which man can exercise, and of the merit which he can gain in his own strength, he was softening the offence of his Pelagian principles and moving closer to the Augustinian position, which denies all merit and ascribes salvation wholly to God. Not at all, says Luther; all that Erasmus and those whom he follows are really doing here is cheapening and debasing their own Pelagianism, by reducing the price of salvation. 'This hypocrisy of theirs results in their valuing and seeking to purchase the grace of God at a much cheaper rate than the Pelagians. The latter assert that it is not by a feeble something within us that we obtain grace, but by efforts and works that are complete, entire, perfect, many and mighty; but our friends here tell us that it is by something very small, almost nothing, that we merit grace. Now, if there must be error, those who say that the grace of God is priced high, and account it dear and costly, err less shamefully and presumptuously than those who teach that its price is a tiny trifle, and account it cheap and contemptible' (pp. 293f.). To be an inferior kind of Pelagian in this way, however, is not, as Luther points out, to approach any nearer to the Augustinian position; it is merely to advertise to the world that, in addition to holding an unwarrantably high opinion of the natural powers of man, one also holds a shockingly low opinion of the moral demands of God's character. The semi-Pelagian compromise, says Warfield, amplifying Luther's thought at this point, 'while remaining Pelagian in principle, yet loses the high ethical position of Pelagianism. Seeking some middle-place between grace and works and fondly congratulating itself that it retains both, it merely falls between the stools and retains neither. It depends as truly as Pelagianism on works, but reduces those works on which it nevertheless depends to a vanishing point.'[1] Pure Pelagianism is bad enough, for it tells us that we are able to earn our salvation, and this is to flatter man; but semi-Pelagianism is worse, for it tells us that we need hardly do anything to earn our salvation, and that is to belittle salvation and to insult God.

But, says Luther, no form of Pelagianism can be true, for two reasons. In the first place, fallen man *in puris naturalibus* can do nothing but sin. He is a member of Satan's kingdom and in all his actions is under Satan's sway. His reason (*ratio*) is blinded; his will (*voluntas*) is hostile to God; he wants only to sin, and his choice (*arbitrium*) is thus always sinful. No possibility of merit exists for him, therefore; all that he does is sinfully motivated and deserves the just judgment of God. The deepest truth about him is that his *arbitrium*, his power and exercise of choice, is

[1] *op. cit.*, p. 470.

enslaved—to sin and Satan; and his natural condition is one of total inability to merit anything other than wrath and damnation. But there is a deeper reason why the doctrine of merit, in all its shapes and forms, must be rejected. The idea of a *meritorious* act is an idea of an *independent* act which is in no way necessitated by God for man or performed by God in man, but is carried out by man acting in some sense apart from God. And there is no such action as this in God's universe. The Creator directly energises and controls all the acts of His creatures. All events are necessitated by His immutable, sovereign will. Human actions are genuinely spontaneous, and authentically express each man's nature, for God works in all things according to their nature; but the fact that it is God who works all man's works in him means that human action can never be independent of God in the sense required for it to acquire merit in the manner which the Pelagians envisage. Man cannot put God in his debt, because man does not stand apart from God as a free and independent agent. Luther thus undercuts the whole conception of merit by affirming the direct sovereignty of God over His world. What he is saying is that the Pelagian idea of merit is a Deistic idea, and has no place in a Theistic order of things such as the Bible depicts, in which God works all in all according to the counsel of His own will. Luther does not shrink from stating this truth in its bluntest form. God, he says, works every human deed, whether good or evil. He works in the evil man according to that man's nature, as He finds it. It is true that the evil man is proximately and directly governed by Satan, the strong man who keeps his goods in peace; yet it is God the Creator who energises Satan, according to his nature, and such power as Satan has is held and exercised by God's own appointment. When Satan acts, according to his nature, as God's enemy, he is being used, according to God's purpose, as God's own agent. Behind the revealed dualism of cosmic conflict between the devil and God lies the hidden mystery of absolute Divine sovereignty; evil is brought to expression only by the omnipotent working of the good God. 'Since God moves and works all in all, He moves and works of necessity even in Satan and the ungodly. But He works according to what they themselves are, and what He finds them to be; which means, since they are evil and perverted themselves, that when they are impelled to action by this movement of Divine omnipotence they do only that which is perverted and evil. It is like a man riding a horse with only three, or two, good feet; his riding corresponds with what the horse is, which means that the horse goes badly . . . and so it is bound to be, unless the horse is healed. Here you see that when God works in and by evil men, evil deeds result; yet God . . . is good, and cannot do evil; but he uses evil instruments. . . . The fault which accounts for evil being done when God moves to action lies in these instruments, which God does not allow to be idle . . .' (p. 204). Mysterious though this is in detail, yet if God is absolutely sovereign and omnipotent, working all in all, then it must in some form be true; and therefore we must reject out of hand all forms of the Deistic notion of God as an onlooker, passively watching the acts of man, in whose performance He plays no direct part. But that means that 'free-will' in Erasmus' sense of an inherent power in man to act apart from God, simply does not exist. Only God has 'free-will', for He is the only independent agent that there is. Man does not act independently of God's necessitating purpose (though he likes to think he does), and therefore 'free-will' is an 'empty name,' an inapplicable title, when predicated of him.

Here, says Luther, is Erasmus' deepest mistake. More than once he complains of the Deistic tinge of Erasmus' thinking about the relations of man and God. 'You, who imagine that the human will is something placed in an intermediate position of "freedom" and left to itself . . . imagine that both God and the devil are far away, mere spectators, as it were, of this mutable "free-will"; you do not believe that they are the prompters or drivers of an *enslaved* will, and each waging relentless war on the other! . . . Either the kingdom of Satan in man is unreal, in which case Christ will be a liar; or else, if this kingdom is as Christ describes it, "free-will" will be merely a beast of burden, Satan's prisoner, which cannot be freed unless the devil is first cast out by the finger of God' (p. 262). And Luther invokes against his opponent Augustine's illustration of the point: 'Man's will is like a beast standing between two riders. If God rides, it wills and goes where God wills. . . . If Satan rides, it wills and goes where Satan wills. Nor may it choose to which rider it will run, or which it will seek; but the riders themselves fight to decide who shall have and hold it' (pp. 103f.). If man could choose his own rider, his will would indeed be free, and he would be sovereign in his own salvation. But this is just what he cannot do. As a sinner, he is in the devil's kingdom, and can do nothing but choose to remain there; it is not in his nature to do anything else. As a creature, he is in the hand of God, who leaves him under the power of sin, or rescues him from its clutches by renewing his nature, according to His own free and sovereign will. As a sinner, he cannot merit salvation in fact for he can do nothing good; as a creature, he could not do so in principle, for the creature can never make the Creator his debtor; man's destiny depends entirely upon the free decision of God. Thus, Luther substitutes for Erasmus' Deistic doctrine of human 'free-will' and salvation by meritorious action a genuinely Theistic doctrine of Divine Lordship and salvation by sovereign mercy. Erasmus affirms that God's mercy is won by works; Luther, that it is recognised and received by faith. Erasmus holds that internal grace is elicited by merit; Luther, that it is freely given without merit and in defiance of demerit. Erasmus thinks of internal grace as the mere strengthening of a will that has already done well to help it do better; Luther thinks of it as a total renewal of corrupt nature by the Holy Spirit, which takes place when God 'calls' a man to faith in Jesus Christ and which makes him capable of good works for the first time in his life. Having changed man's nature, God now works in him according to his new nature, and good works result. Salvation, both as secured for man by Christ, and as applied to and wrought in man by the Spirit, is God's own supernatural work throughout. So Luther explains it:

'What I say on this point is as follows: Man, before he is created to be man, does and endeavours nothing towards his being made a creature, and when he is made and created he does and endeavours nothing towards his continuance as a creature; both his creation and his continuance come to pass by the sole will of the omnipotent power and goodness of God, who creates and preserves us without ourselves. . . . So, too,

I say that man, before he is renewed into the new creation of the Spirit's kingdom, does and endeavours nothing to prepare himself for that new creation and kingdom, and when he is re-created he does and endeavours nothing towards his perseverance in that kingdom; but the Spirit alone works both blessings in us, regenerating us, and preserving us when regenerate, without ourselves. . . . But He does not work in us without us, for He re-created and preserves us for this very purpose, that He might work in us and we might co-operate with Him. Thus he preaches, shows mercy to the poor, and comforts the afflicted by means of us. But what is hereby attributed to "free-will"? What, indeed, is left it but—nothing! In truth, nothing!' (p. 268).

Are there problems raised by this Biblical doctrine of the absolute sovereignty of God in providence and grace? Of course there are. Everything that God reveals of Himself transcends man's comprehension; every doctrine, therefore, must of necessity terminate in mystery, and man must humbly acquiesce in having it so. God does not tell men more of His purpose than man needs to know; and, just because man's knowledge of what God is doing is always incomplete, His actions will often appear to man to have precisely opposite characteristics to those which He Himself ascribes to them. But in such cases it is man's part deliberately to accept God's interpretation in preference to his own. Faith will not lean to its own understanding of the appearance; faith will take God's word as a safe index to the reality, and will wait patiently till contrary appearances dissolve away with the coming of greater light. The problem that presses in this case concerns the justice of God. Luther has full sympathy with the agonies of doubt and despair which this problem can cause to sensitive and realistic souls; he had been through the mill himself. 'God conceals His eternal mercy and loving kindness beneath eternal wrath, His righteousness beneath unrighteousness,' he writes. 'Now, the highest degree of faith is to believe that He is merciful, though He saves so few and damns so many; to believe that He is just, though of His own will He makes us perforce proper subjects for damnation, and seems (in Erasmus' words) "to delight in the torments of poor wretches and to be a fitter object for hate than for love." If I could by any means understand how this same God, who makes such a show of wrath and unrighteousness, can yet be merciful and just, there would be no need for faith. But as it is, the impossibility of understanding makes room for the exercise of faith . . .' (p. 101). And it is here, when faced with appearances that seem to contradict God's own Word, that faith is tried; for here reason rises up in arms against it. 'Doubtless it gives the greatest possible offence to common sense or natural reason, that God, who is proclaimed as being full of mercy and goodness, and so on, should of His own mere will abandon, harden and damn men. . . . It seems an iniquitous, cruel, intolerable thought to think of God; and it is this that has been a stumbling block to so many great men down the ages. And who would not stumble at it? I have stumbled at it myself more than once, down to the deepest pit of despair, so that I wished I had never been made a man. (That was before I knew how health-giving that despair was, and how close to grace.) This is why so much toil and trouble has been devoted to clearing the goodness of God, and throwing the blame on man's will' (p. 217). But the facts remain what they were: the cause of salvation and damnation alike is the sovereign will of God. Both nature and Scripture, if read aright, leave no doubt as to that.

What then shall we do? Luther has two pieces of advice for the man who is tempted to despair, and to deny God's justice altogether. The first is that he should leave alone all speculation and enquiry as to the hidden purposes of God, and confine his attention to what God has revealed and affirmed in His Word. Luther makes this point by developing the distinction between 'God preached' and 'God not preached,' 'God hidden' (*Deus absconditus*). 'Wherever God hides Himself, and wills to be unknown to us, there we have no concern . . . God in His own nature and majesty is to be left alone; in this regard, we have nothing to do with Him, nor does He wish us to deal with Him. We have to do with Him as clothed and displayed in His Word. . . . God does many things which He does not show us in His Word, and He wills many things which He does not in His Word show us that He wills. . . . We must keep in view his Word and leave alone His inscrutable will; for it is by His Word, and not by His inscrutable will, that we must be guided' (pp. 170f.). And this means simply that we must listen to, and deal with, God as He speaks to us in Christ, and not attempt to approach or deal with Him apart from Christ. 'We may not debate the secret will of Divine Majesty. . . . But let man occupy himself with God Incarnate, that is, with Jesus crucified, in whom, as Paul says, are all the treasures of wisdom and knowledge. . . .' In Christ, God comes seeking the salvation of all men; He offers Himself to all; He weeps over Jerusalem because Jerusalem rejects Him. Hear Him, says Luther; rest on His word without fear; they who trust Him always find Him true. Shelve your problems about providence and predestination; be humble enough to receive as God's word the word which God speaks to you in Christ, and to trust yourself to Christ on the basis of it, however unable you may be to square that word with what you know, or think you know, of God's dreadful hidden purposes. Commenting on Christ's lament over Jerusalem (Matt. 23:27), Luther writes: 'Here, God Incarnate says: "I would, and thou wouldest not." God Incarnate, I repeat, was sent for this purpose, to will, say, do, suffer and offer to all men, all that is necessary for salvation; albeit He offends many who, being abandoned or hardened by God's secret will of Majesty, do not receive him thus willing, speaking, doing and offering. . . . It belongs to the same God Incarnate to weep, lament, and groan over the perdition of the ungodly, though that will of Majesty purposely leaves and reprobates some to perish. Nor is it for us to ask why He does so, but to stand in awe of God, Who can do, and wills to do, such things' (p. 176).

The second piece of advice to those in temptation and turmoil (*Anfechtung*) over God's justice is that they should remember that, as men, they cannot at present fully apprehend God; but that, though men, they may hope fully to understand in glory things that were hidden from them on earth. Luther develops these thoughts at the end of the book, in a noble passage of which we quote the conclusion:

'I will give a parallel case, in order to strengthen our faith in God's justice. . . . Behold! God governs the external affairs of the world in such a way that, if you regard and follow the judgment of human reason, you are forced to say, either that there is no God, or that God is unjust. . . . See the great prosperity of the wicked, and by contrast the great adversity of the good. . . . Yet all this, which looks so much like injustice in God, and is traduced as such by arguments which no reason or light of nature can resist, is most easily cleared up by the light of the gospel and the knowledge of grace . . . in a single little word: *There is a life after this life; and all that is not punished and repaid here will be punished and repaid there.* . . .

'If, now, this problem . . . is swept away and settled so easily by the light of the gospel, which shines only in the Word and to faith, how do you think it will be when the light of the Word and faith shall cease, and the real facts, and the majesty of God, shall be revealed as they are? . . .

'Keep in view three lights: the light of nature, the light of grace, and the light of glory. . . . By the light of nature, it is inexplicable that it should be just for the good to be afflicted and the bad to prosper; but the light of grace explains it. By the light of grace, it is inexplicable how God can damn him who by his own strength can do nothing but sin and become guilty. Both the light of nature and the light of grace here insist that the fault lies not in the wretchedness of man, but in the injustice of God. . . . But the light of glory insists otherwise, and will one day reveal God, to Whom alone belongs a judgment whose justice is incomprehensible, as a God Whose justice is most righteous and evident—provided only that in the meanwhile we *believe* it, as we are instructed and encouraged to do . . .' (pp. 315f.).

V. CONCLUSION

What is the modern reader to make of *The Bondage of the Will*? That it is a brilliant and exhilarating performance, a masterpiece of the controversialist's difficult art, he will no doubt readily admit; but now comes the question, is Luther's case any part of God's truth? and, if so, has it a message for Christians to-day? No doubt the reader will find the way by which Luther leads him to be a strange new road, an approach which in all probability he has never considered, a line of thought which he would normally label 'Calvinistic' and hastily pass by. This is what Lutheran orthodoxy itself has done[1]; and the present-day Evangelical Christian (who has semi-Pelagianism in his blood) will be inclined to do the same. But both history and Scripture, if allowed to speak, counsel otherwise.

Historically, it is a simple matter of fact that Martin Luther and John Calvin, and, for that matter, Ulrich Zwingli, Martin Bucer, and all the leading Protestant theologians of the first epoch of the Reformation, stood on precisely the same ground here. On other points, they had their differences; but in asserting the helplessness of man in sin, and the sovereignty of God in grace, they were entirely at one. To all of them, these doctrines were the very life-blood of the Christian faith. A modern editor of Luther's great work underscores this fact: 'Whoever puts this book down without having realised that evangelical theology stands or falls with the doctrine of the bondage of the will has read it in vain.'[2] The doctrine of free justification by faith only, which became the storm-centre of so much controversy during the Reformation period, is often regarded as the heart of the Reformers' theology, but this hardly accurate. The truth is that their thinking was re？ centred upon the contention of Paul, echoed with var degrees of adequacy by Augustine, and Gottschalk, Bradwardine, and Wycliffe, that the sinner's entire salvation is by free and sovereign grace only. The doctrine of justification by faith was important to them because it safeguarded the principle of sovereign grace; but it actually expressed for them only one aspect of this principle, and that not its deepest aspect. The sovereignty of grace found expression in their thinking at a profounder level still, in the doctrine of monergistic regeneration—the doctrine, that is, that the faith which receives Christ for justification is itself the free gift of a sovereign God, bestowed by spiritual regeneration in the act of effectual calling. To the Reformers, the crucial question was not simply, whether God justifies believers without works of law. It was the broader question, whether sinners are wholly helpless in their sin, and whether God is to be thought of as saving them by free,

---

[1] See H. J. Iwand in *Vom unfreien Willen*, p. 253.   [2] *loc. cit.*

unconditional, invincible grace, not only justifying them for Christ's sake when they come to faith, but also raising them from the death of sin by His quickening Spirit in order to bring them to faith. Here was the crucial issue: whether God is the author, not merely of justification, but also of faith; whether, in the last analysis, Christianity is a religion of utter reliance on God for salvation and all things necessary to it, or of self-reliance and self-effort. 'Justification by faith only' is a truth that needs interpretation. The principle of *sola fide* is not rightly understood till it is seen as anchored in the broader principle of *sola gratia*. What is the source and status of faith? Is it the God-given means whereby the God-given justification is received, or is it a condition of justification which it is left to man to fulfil? Is it a part of God's gift of salvation, or is it man's own contribution to salvation? Is our salvation wholly of God, or does it ultimately depend on something that we do for ourselves? Those who say the latter (as the Arminians later did) thereby deny man's utter helplessness in sin, and affirm that a form of semi-Pelagianism is true after all. It is no wonder, then, that later Reformed theology condemned Arminianism as being in principle a return to Rome (because in effect it turned faith into a meritorious work) and a betrayal of the Reformation (because it denied the sovereignty of God in saving sinners, which was the deepest religious and theological principle of the Reformers' thought). Arminianism was, indeed, in Reformed eyes a renunciation of New Testament Christianity in favour of New Testament Judaism; for to rely on oneself for faith is no different in principle from relying on oneself for works, and the one is as un-Christian and anti-Christian as the other. In the light of what Luther says to Erasmus, there is no doubt that he would have endorsed this judgment.

These things need to be pondered by Protestants to-day. With what right may we call ourselves children of the Reformation? Much modern Protestantism would be neither owned nor even recognised by the pioneer Reformers. *The Bondage of the Will* fairly sets before us what they believed about the salvation of lost mankind. In the light of it, we are forced to ask whether Protestant Christendom has not tragically sold its birthright between Luther's day and our own. Has not

Protestantism to-day become more Erasmian than Lutheran? Do we not too often try to minimise and gloss over doctrinal differences for the sake of inter-party peace? Are we innocent of the doctrinal indifferentism with which Luther charged Erasmus? Do we still believe that doctrine matters? Or do we now, with Erasmus, rate a deceptive appearance of unity as of more importance than truth? Have we not grown used to an Erasmian brand of teaching from our pulpits—a message that rests on the same shallow synergistic conceptions which Luther refuted, picturing God and man approaching each other almost on equal terms, each having his own contribution to make to man's salvation and each depending on the dutiful co-operation of the other for the attainment of that end?—as if God exists for man's convenience, rather than man for God's glory? Is it not true, conversely, that it is rare to-day to hear proclaimed the diagnosis of our predicament which Luther—and Scripture —put forward: that man is hopeless and helpless in sin, fast bound in Satan's slavery, at enmity with God, blind and dead to the things of the Spirit? And hence, how rarely do we hear faith spoken of as Scripture depicts it—as it is expressed in the cry of self-committal with which the contrite heart, humbled to see its need and made conscious of its own utter helplessness even to trust, casts itself in the God-given confidence of self-despair upon the mercy of Christ Jesus—'Lord, I believe; help Thou my unbelief!' Can we deny the essential rightness of Luther's exegesis of the texts? And if not, dare we ignore the implications of his exposition?

To accept the principles which Martin Luther vindicates in *The Bondage of the Will* would certainly involve a mental and spiritual revolution for many Christians at the present time. It would involve a radically different approach to preaching and the practice of evangelism, and to most other departments of theology and pastoral work as well. God-centred thinking is out of fashion to-day, and its recovery will involve something of a Copernican revolution in our outlook on many matters. But ought we to shrink from this? Do we not stand in urgent need of such teaching as Luther here gives us—teaching which humbles man, strengthens faith, and glorifies God—and is not the contemporary Church weak for the lack of it? The issue is clear. We are compelled to ask ourselves: If the Almighty God of the Bible is to be our God, if the New Testament gospel is to be our message, if Jesus Christ is the same yesterday, to-day and for ever—is any other position than Luther's possible? Are we not in all honesty bound to stand with him in ascribing all might, and majesty, and dominion, and power, and all the glory of our salvation to God alone? Surely no more important or far-reaching question confronts the Church to-day.

Sola fide
Sola gratia
SOLI DEO GLORIA.

I

INTRODUCTION (*W.A.* 600-602)

To the Venerable Master Erasmus of Rotterdam, Martin Luther wishes Grace and Peace in Christ.

NOBODY expected, venerable Erasmus, that I should take so long to answer your Diatribe on 'Free-will'. Nor is it like me to have delayed; for thus far I have shown myself as one who has gladly seized all such opportunities for writing and, indeed, gone out of his way to look for them. Some, perhaps, will wonder at this new and strange forbearance—or fright!—on Luther's part. His opponents crow over him and write to congratulate Erasmus on conquering him; they sing their champion's triumph-song—'So at last that Maccabaeus, that most obstinate assertor, has met his match, and dares not open his mouth against him!'—and Luther does not stir! Well, I do not blame them for their surprise; I yield you the palm—an unprecedented thing for me!—not merely for far outstripping me in literary power and intellectual ability (we all grant you that as your due, the more so since I am an uncivilized fellow who has lived his life in the backwoods[1]), but also because you checked my zeal for battle and drained my strength before the fight began. That was due to two things: first, your skill in debate—for you discuss the matter throughout with quite remarkable restraint, by which you have prevented my wrath waxing hot against you; and, second, the fact that Fortune (or Chance, or Fate, if you prefer) has led you to say nothing at all on this whole vast topic that has not been said before, and to say so much less about, and assign so much more to, 'free-will' than the Sophists[2] did before you (I shall say more about that later), that it seemed a complete waste of time to reply to your arguments. I have already myself refuted them over and over again, and Philip Melanchthon, in his unsurpassed volume on

---

[1] *barbarus in barbarie semper versatus.*   [2] i.e. the Scholastics.

the doctrines of theology,[1] has trampled them in the dust. That book of his, to my mind, deserves not merely to live as long as books are read, but to take its place in the Church's canon; whereas your book, by comparison, struck me as so worthless and poor that my heart went out to you for having defiled your lovely, brilliant flow of language with such vile stuff. I thought it outrageous to convey material of so low a quality in the trappings of such rare eloquence; it is like using gold or silver dishes to carry garden rubbish or dung. You seem to have had more than an inkling of this yourself, for you were reluctant to undertake the task of writing; because, I suppose, your conscience warned you that, whatever literary resources you might bring with you into the fray, you would not be able to impose on me, but I should see through all your meretricious verbiage to the vile stuff beneath. For 'though I am rude in speech, yet'—by the grace of God—'I am not rude in understanding' (cf. 2 Cor. 11.6.); with Paul, I dare to claim that I have understanding, and that you have not—though I freely grant, as I must, that you have eloquence and I have not.

That made me think like this: my doctrines are fortified with mighty Scripture proofs; now, if there is anyone who has not drunk so deep of them and is not so firmly attached to them as to be impervious to the trivial, nonsensical arguments which Erasmus puts up, however elegantly expressed they may be— well, no reply from me can put him right. For people of that sort you could never speak or write enough about anything, however many thousand books you turned out. You might as well plough the beach and sow seed in the sand, or try to fill a leaking cask with water. To those who have drunk in the Spirit's teaching in my books, we have given enough and to spare already, and such find no difficulty in dismissing your arguments. But it is not surprising if those who read without the Spirit are tossed hither and thither, as a reed is tossed by every wind that blows. God would not have said enough for them if all His creatures were turned into tongues; and it might have been wisdom to leave such as were disturbed by your book in the company of those who glory in you and hail you conqueror.

So, you see, what kept me from rushing in with an answer to

[1] *Loci Communes*, first ed. 1521.

you was not the difficulty of so doing, nor pressure of other work, nor the grandeur of your eloquence, nor fear of you, but simply disgust, disinclination, and distaste—which, if I may say so, express my judgment of your Diatribe. I forbear at the moment to mention the further fact that, in your usual way, you have taken vast pains throughout to be slippery and evasive. You are more canny than Ulysses in the way you suppose yourself to be steering between Scylla and Charybdis —you would have nothing actually asserted, while yet you would seem to assert something! Who, I ask, but one who could catch Proteus himself could bring forward anything to touch people like you? But with Christ's help I shall show you later how much I can do, and how little your twisting has gained you.

But you must not think that I have no reason at all for writing this present reply. Faithful brethren in Christ press me to it, telling me that everyone expects it, seeing that Erasmus' authority may not be treated lightly, and Christian truth is in danger in many hearts. And I myself have begun to think that my silence has not been altogether right. I suspect that I have been led astray by carnal policy,[1] or ill-will, and am not sufficiently mindful of my office, which makes me debtor both to the wise and to the unwise (cf. Rom. 1.14); especially when the prayers of so many brethren call me to fulfil that office now. It is true, as first thoughts told me, that our cause is such that external instruction is not enough, but over and above him who plants and waters without there is need of the Spirit of God within, the living Teacher whose teaching is life, to give the increase (cf. 1 Cor. 3.7); yet since that Spirit is free, and blows, not where we will, but where He wills, I ought to have observed Paul's rule, 'Be instant in season, and out of season' (2 Tim. 4.2), for we know not at what hour the Lord comes. Granted, there are some who have not yet felt the teaching of the Spirit in my writings and have been overthrown by your Diatribe; perhaps their hour had not yet come. And who knows but that God may even condescend to visit you, most excellent Erasmus, by me, His poor weak vessel, and I may come to you by this book in a happy hour and gain a beloved brother. From my heart I beseech the Father of mercies through Christ our Lord that it

---

[1] *carnis meae prudentiae.*

may be so. For though what you think and write about 'free-will' is wrong, I owe you no small debt of thanks for making me far surer of my own view; as I have been since I saw the case for 'free-will' argued with all the resources that your brilliant gifts afford you—and to such little purpose that it is now in a worse state than before. That in itself is clear proof that 'free-will' is an utter fallacy. It is like the woman in the Gospel; the more the doctors treat the case, the worse it gets (cf. Mark 5.26). So it will be the highest token of gratitude that I can give you, if I bring conviction to you, as you brought assurance to me. But conviction in these matters is the Spirit's gift, and not a work of my own office. So we should pray to God that He will open my mouth and your heart and all men's hearts; that He Himself will be our Teacher in the midst of us, working in us both our speaking and our hearing.[1]

But may I ask you, my dear Erasmus, to bear with my want of eloquence, as I in these matters bear with your want of knowledge. God does not give everything to any single man, and we cannot all do everything—as Paul says, 'there are diversities of gifts, but the same Spirit' (1 Cor. 12.4). It remains, therefore, for these gifts to render mutual service, and for one with his gifts to bear the burden of the other's lack; so shall we fulfil the law of Christ (cf. Gal. 6.2).

[1] *qui in nobis loquatur et audiat.*

II

REVIEW OF ERASMUS' PREFACE (*W.A.* 603-639)

(i) *Of the necessity of assertions in Christianity* (603-605)

FIRST, I would run through some of the points in your Preface, where you make some attempt to prejudice our cause and embellish your own. To start with, I observe that, as elsewhere you censure me for being over-bold in making assertions, so here in this book you say that *you find so little satisfaction in assertions that you would readily take up the Sceptics' position wherever the inviolable authority of Holy Scripture and the Church's decisions permit; though you gladly submit your judgment to these authorities in all that they lay down, whether you follow it or not.* That is the outlook which appeals to you.

I assume (as in courtesy bound) that it is your charitable mind and love of peace that prompts such sentiments. Were anyone else to express them, perhaps I should fall on him in my usual way! Nor ought I to allow even you, well-meaning as you are, to go astray any longer with such an idea. To take no pleasure in assertions is not the mark of a Christian heart; indeed, one must delight in assertions to be a Christian at all. (Now, lest we be misled by words, let me say here that by 'assertion' I mean staunchly holding your ground, stating your position, confessing it, defending it and persevering in it unvanquished. I do not think that the term has any other meaning, either in classical authors[1] or in present-day usage. And I am talking about the assertion of what has been delivered to us from above in the Sacred Scriptures. Outside that field, we do not need Erasmus or any other teacher to tell us that over matters which are doubtful, or unprofitable and unnecessary, assertions and contentions are not merely stupid, but positively impious; Paul condemns them often enough! But I do not think you are speaking here about those things, unless

---

[1] *latinis.*

like a comic orator you were intending to take up one subject and then deal with another, as the man did over the turbot; or unless you are godless and crazy enough to maintain that the article concerning 'free-will' is doubtful, or unnecessary.)

Away, now, with Sceptics and Academics from the company of us Christians; let us have men who will assert, men twice as inflexible as very Stoics! Take the Apostle Paul—how often does he call for that 'full assurance'[1] which is, simply, an assertion of conscience, of the highest degree of certainty and conviction. In Rom. 10 he calls it 'confession'—'with the mouth confession is made unto salvation' (v. 10). Christ says, 'Whosoever confesseth me before men, him will I confess before my Father' (Matt. 10.32). Peter commands us to give a reason for the hope that is in us (1 Pet. 3.15). And what need is there of a multitude of proofs? Nothing is more familiar or characteristic among Christians than assertion. Take away assertions, and you take away Christianity. Why, the Holy Spirit is given to Christians from heaven in order that He may glorify Christ and in them confess Him even unto death—and is this not assertion, to die for what you confess and assert? Again, the Spirit asserts to such purpose that He breaks in upon the whole world and convinces it of sin (cf. John 16.8), as if challenging it to battle. Paul tells Timothy to reprove, and to be instant out of season (2 Tim. 4.2); and what a clown[2] I should think a man to be who did not really believe, nor unwaveringly assert, those things concerning which he reproved others! I think I should send him to Anticyra![3]

But I am the biggest fool of all for wasting time and words on something that is clearer to see than the sun. What Christian can endure the idea that we should deprecate assertions? That would be denying all religion and piety in one breath— asserting that religion and piety and all dogmas are just nothing at all. Why then do you—you!—*assert that you find no satisfaction in assertions* and that you *prefer an undogmatic temper to any other?*

You would have it understood, no doubt, that you were not here referring at all to the confession of Christ and His

---

[1] *plerophoriam* (πληροφορίαν): cf. Col. 2.2; 1 Thess. 1.5; Heb. 6.11,10.22.
[2] *festivus.*
[3] A health resort on the Aegean coast, famous for hellebore, which was used in treating mental illness.

doctrines. A correct reminder; and in deference to you I waive the right of which I normally avail myself and eschew all conjecture as to your real thoughts and motives. That I leave for another occasion, perhaps for other writers. Meanwhile, I advise you to correct your tongue and your pen, and refrain from using such expressions in future. Your heart may be upright and honest, but your words—which mirror the heart, they say—are neither. If you really think that the subject of 'free-will' is not necessary knowledge and does not relate to Christ, then your language is correct (for it expresses your meaning), but your thought is blasphemous; if you think this knowledge essential, then your language is blasphemous (for it seems to say the opposite) though your thought is correct. (And in that case all your great heap of complaints about useless assertions and contentions was out of place and beside the point.)

But what will you say about the words I quoted, in which you did not confine yourself to the specific matter of 'free-will', but spoke quite generally of all religious dogmas whatsoever? There you said that *you would take up the Sceptics' position if the inviolable authority of Holy Scripture and the Church's decisions permitted you to do so, so little do you like assertions.* What a Proteus the man is to talk about 'inviolable authority' and 'the Church's decisions'! —as if you had a vast respect for the Scriptures and the Church, when in the same breath you tell us that you wish you had liberty to be a sceptic! What Christian could talk like that? If you are speaking of doctrines that are unprofitable and uncertain, what news do you bring us? Does not everyone wish for liberty to be a sceptic in such matters? Does not every Christian in fact freely avail himself of such liberty, and censure those who become slavish devotees of any opinion? Or perhaps you think (as your words certainly suggest) that all Christians are people whose dogmas are useless things, for which it is absurd of them to quarrel and fight with their assertions! But if you are referring to essential truths—why, what more irreligious assertion could a man possibly make than that he wants to be free to assert precisely *nothing* about such things? The Christian will rather say this: 'So little do I like sceptical principles, that, so far as the weakness of my flesh permits, not merely shall I make it my invariable rule steadfastly to adhere to the sacred text in all that it teaches, and to assert that teaching, but I also want to be as positive as I can about those non-essentials which Scripture does not determine; for uncertainty is the most miserable thing in the world.' What, now, shall we say of your next clause—'*I gladly submit my judgment to these authorities in all that they lay down, whether I follow it or not.*' What do you mean, Erasmus? Is it not enough to have submitted your judgment to Scripture? Do you submit it to the Church as well?—why, what can the Church settle that Scripture did not settle first? And what room do you leave for that liberty and authority to judge the framers of these decisions of which Paul speaks in 1 Cor. 14, when he says: 'let the others judge' (v. 29)? Do you object to there being a judge of the Church's decisions, when Paul lays it down that there must be? What is this new-fangled religion of yours, this novel sort of humility, that, by your own example, you would take from us power to judge men's decisions and make us defer uncritically to human authority? Where does God's written Word tell us to do that? And what Christian would so throw to the winds the commands of both Scripture and the Church as to say '*whether I follow or not*'? You defer to them, and yet you do not at all care whether you follow them or not? Woe to the Christian who doubts the truth of what is commanded him and does not follow it!—for how can he believe what he does not follow? Perhaps you are going to tell us that by 'follow' here you mean 'hold with absolute certainty, without doubting in the Sceptical manner.' But if 'follow' means 'see and comprehend perfectly,' what is there in any creature that any man could follow? And then it would never be the case that one who could follow some things could yet not follow other things; for he who followed one thing (I mean, God) would follow everything, whereas he who does not follow God never follows any part of His creation.

In a word, what you say comes to this: that you do not think it matters a scrap what anyone believes anywhere, so long as the world is at peace; you would be happy for anyone whose life, reputation, welfare or influence was at stake to emulate him who said 'if they affirm, I affirm; if they deny, so do I;'[1] and

---

[1] Ter., *Eun.*, II. 2.21.

you would encourage him to treat Christian doctrines as no better than the views of human philosophers—about which, of course, it is stupid to wrangle and fight and assert, since nothing results but bad feeling and breaches of outward peace. 'What is above us does not concern us'—that is your motto. So you intervene to stop our battles; you call a halt to both sides, and urge us not to fight any more over issues that are so stupid and sterile. That, I repeat, is the meaning of your words. And I think you know what I am driving at here, my dear Erasmus. But, as I said, let the words go; for the moment, I acquit your heart; but you must write no more in this strain. Fear the Spirit of God, who searches the reins and heart, and is not deceived by stupid speeches. I say this in order that from now on you may stop accusing our side of obstinacy and stubbornness. By so doing, you merely let us see that in your heart you cherish a Lucian, or some other hog of Epicurus' herd, who, because he is an atheist himself, finds in all who believe in God and confess Him a subject for secret amusement. Leave us free to make assertions, and to find in assertions our satisfaction and delight; and you may applaud your Sceptics and Academics—till Christ calls you too! The Holy Spirit is no Sceptic, and the things He has written in our hearts are not doubts or opinions, but assertions—surer and more certain than sense and life itself.

(ii) *Of the perspicuity of Scripture* (606-609)

Now I come to another point, which is linked with this. You divide Christian doctrines into two classes, and make out that we need to know the one but not the other. '*Some,*' you say, '*are recondite, whereas others are quite plain.*' Surely at this point you are either playing tricks with someone else's words, or practising a literary effect! However, you quote in your support Paul's words in Rom. 11: 'O the depth of the riches both of the wisdom and knowledge of God!' (v. 33); and also Isa. 40: 'Who gave help to the Spirit of the Lord, or who hath been his counsellor?' (v. 13). It was all very easily said, either because you knew that you were writing, not just to Luther, but for the world at large, or else because you failed to consider that it

was against *Luther* that you were writing! I hope you credit
Luther with some little scholarship and judgment where the
sacred text is concerned? If not, behold! I will wring the
admission out of you! Here is my distinction (for I too am going
to do a little lecturing—or chop a little logic, should I say?):
God and His Scripture are two things, just as the Creator and
His creation are two things. Now, nobody questions that there
is a great deal hid in God of which we know nothing. Christ
himself says of the last day: 'Of that day knoweth no man, but
the Father' (Matt. 24.36); and in Acts 1 he says: 'It is not for
you to know the times and seasons' (v. 7); and again, he says:
'I know whom I have chosen' (John 13. 18); and Paul says:
'The Lord knoweth them that are his' (2 Tim. 2.19); and the
like. But the notion that in Scripture some things are recondite
and all is not plain was spread by the godless Sophists (whom
now you echo, Erasmus)—who have never yet cited a single
item to prove their crazy view; nor can they. And Satan has
used these unsubstantial spectres to scare men off reading the
sacred text, and to destroy all sense of its value, so as to ensure
that his own brand of poisonous philosophy reigns supreme in
the church. I certainly grant that many *passages* in the Scriptures are obscure and hard to elucidate, but that is due, not to
the exalted nature of their subject, but to our own linguistic
and grammatical ignorance; and it does not in any way prevent
our knowing all the *contents* of Scripture. For what solemn truth
can the Scriptures still be concealing, now that the seals are
broken, the stone rolled away from the door of the tomb, and
that greatest of all mysteries brought to light—that Christ,
God's Son, became man, that God is Three in One, that Christ
suffered for us, and will reign for ever? And are not these things
known, and sung in our streets? Take Christ from the Scriptures—and what more will you find in them? You see, then,
that the entire content of the Scriptures has now been brought
to light, even though some passages which contain unknown
words remain obscure. Thus it is unintelligent, and ungodly
too, when you know that the contents of Scripture are as clear
as can be, to pronounce them obscure on account of those few
obscure words. If words are obscure in one place, they are clear
in another. What God has so plainly declared to the world is

in some parts of Scripture stated in plain words, while in other parts it still lies hidden under obscure words. But when something stands in broad daylight, and a mass of evidence for it is in broad daylight also, it does not matter whether there is any evidence for it in the dark. Who will maintain that the town fountain does not stand in the light because the people down some alley cannot see it, while everyone in the square can see it? There is nothing, then, in your remark about the 'Corycian cavern';[1] matters are not so in the Scriptures. The profoundest mysteries of the supreme Majesty are no more hidden away, but are now brought out of doors and displayed to public view. Christ has opened our understanding, that we might understand the Scriptures, and the Gospel is preached to every creature. 'Their sound is gone out into all lands' (Ps. 19.4). 'All things that are written, are written for our instruction' (Rom. 15.4). Again: 'All Scripture is given by inspiration of God, and is profitable for instruction' (2 Tim. 3.16). Come forward then, you, and all the Sophists with you, and cite a single mystery which is still obscure in the Scripture. I know that to many people a great deal remains obscure; but that is due, not to any lack of clarity in Scripture, but to their own blindness and dullness, in that they make no effort to see truth which, in itself, could not be plainer. As Paul said of the Jews in 2 Cor. 4: 'The veil remains on their heart' (2 Cor. 3.15); and again, 'If our gospel be hid, it is hid to them that are lost, whose heart the god of this world hath blinded' (2 Cor. 4.3-4). They are like men who cover their eyes, or go from daylight into darkness, and hide there, and then blame the sun, or the darkness of the day, for their inability to see. So let wretched men abjure that blasphemous perversity which would blame the darkness of their own hearts on to the plain Scriptures of God!

When you quote Paul's statement, 'his judgments are incomprehensible,' you seem to take the pronoun 'his'[2] to refer

---

[1] '*Pomponius Mela tells of a certain Corycian cavern which at first allures by its charming loveliness and draws one into itself, until, as one enters deeper and deeper, a trembling awe at the majesty of the god who dwells there sends one back. So, when we reach this point, it would in my judgment be more prudent and reverent to cry with Paul: "O the depth of the riches of the wisdom and knowledge of God! How incomprehensible are his judgments, and his ways past finding out!" (Rom. 11.33).*' The cave was on Mt. Parnassus, some three miles north of Delphi, and was sacred to Pan and the nymphs.

[2] *eius.*

to Scripture; whereas the judgments which Paul there affirms to be incomprehensible are not those of Scripture, but those of God. And Isaiah 40 does not say: 'who has known the mind of Scripture?' but: 'who has known the mind of the Lord?' (Paul, indeed, asserts that Christians do know the mind of the Lord; but only with reference to those things that are given to us by God, as he there says in 1 Cor. 2 (v. 12)). You see, then, how sleepily you examined those passages, and how apt is your citation of them—as apt as are almost all your citations for 'free-will'! So, too, the examples of obscurity which you allege in that rather sarcastic passage are quite irrelevant—the distinction of persons in the Godhead, the union of the Divine and human natures of Christ, and the unpardonable sin. *Here,* you say, *are problems which have never been solved.* If you mean this of the enquiries which the Sophists pursue when they discuss these subjects, what has the inoffensive Scripture done to you, that you should blame such criminal misuse of it on to its own purity? Scripture makes the straightforward affirmation that the Trinity, the Incarnation and the unpardonable sin are facts. There is nothing obscure or ambiguous about that. You imagine that Scripture tells us *how* they are what they are; but it does not, nor need we know. It is here that the Sophists discuss their dreams; keep your criticism and condemnation for them, but acquit the Scriptures! If, on the other hand, you mean it of the facts themselves, I say again: blame, not the Scriptures, but the Arians and those to whom the Gospel is hid, who, by reason of the working of Satan, their god, cannot see the plainest proofs of the Trinity in the Godhead and of the humanity of Christ.

In a word: The perspicuity[1] of Scripture is twofold, just as there is a double lack of light. The first is external, and relates to the ministry of the Word; the second concerns the knowledge of the heart. If you speak of *internal* perspicuity, the truth is that nobody who has not the Spirit of God sees a jot of what is in the Scriptures. All men have their hearts darkened, so that, even when they can discuss and quote all that is in Scripture, they do not understand or really know any of it. They do not believe in God, nor do they believe that they are God's creatures, nor

---

[1] *claritas.*

anything else—as Ps. 13 puts it, 'The fool hath said in his heart, there is no God' (Ps. 14.1). The Spirit is needed for the understanding of all Scripture and every part of Scripture. If, on the other hand, you speak of *external* perspicuity, the position is that nothing whatsoever is left obscure or ambiguous, but all that is in the Scripture is through the Word brought forth into the clearest light and proclaimed to the whole world.

(iii) *Of the importance of knowing what power 'free-will' has* (609-614)

Still more intolerable is your classifying 'free-will' among the *'useless doctrines that we can do without'*. In its stead you give us a list of what you consider to be sufficient for Christian piety—a draft, indeed, which a Jew, or a Gentile who knew nothing of Christ, could easily draw up; for you do not mention Christ in a single letter—as if you think that Christian piety is possible without Christ, so long as God, (*'who is kindness itself,'* you say) is whole-heartedly served.

What shall I say here, Erasmus? You ooze Lucian from every pore; you swill Epicurus by the gallon. If you do not think this topic a necessary concern for Christians, kindly withdraw from the lists; we have no common ground; I think it vital. If it is *'irreligious'*, *'idle'*, *'superfluous'*—your words—to know whether or not God foreknows anything contingently; whether our will is in any way active in matters relating to eternal salvation, or whether it is merely the passive subject of the work of grace; whether we do our good and evil deeds of mere necessity— whether, that is, we are not rather passive while they are wrought in us—then may I ask what *does* constitute godly, serious, useful knowledge? This is weak stuff, Erasmus; it is too much. It is hard to put it down to ignorance on your part, for you are no longer young,[1] you have lived among Christians, and you have long studied the sacred writings; you leave me no room to make excuses for you or to think well of you. And yet the Papists pardon and put up with these outrageous statements, simply because you are writing against Luther! If Luther were not involved, and you wrote so, they would tear you limb from

[1] *senex.*

limb! Plato and Socrates may be good friends, but truth must be honoured above all. And, limited though your understanding of the Bible and the Christian life may be, even one who opposes Christians should know what they do and do not consider profitable and necessary. Here you are, a theologian, a teacher of Christians, now about to write for their guidance an outline of Christianity, and not merely do you vacillate, in your sceptical way, as to what is profitable and necessary for them; you go back on yourself, defy your own principles and make an *assertion*—an unheard-of assertion!—that here is something non-essential; when, in fact, if it is not really essential, and is not surely known, then neither God, Christ, the gospel, faith nor anything else even of Judaism, let alone Christianity, is left! God Immortal, Erasmus, how vulnerable you make yourself, how wide you lay yourself open to assault and obloquy! What could you write about 'free-will' that was good or correct, when you betray by these words of yours such utter ignorance of Scripture and of godliness? But I shall furl my sails; I will not here use my own words to deal with you (that I may do later); I shall stick to yours.

The outline of Christianity which you have drawn up contains, among other things, this: '*We should strive with all our might, resort to the healing balm of penitence,*[1] *and try by all means to compass the mercy of God, without which man's will and endeavour is ineffective.*' And this: '*Nobody should despair of pardon from a God who by nature is kindness itself.*' These Christ-less, Spirit-less words of yours are chillier than very ice; indeed, they spoil the beauty of your eloquence. Perhaps they are reluctant admissions dragged out of you (poor fellow!) by fear of a tyrannical hierarchy,[2] lest you should seem an utter atheist! Anyway, this is what your words assert: that there is strength within us; there is such a thing as striving with all one's strength; there is mercy in God; there are ways of compassing that mercy; there is a God who is by nature just, and kindness itself; and so on. But if one does not know what this 'strength' is—what men can do, and what is done to them—what this 'striving' is, what is the extent and limit of its effectiveness—then what should he do? What will you tell him to do? Let us see.

[1] *poenitentiae.* [2] *pontificum.*

'*It is irreligious, idle and superfluous*' (you say) '*to want to know whether our will effects anything in matters pertaining to eternal salvation, or whether it is wholly passive under the work of grace.*' But here you speak to the contrary, saying that Christian piety consists in '*striving with all our might*', and that '*apart from the mercy of God our will is ineffective.*' Here you plainly assert that the will is in some respect active in matters pertaining to eternal salvation, for you represent it as striving; and, again, you represent it as the object of Divine action when you say that without God's mercy it is ineffective. But you do not define the limits within which we should think of the will as acting and as acted upon; you take pains to engender ignorance as to what God's mercy and man's will *can* effect by your very teaching as to what man's will and God's mercy *do* effect! Thus that caution of yours sends you round in circles; it has made you resolve to side with neither party, to emerge from between Scylla and Charybdis unscathed—so that if the waves in the open sea upset and overwhelm you, you can then assert all that you now deny, and deny all that you now assert!

I will set your theology before your eyes by a few analogies.[1] Suppose a would-be poet or speech-maker never thought to ask what ability he had, what he could and could not do, and what the subject he was tackling demanded of him—never considered Horace's adage about 'What the shoulders can sustain, and what they will not bear'[2]—but went straight to work, thinking: 'I must strive to get it done; it is *idle* and *superfluous* to ask whether I have enough learning and eloquence and ability'—what would you think of him? And if someone who wanted a rich crop from his land was not *idle* enough to perform the *superfluous* task of investigating the nature of the soil (as Virgil in the Georgics so *idly* and *pointlessly* advises), but rushed precipitately into action, thinking of nothing but the work, and ploughed the seashore and cast his seed wherever there was room, whether in the sand or in the mud—what would you think of him? And what if a man who purposed war, and wanted a glorious victory, or carried responsibility for some other piece of public service, was not so *idle* as to reflect upon what was in his power, whether the treasury could finance him,

---

[1] *similitudinibus.*   [2] *De Arte Poetica*, 39f.

whether the soldiers were fit, whether there was opportunity
for action; but disregarded the historian's advice[1] ('Before acting, deliberate, and when you have deliberated, act speedily'),
and charged ahead with eyes shut and ears stopped, shouting
nothing but 'War! War!'—pressing on with the work? Tell me,
Erasmus, what would you think of such poets, farmers, generals
and statesmen? I will add a text from the Gospel: 'If anyone,
intending to build a tower, does not first sit down and count
the cost, whether he has sufficient to finish it'—well, what is
Christ's judgment on that man? (cf. Luke 14.28).

In just this way, you prescribe for us nothing but things to
do, and yet you forbid us to examine, measure and take knowledge of the limits of our ability, as if this were an idle, superfluous and irreligious enquiry. In this, for all that horror of
imprudence and that ostentatious sobriety to which your vast
caution prompts you, we find you teaching imprudence at its
worst. The Sophists are fools and madmen, in fact, to pursue
their idle enquiries; yet they sin less than you, who actually
instruct men to cultivate madness and give themselves over to
folly. And your madness is greater still, in that you assure us
that this folly is the loveliest Christian piety, gravity, serious
godliness—and salvation! And if we do not do as you tell us,
you *assert* (you, the sworn foe of assertions!) that we are irreligious, idle and empty!—and thus you admirably dodge Scylla
and escape Charybdis too! Confidence in your own ability
drives you along here; you think that by your eloquence you
can so dupe the public that nobody will realise what you cherish
in your heart and what you are trying to achieve by these
slippery writings of yours. But God is not mocked, and it is not
good policy to run against Him!

Furthermore: were it with reference to writing poetry, or
preparing for harvest, or military or public service, or building
houses, that you taught us such folly, it would still be outrageous, particularly in so great a man as yourself, yet it could
have been forgiven you—at any rate, by Christians, who pay
no regard to these temporal things. But when you tell Christian
people to let this folly guide them in their labours, and charge
them that in their pursuit of eternal salvation they should not

---

[1] Sallust, *De coniuratione Cat.*, 1.

concern themselves to know what is in their power and what is not—why, this is plainly the sin that is really unpardonable. For as long as they do not know the limits of their ability, they will not know what they should do; and as long as they do not know what they should do, they cannot repent when they err; and impenitence is the unpardonable sin. This is where your moderate, sceptical theology leads us!

So it is not irreligious, idle, or superfluous, but in the highest degree wholesome and necessary, for a Christian to know whether or not his will has anything to do in matters pertaining to salvation. Indeed, let me tell you, this is the hinge on which our discussion turns, the crucial issue between us; our aim is, simply, to investigate what ability 'free-will' has, in what respect it is the subject of Divine action and how it stands related to the grace of God. If we know nothing of these things, we shall know nothing whatsoever of Christianity, and shall be in worse case than any people on earth! He who dissents from that statement should acknowledge that he is no Christian; and he who ridicules or derides it should realise that he is the Christian's chief foe. For if I am ignorant of the nature, extent and limits of what I can and must do with reference to God, I shall be equally ignorant and uncertain of the nature, extent and limits of what God can and will do in me—though God, in fact, works all in all (cf. 1 Cor. 12.6). Now, if I am ignorant of God's works and power, I am ignorant of God himself; and if I do not know God, I cannot worship, praise, give thanks or serve Him, for I do not know how much I should attribute to myself and how much to Him. We need, therefore, to have in mind a clear-cut distinction between God's power and ours, and God's work and ours, if we would live a godly life.

So, you see, this point is a further item in any complete summary of Christianity. Self-knowledge, and the knowledge and glory of God, are bound up with it. Which means, my dear Erasmus, that it is simply intolerable of you to call the know-ledge of it irreligious, idle, and vain. Your claims upon us are many, but the fear of God claims of us everything. Indeed, you yourself see that all good in us is to be ascribed to God, and assert as much in your outline of Christianity; and this assertion certainly involves a second, namely, that God's mercy alone works everything, and our will works nothing, but is rather the object of Divine working, else all will not be ascribed to God. And yet a little further on you deny that it is religious, godly, or wholesome, to assert or know these things! But an inconsistent thinker, unsure and inexperienced in the things of God, cannot help talking in this fashion.

(iv) *Of the necessitating foreknowledge of God* (614-618)

Another item in the summary of Christianity is knowing whether God foresees anything contingently, or whether we do all things of necessity. This knowledge also you represent as something irreligious, idle, and vain, just as all the ungodly do —indeed, the devils and the damned also represent it as hateful and abhorrent! You are wise to keep clear of such questions as far as you can; but you are a very poor rhetorician and theologian if you venture to open your mouth and instruct us about 'free-will' without any reference to these matters. I will act as your whetstone; though I am no rhetorician myself, I will dare to tell an excellent rhetorician his business. Suppose that Quintilian, having chosen to write on Oratory, were to say, 'In my judgment, all that superfluous nonsense about invention, arrangement, elocution, memory and pronunciation, should be left out; it is enough to know that Oratory is the ability to speak well'—would you not laugh at such an author? Yet, in just the same way, you first choose to write on 'free-will' and then exclude from consideration the entire substance and all the constituent parts of the topic you are going to write about! For you cannot know what 'free-will' is without knowing what ability man's will has, and what God does, and whether He foreknows of necessity.

Surely your rhetoricians teach that he who would speak about a subject should first say whether it exists, then what it is, what its parts are, what is contrary to it, allied to it, like it, and so on? But you deprive poor 'free-will' of all these advantages, and settle no single question relating to it save the first, i.e. whether it exists (and we shall see how worthless your arguments on *that* point are)—so that a more incompetent book on 'free-will' (apart from the elegance of its language) I never saw!

In fact, the Sophists argue on this subject better than you, innocent though they are of rhetorical skill; for, when they tackle 'free-will', they do try to settle all the questions concerning it (whether it exists, what it is, what it does, how it exists, etc.) —even though they too fail to achieve their object. In this book of mine, therefore, I shall harry you and all the Sophists till you tell me exactly what 'free-will' can and does do; and I hope so to harry you (Christ helping me) as to make you repent of ever publishing your Diatribe.

It is, then, fundamentally necessary and wholesome for Christians to know that God foreknows nothing contingently, but that He foresees, purposes, and does all things according to His own immutable, eternal and infallible will. This bombshell knocks 'free-will' flat, and utterly shatters it; so that those who want to assert it must ether deny my bombshell, or pretend not to notice it, or find some other way of dodging it. Before I establish this point by my own arguments and Scriptural authority, I shall first state it with the aid of *your* words.

Surely it was you, my good Erasmus, who a moment ago asserted that *God is by nature just, and kindness itself*? If this is true, does it not follow that He is *immutably* just and kind? that, as His nature remains unchanged to all eternity, so do His justice and kindness? And what is said of His justice and kindness must be said also of His knowledge, His wisdom, His goodness, His will, and the other Divine attributes. But if it is religious, godly and wholesome, to affirm these things of God, as you do, what has come over you, that now you should contradict yourself by affirming that it is irreligious, idle and vain to say that God foreknows by necessity? You insist that we should learn the immutability of God's will, while forbidding us to know the immutability of His foreknowledge! Do you suppose that He does not will what He foreknows, or that He does not foreknow what He wills? If He wills what He foreknows, His will is eternal and changeless, because His nature is so. From which it follows, by resistless logic, that all we do, however it may appear to us to be done mutably and contingently, is in reality done necessarily and immutably in respect of God's will. For the will of God is effective and cannot be impeded, since power belongs to God's nature; and His wisdom is such that He cannot be deceived. Since, then His will is not impeded, what is done cannot but be done where, when, how, as far as, and by whom, He foresees and wills. If the will of God were such that, when the work had been done and while it yet remained in being, the will ceased (as is the case with the will of a man, who, when he has built, say, the house he wants, ceases to will just as really as he does in death), then it could truly be said that things happen contingently and mutably. But the contrary is in fact true: the work ceases to be and the will remains in being— so far beyond the bounds of possibility is it that the production and continued existence of anything can be contingent. Lest we be deceived over our terms, let me explain that *being done contingently* does not, in Latin, signify that the thing done is itself contingent, but that it is done by a contingent and mutable will—such as is *not* to be found in God! And a deed cannot be called *contingent* unless we do it 'contingently', i.e. by chance (as it were) and without premeditation; that is, when our will or hand fastens on something presented to us as if by chance, without our having previously thought or planned anything about it.

I could wish, indeed, that a better term was available for our discussion than the accepted one, *necessity*, which cannot accurately be used of either man's will or God's. Its meaning is too harsh, and foreign to the subject; for it suggests some sort of compulsion, and something that is against one's will, which is no part of the view under debate. The will, whether it be God's or man's, does what it does, good or bad, under no compulsion, but just as it wants or pleases, as if totally free. Yet the will of God, which rules over our mutable will, is changeless and sure —as Boetius sings, 'Immovable Thyself, Thou movement giv'st to all;' and our will, principally because of its corruption, can do no good of itself. The reader's understanding, therefore, must supply what the word itself fails to convey, from his knowledge of the intended signification—the immutable will of God on the one hand, and the impotence of our corrupt will on the other. Some have called it *necessity of immutability*, but the phrase is both grammatically and theologically defective.[1]

This is a point over which the Sophists have toiled for many

[1] This paragraph appears only in the Jena edition of Luther's works (1567).

years now (and have been defeated at last, and forced to give in): they maintained that *all things take place necessarily, but by necessity of consequence* (as they put it), *and not by necessity of the thing consequent.* By this distinction they eluded the force of their own admission—or, rather, *de*luded themselves! I shall not find it hard to show how unreal the distinction is. By *necessity of consequence*, they mean, roughly speaking, this: If God wills something, then it must needs be; but that which thus comes to be is something which of itself need not be; for only God exists necessarily, and everything else can cease to be, if God so wills. This is to say that God's action is necessary, if He wills it, but the thing done is not in itself necessary. But what do they establish by this play on words? This, I suppose—the thing done is not necessary; that is, it has no necessity in its own essential nature: which is just to say, that the thing done is not God Himself! Nonetheless, it remains true that each thing *does* happen necessarily, if God's action is necessary or there is a necessity of consequence, however true it may be that it does *not* happen necessarily, in the sense that it is not God and has no necessity of its own essential nature. If I come to exist of necessity, it does not much worry me that my existence and being are in themselves mutable; contingent and mutable as I am (and I am not God, the necessary Being), yet I still come to exist!

So their absurd formula, *all things take place by necessity of consequence, but not by necessity of the thing consequent*, amounts merely to this: everything takes place by necessity, but the things that take place are not God Himself. But what need was there to tell us that?—as though there were any fear of our claiming that things which happen are God, or possess a divine and necessarily existent nature! So our original proposition still stands and remains unshaken: all things take place by necessity. There is no obscurity or ambiguity about it. In Isaiah, it says 'My counsel shall stand, and my will shall be done' (46.10); and any schoolboy knows the meaning of 'counsel', 'will', 'shall be done', 'shall stand'!

And why should these matters be thought so recondite for us Christians that it is irreligious, idle, and vain to study and know them, when they are on the lips of heathen poets and ordinary people so frequently? How often does Vergil, for one, mention Fate? 'All things stand fixed by law immutable.' Again, 'Fixed is the day of every man.' Again, 'If the Fates summon you.' Again, 'If thou shalt break the binding cord of Fate.'[1] The poet simply seeks to show that in the destruction of Troy and the beginning of the Roman empire Fate did more than all the efforts of men. Indeed, he makes even his immortal gods subject to Fate. Jupiter and Juno themselves needs must yield to it. Hence the poets represented the three Fates[2] as immutable, implacable and irrevocable in their decrees. Those wise men knew, what experience of life proves, that no man's purposes ever go forward as planned, but events overtake all men contrary to their expectation. 'Could Troy have stood by human arm, it should have stood by mine,' says Vergil's Hector.[3] Hence that commonest of all remarks, which is on everyone's lips—'God's will be done'; and: 'If God will, we will do it'; and: 'God so willed,' 'such was the will of those above.' 'Such was your will,' says Vergil. Whence we see that the knowledge of predestination and of God's prescience has been left in the world no less certainly than the notion of the Godhead itself. But those who wished to seem wise argued themselves out of it till their hearts grew dark and they became fools, as Rom. 1 says (vv. 21-2), and denied, or pretended not to know, things which the poets, and the common people, and even their own consciences held as being most familiar, most certain, and most true.

(v) *Of the importance of knowing that God necessitates all things*
     (618-620)

I would also point out, not only how true these things are (I shall discuss that more fully from Scripture on a later page), but also how godly, reverent and necessary it is to know them. For where they are not known, there can be no faith, nor any worship of God. To lack this knowledge is really to be ignorant of God—and salvation is notoriously incompatible with such ignorance. For if you hesitate to believe, or are too proud to acknowledge, that God foreknows and wills all things, not

---

[1] Vergil, *Aeneid*, 2.324, 6.883, 7.314, 10.465.   [2] *Parcae*.   [3] *Aen.*, 2.291f.

contingently, but necessarily and immutably, how can you believe, trust and rely on His promises? When He makes promises, you ought to be out of doubt that He knows, and can and will perform, what He promises; otherwise, you will be accounting Him neither true nor faithful, which is unbelief, and the height of irreverence, and a denial of the most high God! And how can you be thus sure and certain, unless you know that certainly, infallibly, immutably and necessarily, He knows, wills and will perform what He promises? Not only should we be sure that God wills, and will execute His will, necessarily and immutably; we should glory in the fact, as Paul does in Rom. 3—'Let God be true, but every man a liar' (v. 4), and again, 'Not that the word of God has failed' (Rom. 9.6), and in another place, 'The foundation of God standeth sure, having this seal, the Lord knoweth them that are his' (2 Tim. 2.19). In Tit. 1 he says: 'Which God, that cannot lie, promised before the world began' (v. 2). And Heb. 11 says: 'He that cometh, must believe that God is, and that he is a rewarder of them that hope in him' (v. 6).

If, then, we are taught and believe that we ought to be ignorant of the necessary foreknowledge of God and the necessity of events, Christian faith is utterly destroyed, and the promises of God and the whole gospel fall to the ground completely; for the Christian's chief and only comfort in every adversity lies in knowing that God does not lie, but brings all things to pass immutably, and that His will cannot be resisted, altered or impeded.

Observe now, my good Erasmus, where that cautious, peace-loving theology of yours leads us! You call us back, and prohibit our endeavours to learn about God's foreknowledge and the necessity which lies on, men and things, and advise us to leave behind, and avoid, and look down on such enquiries; and in so doing you teach us your own ill-advised principles—that we should seek after ignorance of God (which comes to us without our seeking, and indeed is born in us), and so should spurn faith, abandon God's promises, and discount all the consolations of the Spirit and convictions of our consciences. Epicurus himself would hardly give such advice! Moreover, not content with this, you call those who are concerned to acquire the knowledge in question godless, idle and empty, and those who care nothing for it you call godly, pious and sober. What do you imply by these words, but that Christians are idle, empty and godless fellows? and that Christianity is a trivial, empty, stupid and downright godless thing? So here again, in your desire to discourage us from anything rash, you allow yourself to be carried to the contrary extreme (as fools do) and teach the very quintessence of godless, suicidal folly. Do you see, now, that at this point your book is so godless, blasphemous and sacrilegious, that its like cannot be found anywhere?

I do not speak of your heart, as I said before; for I do not think you are so abandoned that you honestly want to teach these principles or see them applied. But I wanted to make you realise what appalling sentiments the champion of a bad cause finds himself constrained unguardedly to blurt out; and also what it means to go against God's facts and God's Word when we dissemble to oblige others, and defy conscience by acting a part at their bidding. It is no game and no joke[1] to teach the holy Scriptures and godliness, for it is so very easy to fall here in the way that James described: 'he that offends in one point becomes guilty of all' (2.10). For when we show ourselves disposed to trifle even a little and cease to hold the sacred Scriptures in sufficient reverence, we are soon involved in impieties and overwhelmed with blasphemies—as you are here, Erasmus. May the Lord pardon and have mercy on you!

I know, and join you in affirming, that the Sophists have raised a host of questions on these topics, and mixed in with them a great deal of unprofitable matter besides, much of which you specify; indeed, I have attacked them more vigorously and fully than you. But you are ill-advised and over-hasty to confuse and lump together the purity of sacred truth with the profane and foolish questions of the ungodly. 'They have defiled the gold with dung, and changed its good colour,' as Jeremiah says (Lam. 4.1). But the gold should not be equated with the dung and thrown away with it, as you are doing. The gold must be reclaimed from their hands, the pure Scripture must be separated from their own rotten rubbish; which is what I have always tried to do, so that divine truth may be

---

[1] *iocus.*

kept distinct from their nonsense. Nor should it disturb us that nothing has been established through their investigations save that a great loss of unity and decline in affection results when we aspire to be over-wise. Our question is not, what have the Sophistical enquirers achieved? but, how may we become good men and Christians? And you should not blame on to Christian doctrine the evil doings of the godless; all that is quite irrelevant, and you could well speak of it elsewhere and save paper.

(vi) *Of the alleged advantages of suppressing certain truths* (620-630)

Under your third head, you try to turn us into unassuming, idle Epicureans. This is a different kind of advice, but no sounder than the two pieces of your mind already quoted. *'Some things'* (you say) *'are of such a kind that, even if they were true and could be known, it would be imprudent to expose them to everyone's hearing.'* Here again, as usual, you muddle everything up, equating what is holy with what is not, not distinguishing them at all; and so you fall once more to insulting and dishonouring Scripture and God. As I said above, what may be found in or proved by the sacred writings is both plain and wholesome, and so may safely be published, learned and known—and, indeed, should be. So your statement, that some things should not be exposed to everyone's hearing, if made with reference to the contents of Scripture, is false; and if you spoke of other things, your remark was irrelevant and out of place, and a waste of your paper and time. Moreover, you know that I disagree with the Sophists in everything; you might well spare me, therefore, and not lay their perversities at my door. It was against me, remember, that you were supposed to be writing in your book! I know where the Sophists go wrong; I do not need you to tell me; I have criticised them enough myself. I should like that said once for all, and repeated as often as you class me with the Sophists and dilate on their madness to prejudice my case. You are acting unscrupulously, as you very well know.

Now let us look at your reasons for giving this advice. *It is true*, you say, *that, God's nature being what it is, He is no more really in Heaven than He is in a beetle's hole, or even down a drain* (which you yourself scruple to say; you blame the Sophists for blathering about such things)—*yet*, you suggest, *it would be un-reasonable to talk about it in public.*

Now, in the first place, let them blather who will—we are not dealing here with what men do, but with what is right and ought to be done; not with how we do live, but how we should live. Who among us always lives and behaves as he should? But duty and doctrine are not therefore condemned; rather, they condemn us! The truth is, you fetch from afar and rake together all these irrelevances simply because you are embarrassed on this one point, the foreknowledge of God; and, since you cannot overthrow it by any argument, you try meantime to tire out the reader with a flow of empty verbiage. But enough of that; back to the point.

What is the bearing of your statement that some things should not be made public? Do you include the subject of 'free-will' among them? If so, all I said above about the necessity of understanding 'free-will' will round upon you. And why, in that case, have you not followed your own principles, and left your Diatribe unwritten? If you do well to discuss 'free-will', why do you censure such discussion? If it is a bad thing to do, why do you do it? If, on the other hand, you do not put 'free-will' into this category, then once more you are all this time evading the issue, lavishing your long-winded rhetoric on red herrings!

Nor are you right in your treatment of this example, nor in condemning as useless public discussion of the fact that God is in a hole or down a drain. Your thoughts of God are too human. I certainly admit that there are some giddy preachers, who, from no religious or godly motive, but because they want applause, or hanker after novelty, or just cannot keep their mouths shut, talk the most frivolous nonsense; but such please neither God nor men, even by affirming that God is in the heaven of heavens! Where, however, preachers are serious and godly, teaching in sober, pure, sound words, they refer to this sort of thing in public without risk of harm, and, indeed, to much profit. Surely we should all teach that the Son of God was in the Virgin's womb, and born of her belly? And how much does a human belly differ from any other unclean place? One could use foul and disgusting language to describe it;

though we deservedly censure those who do, since an abundance of pure words exists for referring to that necessary subject without either unpleasantness or indecency. Again, Christ's body was human, like our own—and what is more foul than that? Yet surely we should not therefore stop saying that God indwelt that body—*bodily*, as Paul puts it? (cf. Col. 2.9.) What is more foul than death? What is more frightful than hell? Yet the Prophet glories that God is with him in death and near him in hell (cf. Ps. 16.10, 139.8).

So the godly mind is not shocked to hear that God is in death or in hell; though either is more frightful and foul than a hole or a sewer. Indeed, since Scripture testifies that God is everywhere and fills all things, a godly man does not just say that He is in these places; of necessity he learns and knows that He is there—unless we must suppose that, were I ever caught by a tyrant and thrown into a cell or a sewer (as has happened to many saints) I might not there call on God, nor believe that He was with me till I could get into some ornate church? If you teach us this kind of nonsense about God, and are shocked at the places where His Essence resides, you will end by refusing to allow that He dwells with us in heaven—for the heaven of heaven cannot contain Him (cf. 1 Kings 8.27), nor is it worthy to do so. The truth is as I said: you are venting your spleen on us, as usual, in order to prejudice and discredit our cause, because you see that you cannot conquer or overthrow it.

As for your second example, the proposition that '*there are three Gods*,' I admit that this, if taught, is a real stumbling-block. But it is neither true nor Scriptural; it is just a product of the new logic which the Sophists have invented. And what is that to us?

Your treatment of your final example, the case of confession and satisfaction, is a marvellously skilful piece of diplomacy. From first to last (as usual) you tread like a cat on hot bricks,[1] fearful lest you should seem to fail either to condemn our position out of hand or to oppose the Papal tyranny—rather a tight corner for you! So you put God and conscience out of mind for the time being (what does Erasmus care what God wills and conscience sanctions in these matters?); you create a

---

[1] *super aristas graderis.*

diversion; you drag in an irrelevant bogey[1] and assault it. You denounce the people, because their depravity leads them to make the preaching of freedom from confession and satisfaction an excuse for freedom in flesh-pleasing. '*Now*' (you say) '*the necessity of making confession to some extent restrains them.*' Oh, what a fine, noble sentiment! Is this teaching theology? —to bind under laws and, in Ezekiel's phrase (cf. Ezek. 13.18f.) to hunt to death souls which God never bound? Why, by this reasoning you will bring on us once more the entire tyranny of the Papal laws, and defend it as useful and wholesome—for those laws too restrain the depravity of the people! I shall not launch the onslaught which this passage deserves; but, briefly, the truth is this: A good theologian teaches that people should be restrained by the external power of the sword when they do evil, as Paul teaches in Rom. 13 (vv. 1-4). But their consciences must not be ensnared by false laws, and thereby tormented for sins where according to God's will there is no sin. Consciences are bound by God's law alone, and the Papal tyranny, which by its falsehoods frightens and murders souls within, and uselessly exhausts the body from without, is an intruder that should be banished forthwith. Though by external pressure it forces men to make confession and perform other burdensome tasks, it fails to restrain their minds, which are only the more provoked hereby to hate both God and man. Its external butchery of the body is equally futile; it just produces hypocrites. So that the tyrants who impose such laws are nothing but ravening wolves and robbers, stealing souls! And now you, the expert counsellor of souls, recommend to us once more these barbarous soul-murderers, who fill the world with blaspheming, proud-hearted hypocrites solely in order to subject them to a measure of outward restraint!—as if without making hypocrites of them and destroying their consciences there was no way at all of restraining them! as I said.

Now you bring in analogies (for you want to show off your range and mastery of analogies):—'*there are diseases*' (you say) '*which can be borne with less evil than they can be cured, like leprosy*'— and so on. And you quote the example of Paul, who distinguished between what was lawful and what was expedient

---

[1] *larvam externam.*

(cf. 1 Cor. 6.12). *'It is lawful'* (you say) *'to speak the truth, but it is not expedient to do so in every company, nor at every time, nor in every way.'*

What a fulsome speaker you are!—but utterly ignorant of what you are talking about. In a word, you treat this discussion as if the issue at stake between us was the recovery of a debt, or some other trivial item, the loss of which matters far less than the public peace, and therefore should not so upset anyone as to make him hesitate to give and take, yielding the point if need be, in order to ensure that no occasion for public disorder arises. You make it clear that this carnal peace and quiet seems to you far more important than faith, conscience, salvation, the Word of God, the glory of Christ, and God himself. Let me tell you, therefore—and I beg you to let this sink deep into your mind—I hold that a solemn and vital truth, of eternal consequence, is at stake in this discussion; one so crucial and fundamental that it ought to be maintained and defended even at the cost of life, though as a result the whole world should be, not just thrown into turmoil and uproar, but shattered in chaos and reduced to nothingness. If you do not grasp that, if it leaves you unmoved, then mind your own business, and leave those to grasp it and be moved by it to whom it is given of God!

For, thank God, I am not such a silly fool that I would have been willing to sustain and champion this cause for so long, with such fortitude and firmness (obstinacy, you call it), often at the risk of my life, hated and plotted against continually—enduring, in a word, the rage of men and of devils together—merely to gain money (which I neither have nor want), or renown (which I could not have if I wanted it in a world that hates me so), or to protect my life (which is always forfeit now). Do you think that because your heart trembles at these upheavals you are the only one who has a heart? I am not made of stone, either; I am no child of Marpesian crags. But (since it must be one or the other) I would rather be joyful in God's grace and bear the brunt of this temporal uproar for the sake of the Word of God— which demands to be asserted with invincible and unshakeable zeal—rather that, I say, than be ground to powder under the wrath of God by the unbearable torments of the uproar that shall be everlasting! May Christ grant that your heart may not be as your words suggest—I hope and pray that it is not—for you certainly imply that you agree with Epicurus that God's Word and the life to come are fables. For your teaching is designed to induce us, out of consideration for Popes, princes and peace, to abandon and yield up for the present the sure Word of God. But when we abandon that, we abandon God, faith, salvation, and all Christianity! How much sounder is Christ's advice, that we should rather despise the whole world!

You say this sort of thing simply because you have not read, or at any rate have not noticed, that it is regularly the case with the Word of God that the world is thrown into confusion by reason of it. Christ openly affirms as much: 'I came not' (says He) 'to send peace, but a sword' (Matt. 10.34). So in Luke: 'I came to send fire on the earth' (12.49). So Paul, in 1 Cor 6: 'In tumults,' etc. (2 Cor. 6.5). The prophet in the second Psalm bears elaborate testimony to the same truth when he declares that the nations are in uproar, the peoples rage, the kings rise up, the rulers conspire, against the Lord and against Christ— as though to say that the many, the mighty, wealth, power, wisdom, righteousness and all that is exalted in the world opposes the Word of God. Look at the Acts of the Apostles, and see there what happened in the world by reason of the word of Paul alone (to say nothing of the other apostles)—how, single-handed, he threw into confusion Jews and Gentiles alike. As his foes said of him, he turned the world upside down! (Acts 17.6). The kingdom of Israel was thrown into confusion under Elijah, as Ahab complained (1 Kings 18.17). What upheaval was there under the other prophets, when they were all executed or stoned, and Israel was led captive into Assyria, and Judah to Babylon! Was *that* peace? The world and its god cannot and will not bear the Word of the true God, and the true God cannot and will not keep silent. Now these two Gods are at war; so what else can there be throughout the world but uproar?

To want to quell these tumults, therefore, is really to want to remove the Word of God and stop its course. When the Word of God comes, it comes to change and renew the world, and even heathen writers acknowledge that such changes cannot take place without commotion and upheaval—nor, indeed, without bloodshed. Now it is the Christian's part to expect and coolly to endure these things—as Christ says, 'When ye shall hear of wars and rumours of wars, be not dismayed: for these things must first come to pass, but the end is not yet' (Matt. 24.6). Personally, did I not see these upheavals, I should say that the Word of God was not in the world. Now that I see them, I rejoice from my heart and smile at them, knowing for sure that the Pope's kingdom and all its allies will fall; for the Word of God is now in full cry, and these are its principal target.

I see indeed, my good Erasmus, that in many of your books you deplore the loss of peace and concord, and make a series of attempts to heal the breach. Your intentions are of the best (at least, I think so); but the gouty foot laughs at your doctoring. Here, as you yourself admit, you are indeed sailing against the stream; why, you are trying to quench fire with straw! Stop your complaining, stop your doctoring; the origin and continuance of this conflict is from God; and it will not cease till all who oppose the Word have become as the mire of the streets. I can only regret, however, that so great a theologian as yourself needs to go back to school and be taught these things, when you should have been teaching others.

Your elegant dictum that some diseases may be borne with less harm than they can be cured with is in point here; but you misapply it. Give the name of 'diseases which may be borne with less harm' to these tumults, commotions, confusions, dissensions, discords, wars and everything else of that sort with which the world is shaken and buffeted on account of the Word of God! These things, I say, being temporal, may be endured with less harm than inveterate evil ways, which will inevitably ruin all souls that are not changed by the Word of God. If the Word were removed, eternal good, God, Christ, and the Spirit, would be removed with it. How much better, then, is it to lose the world than to lose God, the world's Creator, who can create countless worlds afresh, and is better than infinite worlds! For what are temporal things beside eternal? We should, therefore, endure this leprous outbreak of temporal evils, rather than keep the world at peace and free from these upheavals; for the price of that peace would be the blood and ruin of all souls, who would then be destroyed and damned for ever! For the whole world is not of value enough to redeem a single soul.

You command fine, elegant analogies and epigrams; but the way you apply them when you treat of holy things is childish—indeed, perverse. You grovel on the ground and cannot conceive of anything that is above man's understanding. But there is nothing childish, or merely man-like, about the operations of God; they are Divine, and they exceed man's grasp. And that is why you fail to see that it is by reason of God's will and activity that these tumults and divisions are raging throughout the world—and so you are afraid that the sky will fall! But I, by God's grace, clearly see what you cannot see; indeed, I foresee other, greater upheavals in store for a future generation, compared with which these present are but as the whisper of a faint breeze, or the murmur of a gentle brook.

Now, to return to the doctrine of freedom from confession and satisfaction: you are denying, or at least showing yourself unaware, that there exists a Word of God. This, of course, is a different inquiry. I, for my part, know for sure that there is a Word of God, which asserts Christian liberty and warns us not to let ourselves be snared into bondage by human traditions and laws. This I have taught at length elsewhere; but, if you want to enter the lists, I am ready to discuss it and fight it out with you too. (There are quite a number of books written by myself on this subject.)

'But' (you say) 'the Papal laws should still in charity be borne with and kept, for it may be that eternal salvation through the Word of God will yet prove compatible with the world's peace without any disturbance.'

As I said above, that cannot be. The prince of this world does not permit the laws of the Pope and his pontiffs to be kept in liberty; his intention is to entangle and bind consciences. This the true God cannot bear. So the Word of God and the traditions of men fight each other in implacable opposition. God and Satan are personally engaged in this same conflict, each labouring to destroy the works and subvert the doctrines of the other, like two kings laying waste each other's kingdoms. 'He that is not with me,' said Christ, 'is against me' (Luke 11.23).

As for your fear that many persons of vicious inclination will abuse this liberty, this must be thought of as one of the disturbances aforementioned, part of the temporal leprosy that we must bear and the malady that we must endure. But it must not be held so important as to warrant the removal of the Word of God in order to restrain their abuse of it. If not all can be saved, yet some are saved; the Word of God came for their sake, and so they love it the more fervently and assent to it the more readily. What evil did ungodly men not do before the Word came? and what good did they ever do? Was not the world always full of war, deceit, violence, quarrelling and iniquity of every kind?—so much so that Micah compares the best among them to a thorn hedge! (cf. Mic. 7.4)—and what do you think he would say of the others? Yet now that the gospel is come, men start blaming the world's wickedness on to it!—when the truth is, rather, that the good Gospel brings the world's wickedness to light; for without the gospel the world dwelt in its own darkness. So do the uneducated blame education for the fact that, as education spreads, their own ignorance becomes apparent. Such are the thanks we return for the word of life and salvation! What fear may we suppose there was among the Jews, when the Gospel freed all men from the law of Moses? What scope did not this great liberty appear to give to evil men? Yet the Gospel was not, on that account, taken away; instead, the godly were told not to use their liberty to indulge the flesh (cf. Gal. 5.13), and the ungodly were left to their own devices.

Moreover, there is no force in that part of your advice—panacea, I should say—in which you observe: '*It is lawful to speak the truth; but it is not expedient to do so in every company, nor at every time, nor in every way,*' and quote Paul (inappropriately enough) where he says: 'All things are lawful for me, but all things are not expedient' (1 Cor. 6.12). Paul does not speak there of teaching doctrinal truth; you are wresting his words, forcing them to mean what you want. In fact, Paul would have the truth spoken everywhere, at all times, in any and every way; so that he is delighted even when Christ is preached out of envy and ill-will, and openly declares that he rejoices, however Christ is preached (cf. Phil. 1.15f.). In the text you quote, Paul speaks only of behaviour and the practical application of doctrine; he is dealing with those who, boasting of their Christian liberty, seek their own ends without considering how they offend and injure the weak. No; doctrinal truth should be preached always, openly, without compromise, and never dissembled or concealed. There is no offence in it; it is the staff of uprightness. Who gave you the right and power to confine Christian doctrine to particular persons, places, times and cases, when Christ wills that it should be freely published and reign throughout the world? 'The word of God is not bound,' says Paul (2 Tim. 2.9); and shall Erasmus bind the Word? God did not give us a Word that has respect of times, places, or persons. When Christ says: 'Go ye into all the world' (Matt. 28.19), He does not say, as does Erasmus, 'go to this place, but not that.' Again: 'Preach the Gospel to every creature' (Mark 16.15). He does not say: 'to some, but not to others.' In short, you enjoin in the ministry of God's Word respect of persons, of places, of customs and of seasons; whereas one great part of the glory of the Word is precisely this—that, as Paul says, it does not respect persons, nor is God a respecter of persons (cf. Rom. 2.11; Eph. 6.9; Col. 3.25). You see again how unadvisedly you rush against the Word of God, as though you rated your own thoughts and ideas far above it.

If we should ask you to settle for us the occasions when, and the persons to whom, and the ways in which, the truth is to be spoken, how soon would you give your answer? The world could calculate when time is to stop and its own existence end sooner than you could establish a single reliable rule. What is to happen to the teaching office, the work of soul-instruction, while we are waiting for you? In any case, how could you fix such rules, when you know no general principles governing persons, times or manners? And even if you knew them perfectly, you would not know the hearts of men. Or perhaps the manner, time and person you have in mind are as follows—so to teach the truth that the Pope does not object, Caesar is not enraged, pontiffs and princes are not upset, and no disturbances and upheavals are caused in the world, lest many should stumble and grow worse? What sort of a policy this is, you saw above. But you were pleased to indulge in this unprofitable rhetoric, so that you might avoid saying nothing!

How much more fitting is it for wretched men like ourselves to ascribe to God, Who knows all men's hearts, the glory of settling the way in which, and the persons to whom, and the occasions when, the truth should be spoken! He Himself knows what should be said to each, and when, and how. Now, He has laid it down that His Gospel, which all need, should not be confined to any place or time, but should be preached to all men, at all times and in all places. I proved earlier that what is delivered in the Scriptures is plain to all, and is wholesome, and must be proclaimed abroad—as you stated yourself in your *Paraclesis*, with better judgment than you are showing now. Those who are unwilling for souls to be redeemed, like the Pope and his adherents—leave it for them to bind the Word of God and keep men from life and the kingdom of heaven; for they neither enter in themselves, nor allow others to enter (cf. Matt. 23.13). You only do harm, Erasmus, when you pander to their obsession by this policy of yours.

The same circumspection appears in your next bit of advice, that *wrong decisions made in councils should not be publicly acknowledged, lest grounds for denying the authority of the fathers should thereby be given*. This, of course, is just what the Pope wanted you to say! He finds it sweeter hearing than the Gospel itself; he will be most ungrateful if he does not honour you in return with a cardinal's hat, plus all the attendant revenues! But in the meanwhile, Erasmus, what will those souls do that are bound and butchered by this iniquitous ordinance? Is it nothing to you? Of course, you always think, or pretend to think, that men's ordinances can be observed together with the Word of God without risk. If they could, I would at once come over to your view. But, if you are still in ignorance, I must tell you again: men's ordinances cannot be observed together with the Word of God, because the former bind consciences and the latter looses them. The two things are as much opposed to each other as fire and water. This would not, indeed, be so if men's ordinances could be observed in liberty: that is, as not binding the conscience. But the Pope will not have that, nor can he, unless he wants his kingdom destroyed and ended; for it stands only by ensnaring and binding consciences which the Gospel pronounces free. The authority of the Fathers must therefore be held null and void, and any erroneous decisions they made (as are all that conflict with the Word of God) must be torn up and thrown away; for Christ is a higher authority than the Fathers. In short, then: if you take this position with reference to the Word of God, it is blasphemy; and if with reference to other things only, then your long-winded argument for your policy is nothing to me, for it is precisely with reference to the Word of God that I am arguing!

(vii) *Of the alleged disadvantages of proclaiming that God necessitates all things* (630-634)

In the last part of your Preface, where you earnestly dissuade us from our kind of doctrine, you think victory is almost won. '*What*' (you say) '*can be more useless than to publish to the world the paradox that all we do is done, not by "free-will", but of mere necessity, and Augustine's view that God works in us both good and evil; that He rewards His own good works in us, and punishes His own evil works in us?*' (You are copious here in giving reasons, or, rather, in demanding that we give them.) '*What a flood-gate of iniquity*' (you say) '*would the spread of such news open to people! What wicked man would amend his life? Who would believe that God loved him? Who would fight against his flesh?*' (I wonder that in this furious outburst you did not remember the matter in hand, and say: 'where then will "free-will" be found?'!)

My good Erasmus! I reply as before. If you think these paradoxes are inventions of men, why do you oppose them? why get so heated? against whom are you speaking? Is there any man in the world to-day who has attacked the doctrines of men more strongly than Luther? Your lecture is wasted on me! If, however, you believe these paradoxes to be words of God, then where is your conscience,[1] where is your shame, where is, I will not say your famous moderation, but the fear and reverence which you owe to the true God?—for what you are saying is that there is no information more useless than God's Word! So your Creator must learn from you, His creature, what may usefully be preached and what not? God

[1] *frons.*

was so stupid and thoughtless, was He, that He did not know what should be taught till you came along to tell Him how to be wise, and what to command?—as if without your pointing it out He would not have realised that this paradox involves the consequence you draw? No; if God has willed that these things should be openly proclaimed and published, who are you to forbid it? The apostle Paul, in his epistle to the Romans, frankly discusses these very matters, not in a corner, but openly, publicly, before the whole world, and in harsher terms than those you quote. 'Whom he will he hardeneth,' he says; and again, 'God, willing to show forth his wrath,' etc. (Rom. 9.18, 22). What is harder (to the flesh, at any rate) than Christ's saying, 'Many are called, but few chosen?' (Matt. 22.14). And again, 'I know whom I have chosen?' (John 13.18). On your view, of course, there is no information more useless than all this—your reason being, presumably, that it might drive the ungodly to despair, hatred and blasphemy!

Here, I see, you are taking the view that the truth and usefulness of Scripture should be measured and decided according to the feeling of men—to be precise, of the ungodliest of men; so that nothing henceforth will be true, Divine and wholesome but what these persons find pleasing and acceptable; and what is not so will at once become useless, untrue and harmful. What else do you here plead for, but that the words of God may thus depend on, and stand or fall by, the will and authority of men? But Scripture says the opposite, that all things stand or fall by the will and authority of God, and that all the earth keeps silence before the face of the Lord (cf. Hab. 2.20). One who talks as you do must imagine that the living God is no more than a wild inconsequent ranter shouting from a soap-box,[1] whose words you may interpret, receive or refute as you please, according to their observed effect on the ungodly. Here you make plain, my dear Erasmus, just how little sincerity lay behind your advice, given earlier, that we should revere the majesty of the judgments of God. Then, dealing with the doctrines of Scripture (where there is no need to revere hidden mysteries, since no doctrines in fact are such), you warned us in the most pious language against any inquisitive invasion of

---

[1] *levem et imprudentem rabulam in aliquo suggesto declamantem.*

the Corycian caverns, and well-nigh frightened us off reading the Bible altogether—though Bible-reading is something to which Christ and the Apostles urgently exhort us, as elsewhere you do yourself. But now that we have actually come, not just to the doctrines of Scripture or the Corycian cavern, but to the awful secret of God's Majesty—that is, as was said, the question, why does He work as He does—here you break down the barriers and burst in, all but blaspheming! What indignation against God do you not display, because you may not see the reason and design of His counsel! Why do you not invoke obscurities and ambiguities here? Why do you not restrain yourself, and discourage others, from prying into matters which God wills to keep hidden from us, and has not made known in the Scriptures? Here we should lay our hand on our mouth; here we should revere what lies concealed, and adore the secret decrees of the Divine Majesty, and cry with Paul: 'Who art thou, O man, that contendest with God?' (Rom. 9.20).

'*Who*' (you say) '*will try and reform his life?*' I reply, Nobody! Nobody can! God has no time for your practitioners of self-reformation, for they are hypocrites. The elect, who fear God, will be reformed by the Holy Spirit; the rest will perish un-reformed. Note that Augustine does not say that a reward awaits *nobody's* works, or *everybody's* works, but *some men's* works. So there will be some who reform their lives.

'*Who will believe*' (you say) '*that God loves him?*' I reply, Nobody! nobody can! But the elect shall believe it; and the rest shall perish without believing it, raging and blaspheming, as you describe them. So there will be some who believe it.

You say that *a flood-gate of iniquity is opened by our doctrines.* So be it. Ungodly men are part of that evil leprosy aforementioned, which we must endure. Nevertheless, these are the very doctrines which throw open to the elect, who fear God, a gateway to righteousness, an entrance into heaven, and a road to God! If, as you advise, we should keep off these doctrines, and hide this word of God from men, and leave them all to labour under a false assurance of salvation, never learning the fear of God and true humiliation, and so never coming through that fear to true, saving grace and love—why, then we should have shut your flood-gate to some purpose; for in its place we should set open before ourselves and everyone else broad gates, yes, gaping chasms and raging whirlpools, to take us down not only into sin, but into the very depths of hell! Thus we too should fail to enter heaven ourselves, and hinder others who were entering (cf. Matt. 23.13).

'What use or need is there, then, of publishing such things, when so many harmful results seem likely to follow?'

I reply: It should be enough to say simply that God has willed their publication, and the reason of the Divine will is not to be sought, but simply to be adored, and the glory given to God, Who, since He alone is just and wise, wrongs none and can do nothing foolish or inconsiderate—however much it may seem otherwise to us. This answer will satisfy those who fear God. However (to say a little more than I need, since there is so much more that I can say); there are two considerations which require the preaching of these truths. The first is the humbling of our pride, and the comprehending of the grace of God; the second is the nature of Christian faith.

For the first: God has surely promised His grace to the humbled: that is, to those who mourn over and despair of themselves. But a man cannot be thoroughly humbled till he realises that his salvation is utterly beyond his own powers, counsels, efforts, will and works, and depends absolutely on the will, counsel, pleasure and work of Another—God alone. As long as he is persuaded that he can make even the smallest contribution to his salvation, he remains self-confident and does not utterly despair of himself, and so is not humbled before God; but plans out for himself (or at least hopes and longs for) a position, an occasion, a work, which shall bring him final salvation. But he who is out of doubt that his destiny depends entirely on the will of God despairs entirely of himself, chooses nothing for himself, but waits for God to work in him; and such a man is very near to grace for his salvation.

So these truths are published for the sake of the elect, that they may be humbled and brought down to nothing, and so saved. The rest of men resist this humiliation; indeed, they condemn the teaching of self-despair; they want a little something left that they can do for themselves. Secretly they continue proud, and enemies of the grace of God. This, I repeat, is one reason—that those who fear God might in humility comprehend, claim and receive His gracious promise.

The second reason is this: faith's object is things not seen. That there may be room for faith, therefore, all that is believed must be hidden. Yet it is not hidden more deeply than under a contrary appearance of sight, sense and experience. Thus, when God quickens, He does so by killing; when He justifies, He does so by pronouncing guilty; when He carries up to heaven, He does so by bringing down to hell. As Scripture says in 1 Kings 2, 'The Lord killeth and maketh alive; He bringeth down to the grave and bringeth up' (1 Sam. 2.6). (This is no place for a fuller account of these things; but those who have read my books are well acquainted with them.) Thus God conceals His eternal mercy and loving kindness beneath eternal wrath, His righteousness beneath unrighteousness. Now, the highest degree of faith is to believe that He is merciful, though He saves so few and damns so many; to believe that He is just, though of His own will He makes us perforce proper subjects for damnation, and seems (in Erasmus' words) *'to delight in the torments of poor wretches and to be a fitter object for hate than for love.'* If I could by any means understand how this same God, who makes such a show of wrath and unrighteousness, can yet be merciful and just, there would be no need for faith. But as it is, the impossibility of understanding makes room for the exercise of faith when these things are preached and published; just as, when God kills, faith in life is exercised in death.

And that is enough at present for your Preface!

By our method of open discussion we shall do more good to those who argue about these paradoxes than we should by following your advice, which springs from a desire to humour their impiety by keeping quiet and saying nothing. But you achieve nothing by this advice. For suppose you believe, or suspect, even, that the paradoxes are true—well, they are matters of no small moment, and so insatiable is man's desire to pry into secrets (and the more so the more we want to keep them secret!) that your very dissuasive will make everyone far more eager than before to know whether the paradoxes are true or not! Your own heat will so inflame them that this godly zealous admonition of yours will give them more reason to make the paradoxes common knowledge than anyone on our side has ever done! You would have been far wiser to say nothing at all about avoiding the paradoxes if you wanted your wish granted. Now, however, seeing that you have not directly denied their truth, it will be impossible to keep them hidden; their apparent plausibility will encourage everyone to look into them—and that will be that! You must either deny their truth, or else hold your own tongue first, if you want other people to hold theirs.

(viii) *Of the spontaneity of necessitated acts* (634-635)

As for the other paradox, '*all we do is done, not by free-will, but of mere necessity*'—let us take a brief look at it, for we must not let such a mischievous remark go unchallenged. My comment is simply this: if it be proved that our salvation is not of our own strength or counsel, but depends on the working of God alone (which is something I hope to demonstrate later in the main discussion), does it not clearly follow that when God is not present to work in us, all is evil, and of necessity we act in a way that contributes nothing towards our salvation? For if it is not we, but God alone, who works salvation in us, it follows that, willy-nilly, nothing we do has any saving significance prior to His working in us.

I said 'of necessity'; I did not say 'of compulsion'; I meant, by a necessity, not of *compulsion*, but of what they call *immutability*. That is to say: a man without the Spirit of God does not do evil against his will, under pressure, as though he were taken by the scruff of the neck and dragged into it, like a thief or footpad being dragged off against his will to punishment; but he does it spontaneously and voluntarily. And this willingness or volition is something which he cannot in his own strength eliminate, restrain or alter. He goes on willing and desiring to do evil; and if external pressure forces him to act otherwise, nevertheless his will within remains averse to so doing and chafes under such constraint and opposition. But it would not thus chafe were it being changed, and were it yielding to constraint willingly. This is what we mean by *necessity of immutability*:

that the will[1] cannot change itself, nor give itself another bent, but, rather, is the more provoked to crave the more it is opposed, as its chafing proves; for this would not occur, were it free or had 'free-will'. Ask experience how impervious to dissuasion are those whose hearts are set on anything! If they abandon their quest of it, they only do so under pressure, or because of some counter-attraction, never freely—whereas, when their hearts are not thus engaged, they spare their labour, and let events take their course. On the other hand: when God works in us, the will is changed under the sweet influence of the Spirit of God. Once more it desires and acts, not of compulsion, but of its own desire and spontaneous inclination. Its bent still cannot be altered by any opposition; it cannot be mastered or prevailed upon even by the gates of hell; but it goes on willing, desiring and loving good, just as once it willed, desired and loved evil. Experience proves this too. How firm and invincible are holy men, who, when forcibly constrained to sin, are the more provoked thereby to desire good—even as flames are fanned, rather than quenched, by the wind. Here, too, there is no freedom, no 'free-will', to turn elsewhere, or to desire anything else, as long as the Spirit and grace of God remain in a man.

In a word: if we are under the god of this world, strangers to the work of God's Spirit, we are led captive by him at his will, as Paul said to Timothy (2 Tim. 2.26), so that we cannot will anything but what he wills. For he is a 'strong man armed,' who keeps his palace to such good effect that those he holds are at peace, and raise no stir or feeling against him—otherwise, Satan's kingdom would be divided against itself, and could not stand; but Christ says it does stand. And we acquiesce in his rule willingly and readily, according to the nature of willingness, which, if constrained, is not 'willingness'; for constraint means rather, as one would say, 'unwillingness'.[2] But if a stronger appears, and overcomes Satan, we are once more servants and captives, but now desiring and willingly doing what *He* wills—which is royal freedom (cf. Luke 11.18-22).

So man's will is like a beast standing between two riders. If God rides, it wills and goes where God wills: as the Psalm says,

[1] *voluntas.*   [2] *noluntas.*

'I am become as a beast before thee, and I am ever with thee' (Ps. 73.22-3). If Satan rides, it wills and goes where Satan wills. Nor may it choose to which rider it will run, or which it will seek; but the riders themselves fight to decide who shall have and hold it.

(ix) *That a will which has no power without grace is not free* (635-638)

What if I prove from the very words in which you assert 'free-will' that there is no such thing as 'free-will'? and show that you unwittingly deny what you are trying with such vast sagacity to affirm? Why, if I fail here, I promise you that all I write against you in this book shall be withdrawn, and all that your Diatribe advances and seeks to establish against me shall be ratified!

You describe the power of 'free-will' as small, and wholly ineffective apart from the grace of God.[1] Agreed? Now then, I ask you: if God's grace is wanting, if it is taken away from that small power, what can it do? It is ineffective, you say, and can do nothing good. So it will not do what God or His grace wills. Why? Because we have now taken God's grace away from it, and what the grace of God does not do is not good. Hence it follows that 'free-will' without God's grace is not free at all, but is the permanent prisoner and bondslave of evil, since it cannot turn itself to good. This being so, I give you full permission to enlarge the power of 'free-will' as much as you like; make it angelic, make it divine, if you can!—but when once you add this doleful postscript, that it is ineffective apart from God's grace, straightway you rob it of all its power. What is *ineffective* power but (in plain language) *no* power? So to say that 'free-will' exists and has power, albeit ineffective power, is, in the Sophists' phrase, a contradiction in terms.[2] It is like saying ' "free-will" is something which is not free'—as if you said that fire is cold and earth hot. Fire certainly has power to heat; but if hell-fire (even) was cold and chilling instead of

---

[1] '*As in those who lack grace (special grace, I mean) reason is darkened but not destroyed, so it is probable that their power of will is not wholly destroyed, but has become ineffective for upright actions.*'

[2] *oppositum in adiecto.*

burning and scorching, I would not call it 'fire', let alone 'hot' (unless you meant to refer to an imaginary fire, or a painted one). Note, however, that if we meant by 'the power of free-will' the power which makes human beings fit subjects to be caught up by the Spirit and touched by God's grace, as creatures made for eternal life or eternal death, we should have a proper definition. And I certainly acknowledge the existence of *this* power, this fitness, or 'dispositional quality' and 'passive aptitude' (as the Sophists call it), which, as everyone knows, is not given to plants or animals. As the proverb says, God did not make heaven for geese!

It is a settled truth, then, even on the basis of your own testimony, that we do everything of necessity, and nothing by 'free-will'; for the power of 'free-will' is nil, and it does no good, nor can do, without grace. (Unless you intend 'efficacy' to be taken in a new sense, as implying completion, and are suggesting that 'free-will' can actually will and begin a thing, though it cannot complete it. This I do not believe; I shall say more on the point later.) It follows, therefore, that 'free-will' is obviously a term applicable only to the Divine Majesty; for only He can do, and does (as the Psalmist sings) 'whatever he wills in heaven and earth' (Ps. 135.6). If 'free-will' is ascribed to men, it is ascribed with no more propriety than divinity itself would be—and no blasphemy could exceed that! So it befits theologians to refrain from using the term when they want to speak of human ability, and to leave it to be applied to God only. They would do well also to take the term out of men's mouths and speech, and to claim it for their God, as if it were His own holy and awful Name. If they must at all hazards assign some power to men, let them teach that it must be denoted by some other term than 'free-will'; especially since we know from our own observation that the mass of men are sadly deceived and misled by this phrase. The meaning which it conveys to their minds is far removed from anything that theologians believe and discuss. The term 'free-will' is too grandiose and comprehensive and fulsome. People think it means what the natural force of the phrase would require, namely, a power of freely turning in any direction, yielding to none and subject to none. If they knew that this was not so, and that the term signifies only a tiny spark of power, and that utterly ineffective in itself, since it is the devil's prisoner and slave, it would be a wonder if they did not stone us as mockers and deceivers, who say one thing and mean another—indeed, who have not yet decided what we do mean! For, as the wise man says, 'he who speaks sophistically is hateful' (? Pr. 6.17), especially if he does so in matters of religion, where eternal salvation is at stake.

Since, therefore, we have lost the meaning and the real reference of this glorious term, or, rather, have never grasped them (as was claimed by the Pelagians, who themselves mistook the phrase) why do we cling so tenaciously to an empty word, and endanger and delude faithful people in consequence? There is no more wisdom in so doing than there is in the modern foible of kings and potentates, who retain, or lay claim to, empty titles of kingdoms and countries, and flaunt them, while all the time they are really paupers, and anything but the possessors of those kingdoms and countries. We can tolerate their antics, for they fool nobody, but just feed themselves up— unprofitably enough—on their own vainglory. But this false idea of 'free-will' is a real threat to salvation, and a delusion fraught with the most perilous consequences.

Most people would be amused, or, more likely, infuriated if at this late hour a linguistic revolutionary threw overboard established usage, and tried in its place to introduce the practice of calling a beggar *wealthy*, not because he had any wealth, but because it was possible that a king might give him his—and talked in this way, not as a figure of speech, like sarcasm or irony, but with all apparent seriousness. Thus, he would call one who was sick unto death *perfectly healthy*, on the ground that another might give him his health. Or he would call an unlettered idiot *a learned man*, on the ground that another might give him his learning. It is no different to say, *man has 'free-will'* —merely on the ground that God might grant him His! By thus misusing language, anyone can boast that he has anything: for instance, that he is the lord of heaven and earth—if God would give him that distinction! But such talk is more appropriate to actors and confidence tricksters[1] than to

---

[1] *quadruplatorum.*

theologians! Our words should be correct, pure and sober—in Paul's phrase, 'sound speech, that cannot be condemned' (Tit. 2.8).

If we do not want to drop this term altogether—which would really be the safest and most Christian thing[1] to do—we may still in good faith teach people to use it to credit man with 'free-will' in respect, not of what is above him, but of what is below him. That is to say, man should realise that in regard to his money and possessions he has a right to use them, to do or to leave undone, according to his own 'free-will'—though that very 'free-will' is overruled by the free-will of God alone, according to His own pleasure. However, with regard to God, and in all that bears on salvation or damnation, he has no 'free-will', but is a captive, prisoner and bondslave, either to the will of God, or to the will of Satan.

(x) *Conclusion of this section* (638-639)

These observations of mine on the heads of your Preface cover nearly the whole matter under debate, almost more so than does the body of the book to follow. The essence of what I have said can be put in a nutshell in the following dilemma: Your Preface states objections either to the words of God or to the words of men. If the latter, it is all written to no purpose, and does not touch me. If the former, it is all blasphemy. In view of that, it would have been helpful had it been plainly stated whether it was about the words of God or of men that we were arguing. But maybe that will come up in the Prologue which follows, or in the main discussion.

Your recapitulation at the close of the Preface does not impress me one whit. You call my doctrines *fables and useless things*; you say *that Christ crucified should rather be preached according to Paul's example; that wisdom should be taught among the perfect; that the language of Scripture is accommodated to the various capacities of the hearers; and that you therefore think it is best left to the discretion and charity of the instructor to teach what will profit his neighbour.* Silly, ignorant remarks, all of them! We teach nothing save Christ crucified. But Christ crucified brings all these

---

[1] *religiosissimum.*

doctrines with Him, including 'wisdom also among them that are perfect.' No other wisdom may be taught among Christians than that which is 'hidden in a mystery,' and this belongs only to the 'perfect'—not to the sons of a Judaizing, law-bound generation which has no faith and boasts of its works! So thinks Paul; see 1 Cor. 2 (vv. 6ff.). Do you, I wonder, take preaching Christ crucified to be just a matter of calling out "Christ was crucified," and nothing more?

As for your remark that '*God is represented as angry, furious, hating, grieving, pitying, repenting, none of which passions have any place in him,*' this is mere carping obstructionism.[1] These expressions do not make Scripture obscure, nor do they need adapting to the various capacities of the hearers—unless, of course, one likes creating difficulties where none exist! They are accepted forms of language—figures of speech which even schoolboys know about. What we debate in this case, however, is not linguistic figures, but doctrines.

---

[1] *hic nodus in scirpo quaeritur.*

III

REVIEW OF ERASMUS' INTRODUCTION
(*W.A.* 639-661)

(i) *That the authority of antiquity can be no sure proof of 'free-will'*
(639-649)

AT the outset of the disputation proper, you pledge yourself
*to argue from the canonical Scriptures, since Luther submits to the
authority of no extra-canonical writer.* Thank you! I welcome that
promise, even though you make it merely to save yourself
fruitless labour and not because you judge those other writers
immaterial for the matter in hand. For you do not quite approve
of my—presumption, shall we say? or whatever it is that this
principle of mine should be called. *You are much influenced* (you
tell us) *by the great array of learned men, objects of many centuries'
unanimous acclaim, some of them expert Biblical scholars, some of them
great saints, some martyrs, many renowned for miracles, plus the
theologians of more recent times and an abundance of schools, councils,
bishops and popes beside. In short* (you say) *there stands on your side
scholarship, ability, numbers, dignity, distinction, courage, holiness,
miracles and what not else, while on my side there is just Wycliffe and
Laurentius Valla* (though Augustine, whom you do not mention,
is entirely with me). *But these latter* (you say) *have no weight as
compared with the others. Which leaves only Luther—a man of no standing, a youngster—together with his friends; who can boast no such
scholarship, or ability, or numbers, or dignity, or holiness, or miracles.
Why* (you say) *they could not cure a lame horse! They make a parade
of Scripture, though they are as uncertain about it as their opponents;
they boast of having the Spirit, but nowhere show it forth*—and there
are other things which by dint of copious utterance you are able
to enumerate. *So* (you conclude) *there is really nothing to us; as the
wolf said to the nightingale that he had eaten: 'You're a voice—and*

that's all!' They speak; and for that reason alone (you say) *they expect to be believed!*[1]

I grant, my good Erasmus, that you may well be influenced by these considerations. For more than ten years they so influenced me that I should not think any other mortal was ever so deeply moved by them. I, too, thought it incredible that this Troy of ours, so often assaulted and so long unconquered, could ever be taken. And I call God witness against my soul, that I would have continued so, and would be under their influence to-day, had not constraint of conscience and evidence of facts forced me on to a different road. Doubtless you can appreciate that my heart is not made of stone; and that, had it been stone, it could not but have been softened by the buffeting received in my struggle with the waves and the storms, as I dared to do that which, once done, must, as I saw, bring down the whole weight of the authority of those whom you have listed like a deluge upon my head. But this is no place for composing a history of

---

[1] The section of the Diatribe which Luther here discusses may be quoted at length: '*However, I would like to impress upon the reader that, if I shall appear to be Luther's equal in the matter of testimonies from the Divine Scripture and solid arguments, he should then set before his eyes the very great array of most learned men, acclaimed by many ages down to the present day, many of whom, over and above their admirable skill in the Holy Scriptures, are recommended by godliness of life, and some of whom bore witness with their blood to the doctrine of Christ which they had defended by their writings . . . not to mention the authority of many schools, councils, and supreme pontiffs. From the times of the Apostles to the present day, no writer has so far appeared who would sweep away the power of "free-will" altogether, save only Manichaeus, and John Wycliffe. (The authority of Laurentius Valla, who seems almost to agree with them, does not carry much weight with the theologians.) . . . If the reader sees that the equipage of my argument fights on equal terms with its adversary, then let him ponder whether he thinks that more weight is due to the precedents of so many scholars, saints, martyrs, theologians ancient and modern, schools, councils, bishops and supreme pontiffs, or to the private judgment of one or two individuals. I admit that it is right that the authority of the Divine Scripture alone should prevail above all the judgments of mortal man. But the controversy here does not concern the Scriptures. Each side embraces and does honour to the same Scripture: their conflict concerns the sense of Scripture. . . . I am told: "What need is there of an expositor* (interprete), *when the Scripture is clear?" If it is so clear, why were excellent men blind at this point for so many centuries, and that in a matter of such moment as our opponents would have it thought to be? . . . I am told: "What bearing has weight of numbers* (multitudo) *on the meaning of the Spirit?" I reply: what bearing has lack of numbers* (paucitas)? *. . . The Apostles would not have been believed, had not miracles procured belief for their doctrine . . . When the Apostles shook off vipers, healed the sick, and aroused the dead, then at last they were believed; and yet hardly so, so paradoxical was their teaching. Now, though our opponents put forward teaching that is generally considered to be almost more paradoxical still, none of them has so far appeared who could even cure a lame horse! Leaving miracles aside, would that certain persons would exhibit the sincerity and simplicity of Apostolic character, which for us slowcoaches* (tardiusculis) *would do in place of miracles! I say this, not specifically against Luther* (whom I do not know personally, and whose writings variously* (varie) *affect me as I read them*), *but of certain others of whom I have a nearer knowledge. . . .'*

my life and works. I did not undertake this debate with a view to self-advertisement, but in order that I might exalt the grace of God. What I am, and with what spirit and intent I have been caught up in these issues, I leave to the judgment of Him Who knows that all this has come to pass by His free-will, not mine— as the whole world should have realised long ago. This introduction of yours undoubtedly puts me in an invidious position, from which I cannot easily escape without exalting myself and slighting all these Fathers. Briefly, however, I will speak to it.

I am inferior in learning, ability, numbers, authority and everything else. Even you think so! But now, suppose I should ask you these three questions: what is the manifestation of the Spirit? what are miracles? and what is holiness? As far as I know you from your letters and books, you would stand revealed as such an ignorant simpleton that you could not utter a single syllable of explanation. Or suppose I should press the question, which of all those of whom you boast can you prove for certain to be, or to have been, a saint, or to have possessed the Spirit, or to have wrought miracles? I think you would sweat freely over your answer, and fruitlessly too! You say many things that are commonly accepted and publicly repeated in sermons; but you would not believe how much of their credibility and authority they lose when brought to the judgment of conscience. 'Many are accounted saints on earth, whose souls are in hell,' is a true proverb!

I will grant you, if you like (though you do not request it), that they all were saints, all had the Spirit, and all wrought miracles. But now tell me this: was any one of them a saint, did any one of them receive the Spirit, or work miracles, in the name of 'free-will', or by the power of 'free-wil,'l or to confirm the doctrine of 'free-will'? Far from it, you will say; all these things were done in the name and by the power of Jesus Christ, and to confirm the doctrine of Christ. But why, in that case, do you bring forward their holiness, possession of the Spirit, and miracles, to support the doctrine of 'free-will', which they were not wrought nor given to support? Their miracles, possession of the Spirit, and holiness, therefore, support us, who preach Jesus Christ, and not the strength or works of man.

And now, what wonder is it if those holy, spiritual, marvellous men were sometimes prepossessed by the flesh, and spoke and acted according to the flesh; when the selfsame thing happened more than once to the very apostles under Christ Himself? You do not deny—indeed, you assert—that 'free-will' is something with which neither the Spirit nor Christ have anything to do, but which is man's affair. Therefore, the Spirit, who was promised to extol Christ, certainly cannot preach 'free-will'. If, then, the fathers ever preached 'free-will', their words were certainly of the flesh (for they were but men) and not of the Spirit of God. Much less did they work miracles in confirmation of that doctrine! So your appeal to the holiness, the spirit and the miracles of the fathers is pointless; for what they prove is not 'free-will', but the doctrine of Jesus Christ, which contradicts the doctrine of 'free-will'.

But come now, you that support 'free-will' and claim that the doctrine concerning it is true, that is, that it has come from the Spirit of God—do you here and now show forth the Spirit, work miracles and give evidence of holiness! You who make such a claim owe at least this much to us who deny it. The Spirit, holiness and miracles should not be required of us, who deny, but from you, who assert. A mere negative does not propound anything, is not anything, is not obliged to prove anything, and needs no proof itself; it is the affirmative that needs proving. You assert that the power of 'free-will' is a fact in man. But no miracle from God has ever yet been seen or heard of in support of any doctrine about what is fact in man; miracles are only given to support doctrines that tell us facts about God! And we are instructed in Deut. 18 to receive no doctrine at all that is not first proved by signs from God (v. 22). Indeed, Scripture calls man 'vanity' and 'a lie'; which is just to say that all that is human is vanity, and lies! Come, then, come, I say, and prove that this doctrine of yours about a mere human vanity and lie is true! Where, now, is your demonstration of the Spirit? Where is your holiness? Where are your miracles? I see your abilities, your learning and your authority; but these are things that God has given to all the world alike. Come, then! We shall not compel you to work great miracles, nor to cure a lame horse, lest you should plead in excuse the carnality of the age (though God is wont to confirm His doctrine by miracles without respect to the carnality of the age; what moves Him is not the merits or demerits of a carnal age, but just mercy, and grace, and love of the souls that are to be established by solid truth unto their glory). You may choose to work as tiny a miracle as you like. Indeed, to prod your Baal into action, I here challenge and defy you to create a single frog in the name and by the power of 'free-will'! Why, the godless heathen Magi in Egypt could create frogs in abundance! (Note that I shall not burden you with the task of making lice, which not even they could produce!) I will suggest a more trifling matter still: take a single flea or louse—since you tempt and mock our God with your talk of curing a lame horse—take that, and combine all the powers and concentrate all the energies both of your god and of all your supporters; and if, in the name and by the power of 'free-will', you can kill it, you shall be conquerors, your cause shall be established, and we will at once come and adore that god of yours, the amazing louse-slaughterer! (Not that I would deny that you can remove even mountains; but it is one thing to say that a work was done by the power of 'free-will', and another thing to prove it.)

And what I have said of miracles I say of holiness also: If, out of the great lists of ages, men and all the other things you enumerated, you can point to a single work (if only the lifting of a straw from the ground), or a single word (if only the syllable *my*), or a single thought (if only the faintest sigh), springing from the power of 'free-will', by which men applied themselves to grace, or merited the Spirit, or obtained pardon, or prevailed with God in the slightest degree (I say nothing of being sanctified thereby), once more you shall be the victors, and we the vanquished. *Done in the name and by the power of 'free-will'*, I say; for there is abundant Scripture testimony to what is wrought in men by the power of Divine creation. And your party is unquestionably obliged to point out such a case; lest you should stand revealed as such ludicrous teachers that you broadcast throughout the world, with all the arrogance and authority you can command, doctrines concerning something of whose existence you cannot produce a single token. Your doctrines will be called inconsequential dreams—which is supremely discreditable to the great men of so many centuries, learned, holy, and miraculous, whose support you invoke! And then we shall have more respect for the Stoics than for you; for though they took it on them to describe such a wise man as they never saw, yet they did try to delineate some part of their ideal. But you can delineate nothing at all, not even the shadow of your doctrine!

I say the same of the Spirit too: If out of all the protagonists of 'free-will' you can produce one who had that modicum of strength of mind and heart which he needed to be able to disregard a single farthing, or to go without a single farthing, or to bear a single word or token of affront (I say nothing of despising riches, life and fame), and this in the name and by the power of 'free-will', once more the palm of victory shall be yours, and we will gladly admit defeat.[1] And such a concrete example you, who are so loud and proud in trumpeting forth the power of 'free-will', are bound to show us; otherwise you will once more stand revealed as setting up a will-o'-the-wisp, and doing as did the man who went to see a play in an empty theatre![2]

In fact, I can easily prove to you the exact opposite of your position: namely, that whenever such holy men as you boast of approach God to pray or deal with Him, they approach Him in utter forgetfulness of their 'free-will'; in self-despair they cry to Him for pure grace alone, as something far other than they deserve. Augustine was often thus; so was Bernard when, at the point of death, he said: "I have wasted my time, for I have lived a waster's life."[3] I see no mention here of a power that could apply itself to grace; all power is here condemned, because it was entirely turned away from grace. Admittedly, these selfsame saints, when engaged in argument, spoke of 'free-will' in a different strain. But that just illustrates what I see to be a universal experience: men are different when occupied with words and disputations from what they are when occupied with experience and practice.[4] In the former case, their speech does not accord with what they previously felt; in the latter, their feelings do not accord with what they previously said.

---

[1] *sub hastam libenter ibimus.*   [2] cf. Horace, *Epist.* I.18, 15 and II. 2, 128-130.
[3] *Perdidi tempus meum, quia perdite vixi.*   [4] *affectibus et operibus.*

Men should therefore be assessed, godly and ungodly alike, rather by what they feel than by what they say. But we grant you more yet. We will not ask of you miracles, or the Spirit, or holiness. Let us return to the doctrine itself. We ask of you only this: that you will just explain to us what work, word or thought your power of 'free-will' can evoke, or endeavour, or accomplish, so as to apply itself to grace. It is not enough to say, 'there is power! there is power! there is power in "free-will".' What is more easily said? But this is not the way of those most holy and learned men, the objects of so many centuries' acclaim! You must name the child (as they say in the German proverb); you must define what this power is, what it can do, what is done to it, what happens to it. For instance—I will put it very crudely—we want to know whether this power ought, or whether it tries, to pray, or fast, or work, or weary the body, or give alms. For if it is a power, it must do some work! But here you are more dumb than Seriphian frogs and fishes. And how are you going to define this power, when on your own testimony you yourselves are still undecided about it, differing among each other and inconsistent with yourselves? What can be done about a definition, when the very subject of it is not self-consistent?

And suppose that, after Plato's years have gone by, you find yourselves at last agreed about this power, and its work is then defined as praying, or fasting, or some such thing (perhaps it still lies hid among Plato's ideas)—who will assure us that your view is true, that it pleases God, and that we are right and safe in adopting it? Especially when you yourselves acknowledge that this is a fact about man, with which the testimony of the Spirit does not deal; for it was in the world, and discussed by philosophers, before ever Christ came or the Spirit was sent down from heaven. It is quite certain that this doctrine was not sent down from heaven, but sprang from the earth long before; weighty testimony is therefore needed to establish it as sure and true.

Allowing, then, that we on our side lack standing and are few, while you on yours are public figures and are many; that we lack education, while you are thoroughly learned; that we are stupid, while you are brilliant; that we were born yesterday, while you are older than Deucalion; that we never won public acknowledgment, while you have been acclaimed by many generations; that, in sum, we are sinners, carnal men and dolts, while you, by reason of your holiness, possession of the Spirit, and miracles, are fit to strike awe into the very devils; yet, for all that, grant us at least the right of Turks and Jews, to ask you to give the reason for your doctrine, as your friend Peter told you to do (cf. 1 Pet. 3.15). We make our request with the greatest moderation; that is to say, we do not demand that your doctrine be proved by holiness, or by possession of the Spirit, or by miracles (which yet we could do, by the same right with which you demand these things of others); why, we even grant you that you need not produce a single instance of a work, or word, or thought as evidence for your doctrine; you need only explain the doctrine to us, and just tell us what you would have it taken to mean, and in what form we are to understand it—and if you will not or cannot do this, then at least let us try to produce an example of it ourselves! You are as bad as the Pope and his men, who say: 'Do as we *say*, but don't do as we *do*!' Similarly, you say: 'this power requires that work be done;' so *we* shall prepare for action, while *you* remain at ease! Shall we not gain even this one request from you? The more numerous you are, the longer established you are, the more distinguished you are, the more universal your superiority over us, so much the more is it a disgrace to you that when we, who on all counts are as nothing in your eyes, want to learn and practice your doctrine, you cannot prove it, either by a miracle—even the slaughter of a louse—or by the least motion of the Spirit, or by the tiniest work of sanctity; nor can you point to a single instance, either of word or deed, that exemplifies it; and, further (and this is an unheard-of thing), you cannot even formulate it, nor tell us the meaning of your doctrine! O frivolous teachers of 'free-will'! What are you now, but '*a voice— and that's all*'? Who are they now, Erasmus, who '*boast of the Spirit, but have nothing to show*'; who '*speak only, and straightway want men to believe them*'? Are they not the members of your own party, whom you have exalted thus to high heaven? You do not even speak; yet what grandiose claims and demands you make! In Christ's name, therefore, we entreat you and yours, my good Erasmus, at least to allow us to be terrified at this peril to our conscience, and to tremble for fear, and at any rate to defer our assent to a doctrine which, as you yourself see, is nothing but an empty term and sound of syllables—'There is power in "free-will"'! there is power in "free-will"'!' And even if you completely succeed in proving and establishing all your arguments, it will still be nothing more. Why, it is still a matter of doubt among your own party whether the term means something or nothing; for they differ from each other, and are inconsistent with themselves. It is utterly iniquitous therefore, and the greatest pity in the world by far, that our consciences, which Christ redeemed by His blood, should be troubled by the ghost of this one little word, and a word of no certain meaning at that. And then, if we do not allow ourselves to be thus troubled, we are charged with unheard-of pride for slighting so many Fathers of so many centuries, who affirmed 'free-will'! But, as you see from what has been said, the truth is rather that they never defined anything at all concerning 'free-will', and the doctrine of 'free-will' is erected under cover of their reputation, though they cannot describe it, nor fix its name. Thus with a lying word men befool the world!

And here, Erasmus, I invoke your own advice, given above, that *questions of this kind be left alone, and that Christ crucified, and as much as suffices for Christian piety, be taught instead.* But this is what we have long been desiring, and doing. What else do we contend for, but that the simplicity and purity of Christian doctrine should prevail, and that what men have invented and brought in along with it should be left behind and disregarded? But you, who give us this advice, do not take it yourself; you do the opposite; you write Diatribes; you cry up the decrees of Popes; you vaunt the authority of men; you try every means of carrying us off into these strange pastures and foisting upon us things both unscriptural and unnecessary, so that we may spoil the simplicity and sincerity of Christian piety, and disorder it with man-made additions. From which we easily see that your advice to us did not come from your heart, and that you do not write anything in a serious spirit, but with the self-confidence of one who thinks that by the empty bubbles of his words he can lead the world where he pleases. In fact, however, you lead it nowhere; for you utter nothing at all but unadulterated contradictions, on every subject and at every stage; and one would be absolutely right to call you Proteus, or Vertumnus, in person,[1] and to say to you, in Christ's words, 'Physician, heal thyself!' (Luke 4.23). It is a disgrace to a teacher when his own error confutes himself!

Until you have proved your affirmative, then, we stand fast upon our negative. And we appeal to the judgment of all that company of saints of whom you boast—to the whole world, rather—as we make bold to say, and glory in saying, that we ought not to acknowledge something which is nothing, when no certain demonstration of what it is can be given; and that you are all in the grip of incredible presumption or madness when you demand that we should acknowledge it—and that for no other reason than that you, who are many, mighty and long-established, are pleased to assert something which you yourselves admit to be nothing! As though it were fit conduct for Christian teachers to befool poor people in matters of religion with something which is nothing, as if it were of great moment for their salvation! Where, now, is your shrewd wit of Greek genius? Once you had it, when you used to construct your falsehoods with at least a fair exterior; but here you lie bare-faced and in plain speech! Where is your stylish Latin (laboriously modelled on Greek), now thus fooling, and being fooled, over an utterly empty term? But this is what happens to thoughtless and evil-hearted readers of books: they assign the highest authority to all the things that were marks of infirmity in the fathers and the saints. The fault here is not in the authors, but in the readers. It is as though, on the ground of the holiness and authority of St. Peter, one should argue that all that St. Peter ever said was true, and that it was truth even when, from weakness of the flesh, he urged Christ not to suffer (see Matt. 16 [v. 22]), and when he told Christ to depart from him out of the ship (Luke 5.8), and on the many other occasions when he was rebuked by Christ Himself.

Such men are like those who for fun idly say that not everything that is in the Gospel is true, and pick on the occasion in John 8 (v. 48) when the Jews said to Christ: 'Do we not say well

---

1 Vertumnus was the Etruscan god of the changing seasons.

that thou art a Samaritan and hast a devil?'—or: 'He is guilty of death' (Matt. 26.66)—or: 'We found this fellow perverting our nation, and forbidding to give tribute to Caesar' (Luke 23.2). These protagonists of 'free-will' do the same thing, but with a different end in view; not deliberately, like those I mentioned, but in blindness and ignorance; for they pick on what the fathers, stumbling in the weakness of their flesh, said in favour of 'free-will', and go on to oppose it to what the same fathers, in the power of the Spirit, said elsewhere against 'free-will'; and they so press and force the issue that the better falls before the worse. So it comes to pass that they give authority to the inferior statements, because these make in favour of their own carnal opinion, and deny it to the better statements, because these make against that carnal opinion. But why do we not rather select the better statements? There are many such in the fathers! To take an example: what can be said that is more carnal, more utterly godless, sacrilegious and blasphemous, than what Jerome is wont to say: "Virginity peoples heaven, marriage earth"[1]—as though earth, not heaven, is the right place for the patriarchs, apostles and Christian husbands, and heaven for pagan vestal virgins without Christ! Yet is it these sentiments, and others like them, that the Sophists collect from the fathers to get themselves authority—for their weapon is numbers, rather than judgment. So did that idiotic Faber of Constance, who has just presented the public with his precious jewel, that is, his Augean stable[2]—thus ensuring that there might be something to make the godly learned feel sick, and vomit!

(ii) *That the true church, which is hidden from man's view, does not err* (649-652)

In passing, I will here reply to the passage where you describe it as *unbelievable that God should overlook an error in His church for so many ages, and not reveal to any of His saints a point which we maintain to be fundamental in Christian doctrine.* In the first place, we do not say that God tolerated this error in His church, or in any of His saints. For the church is ruled by the

[1] *ad Eustochium*, ep. 22.19.   [2] J. Faber, *Malleus in Haeresin Lutheranam* (1524).

Spirit of God, and Rom. 8 tells us that the saints are led by the Spirit of God (v. 14). And Christ abides with His church till the end of the world (Matt. 28.20). And the church is the pillar and ground of the truth (1 Tim. 3.15). This we know; for the Creed which we all hold runs thus, 'I believe in the *holy* catholic church.' So it is impossible that she should err in even the least article. Even should we grant that some of the elect are held in error throughout their whole life, yet they must of necessity return into the way before they die; for Christ says in John 8: 'None shall pluck them out of my hand' (John 10.28). But what is hard and problematical is just this: ascertaining whether those whom you call the church were the church—or, rather, whether after their lifetime of error they were at last brought back to the truth before they died. It does not at once follow that, if God suffered all those consummate scholars whom you quote to err throughout so many ages, therefore He suffered His church to err! Look at Israel, the people of God. There, out of a great number of kings over a long period of time, not one king is mentioned who did not err. Under Elijah the prophet, all the people and every public institution among them had gone astray into idolatry, so that he thought he was the only one left; yet, while the kings and princes, priests and prophets, and all that could be called the people and church of God, were going to ruin, God had reserved seven thousand to Himself (cf. 1 Kings 19.18). But who saw them, or knew them to be the people of God? And who will dare to deny that in our day, under these principal men of yours (for you only mention persons of public office and of great name), God has kept to Himself a church among the common people, while allowing all whom you mention to perish like the kingdom of Israel? For it is God's prerogative to bring down the chosen ones of Israel, and, as Ps. 77 says, to slay their fat ones (Ps. 78.31); but to preserve the dregs and remnant of Israel, according to Isaiah's words (cf. Isa. 10.22).

What happened under Christ Himself, when all the apostles were offended at Him, when He was denied and condemned by all the people, and only Joseph, Nicodemus and the thief on the cross were preserved? Was it not the former group who were then called the people of God? Indeed, there was a people of God remaining, but it was not so called; and that which was so called was not it. Who knows whether, throughout the whole course of world history from its beginning, the state of the church has not always been such that some were called the people and saints of God who were not so, while others, who were among them as a remnant, were the people and saints of God, but were not so called?—as appears from the histories of Cain and Abel, Ishmael and Isaac, Esau and Jacob. Look at the time of the Arians, when scarcely five catholic bishops were preserved in the whole world, and they were driven from their sees, while the Arians reigned everywhere, taking to themselves the public name and office of the church. Yet under these heretics Christ preserved His church; though in such a way that it was not for a moment thought or held to be the church.

Or show me a single bishop discharging his office under the kingdom of the Pope. Show me a single council at which they dealt with matter of religion, and not with gowns, rank, revenues and other profane trifles instead, which only a lunatic could consider the province of the Holy Ghost! Yet they are called the church, despite the fact that all who live as they do are lost, and are anything but the church. Even under them, however, Christ has preserved His church, though not so as to be called the church. How many saints do you think the Inquisitors alone have in time past burned and killed for heretical perversions, such as John Hus and those like him? And many holy men of the same spirit doubtless lived in their day.

Why do you not rather marvel at this, Erasmus: Since the world began, there have always been superior talents, greater learning, and a more intense earnestness among pagans than among Christians and the people of God. It is as Christ Himself acknowledges: 'the sons of this world are wiser than the sons of light' (Luke 16.8). What Christian can be compared with Cicero alone (to say nothing of the Greeks) for ability, learning and hard work? What then shall we say hindered them from finding grace? For they certainly exerted 'free-will' to the utmost of their power! Who dare say that not one among them pursued truth with all his heart? Yet we are bound to maintain that not one of them reached it. Will you say in this case too that it is unbelievable that God abandoned so many great men throughout the whole course of history and let them strive in vain? Certainly, if 'free-will' has any being and power at all, its being and power must have been present with such men as these, in some one case at least! But it availed nothing; indeed, it always wrought in the wrong direction; so that by this argument alone it can be proved clearly enough that 'free-will' is nothing at all, inasmuch as one can show no trace of it from beginning to end of the world!

But I return to the matter in hand. What wonder, if God should leave all the great men of the church to go their own ways, when He thus allowed all the nations to go their own ways, as Paul says in Acts (cf. Acts 14.16)? My good Erasmus, God's church is not so common a thing as the term 'God's church'; nor are God's saints so promiscuously found as the phrase 'God's saints.' The saints are pearls and precious jewels, which the Spirit does not cast before swine; but (as Scripture puts it) He keeps them hid, that the wicked may not see the glory of God! Else, if they were open to the recognition of all, how could they be so vexed and afflicted in the world as they are? So Paul says: 'Had they known him, they would not have crucified the Lord of glory' (1 Cor. 2.8).

I do not say this because I deny that those whom you cite are the saints and church of God; but because it cannot be proved that they really are saints, should anyone deny it; it is left completely uncertain; which means that no position is sufficiently guaranteed by their holiness to make good any doctrine. I call them saints, and so regard them; I call them the church, and so judge them—but by the rule of charity, not by the rule of faith. By which I mean that charity, which always thinks the best of everyone, and is not suspicious, but believes and assumes all good of its neighbour, calls every baptized person a saint. There is no danger involved if she is wrong; it is the way of charity to be deceived, for she is open to all the uses and abuses of every man, as being handmaid of all, good and bad, believing and unbelieving, true and false. Faith, however, calls none a saint but him who is proclaimed such by divine sentence; for the way of faith is not to be deceived. Therefore, though we should all look on each other as saints as a matter of charity, none should be declared a saint as a matter of faith, as if it were an article of faith that so-and-so is a saint. (In this way, that adversary of God, the Pope, canonizes as saints men of his own choice, whom he never knew, so setting himself in God's place [cf. 2 Thess. 2.4].) All that I say of those saints of yours—ours, rather—is this: that, since they differ among themselves, those should rather have been followed who spoke best (that is, for grace against 'free-will'), leaving aside those who through weakness of the flesh testified of the flesh rather than of the Spirit. So, too, in the case of those who are inconsistent, the places where they speak from the Spirit should have been picked out and held fast, and those where they savour of the flesh let go. This is the right course for the Christian reader, as being the clean beast that parts the hoof and chews the cud (cf. Lev. 11.3; Deut. 14.6)! But as it is we abandon our judgment and swallow everything indiscriminately; or else (what is more wretched still) we reject the better and acclaim the worse in one and the same author, and proceed to affix to those same worse parts the title and authority of his sanctity—which he gained, not by reason of 'free-will' or the flesh, but by reason of that which is best of all, even of the Spirit only!

(iii) *That all doctrines must be tested and judged by Scripture* (652-653)

What then shall we do? The church is hidden away, the saints are out of sight; what and whom shall we believe? As you yourself argue, and with great point, '*Who gives us assurance? How shall we detect the Spirit? If you regard learning, you find Rabbis in both camps; if you regard life, you find sinners in both camps; if you turn your eyes to Scripture, both sides claim it as their own. Furthermore, our controversy is not merely over Scripture (which is somewhat deficient in clarity at present), but over the precise meaning of Scripture; and here not the numbers, learning and distinction on the one side, much less the paucity, ignorance and lack of distinction on the other, can advance either cause.*' The matter is therefore left in doubt, and the case remains *sub judice*, so that it looks as if our most sensible course is to concur with the views of the Sceptics!—unless we follow

your own masterly policy of saying you are in doubt and professing that you seek truth and are trying to learn it, while at the
same time giving allegiance to the party that asserts 'free-will',
until the truth becomes plain! Here is my answer to you. What
you say is part of the truth, but not all of it. It is true that we
shall not detect the spirits by appeals to learning, life, abilities,
majorities, distinction, or to ignorance and lack of education, or
numbers, or standing. However, I do not applaud those who
take refuge in bragging about the Spirit. I fought last year, and
am still fighting, a pretty fierce campaign against those fanatics
who subject the Scriptures to the interpretation of their own
spirit. On the same account I have thus far hounded the Pope,
in whose kingdom nothing is more commonly said or more
widely accepted than this dictum: 'the Scriptures are obscure
and equivocal; we must seek the interpreting Spirit from the
apostolic see of Rome!' No more disastrous words could be
spoken; for by this means ungodly men have exalted themselves
above the Scriptures and done what they liked, till the Scriptures were completely trodden down and we could believe and
teach nothing but maniacs' dreams. In a word, that dictum is
no mere human invention; it is poison sent into the world by
the inconceivably malevolent prince of all the devils himself!

This is our contention: that spirits must be detected and
tried by a double judgment. The first is internal. By it, through
the enlightening of the Holy Ghost, the special gift of God, one
enjoys complete certainty in judging of and deciding between
the doctrines and opinions of all men as they affect oneself and
one's own personal salvation. Of this judgment it is said in
1 Cor. 1: 'The spiritual man judges all things, but he himself is
judged by no man' (1 Cor. 2.15). It belongs to faith, and is
needful for every Christian, even for a layman. This is what we
earlier spoke of as the *internal perspicuity of Holy Scripture*. Perhaps
this was in the mind of those who answered you by saying that
everything must be decided by the judgment of the Spirit.[1]
But this judgment benefits none but him who has it, and is not
our concern in this present debate. Nor, I think, does anyone
doubt its reality.

[1] '*When asked, by what proof the true interpretation of Scripture may be known, when men*
(homines) *stand on both sides, they reply: "by the judgment of the Spirit."* '

The second is an external judgment. By it, we judge the spirits and doctrines of all men, also with the greatest certainty, and not now for ourselves only, but also for the benefit and salvation of others. This judgment is the province of the public ministry of the Word and the external office, and is the special concern of teachers and preachers of the Word. We employ it when we strengthen the weak in faith and refute opponents. We spoke of this earlier as the *external perspicuity of Holy Scripture.* We hold that all spirits should be proved in the sight of the church by the judgment of Scripture. For it should be settled as fundamental, and most firmly fixed in the minds of Christians, that the Holy Scriptures are a spiritual light far brighter even than the sun, especially in what relates to salvation and all essential matters.

(iv) *That the teaching of Scripture is clear and decisive* (653-658)

But because we have been so long persuaded of the opposite, by that pestilent dictum of the Sophists, that the Scriptures are obscure and equivocal, we are compelled to begin by proving this very first principle of ours, by which all else must be proved (a procedure which to philosophers would seem irrational and impossible!).

First, Moses says in Deut. 17 (v. 8) that, if a difficult matter comes into judgment, men must go to the place which God has chosen for His name, and there consult the priests, who are to judge it according to the law of the Lord. 'According to the law of the Lord,' he says; but how will they thus judge, if the law of the Lord is not, externally, as clear as can be, so that they may be satisfied about it? Else it would have been enough to say: 'according to their own spirit!' Why, under any and every government all issues between all parties are settled by the laws. But how could they be settled if the laws were not perfectly clear, and were truly as lights among the people? If the laws were equivocal and uncertain, not only would no issues be settled, but no sure standards of conduct would exist. It is for this very reason that laws are enacted, that conduct may be regulated according to a definite code and disputes may find settlement. It is necessary, therefore, that that which is to be the measure and yardstick for others, as the law is, should be much clearer and more certain than anything else. If laws need to be luminous and definite in secular societies, where only temporal issues are concerned, and such laws have in fact been bestowed by Divine bounty upon all the world, how should He not give to Christians, His own people and His elect, laws and rules of much greater clarity and certainty by which to adjust and settle themselves and all issues between them? For He wills that His people should not set store by temporal things! 'If God so clothe the grass of the field, which to-day is, and to-morrow is cast into the oven,' how much more us (cf. Matt. 6.30)? But let us go on, and overwhelm this pestilent saying of the Sophists with passages of Scripture.

Ps. 18 (Ps. 19.8) says: 'The commandment of the Lord is clear (or pure), enlightening the eyes.' I am sure that what enlightens the eyes is neither obscure nor equivocal!

Again, Ps. 118 (Ps. 119.130) says: 'The entrance of thy words giveth light; it giveth understanding to babes.' Here it says of God's words, that they are an entrance, something open, which is plainly set before all and enlightens even babes.

Isa. 8 (v. 20) despatches all questions 'to the law and to the testimony,' and threatens that unless we comply the light of dawn must be denied us.

In Zech. 2 (Mal. 2.7), God commands that they should seek the law from the mouth of the priest; 'for he is the messenger of the Lord of Hosts.' But what a fine messenger and spokesman from God would he be, who should deliver messages that were unclear to himself and obscure to the people, so that he did not know what he was saying, nor they what they were hearing!

And what is more commonly said in praise of Scripture through, the whole Old Testament, especially in the 118th Psalm (Ps. 119), than that it is in itself a most clear, sure light? That Psalm makes mention of its clearness in these words 'Thy word is a lamp unto my feet, and a light unto my paths' (v. 105). The Psalmist does not say: 'thy Spirit alone is a lamp unto my feet,' though he assigns to the Spirit His part when he says: 'thy good spirit shall lead me into the land of uprightness' (Ps. 143.10). Thus Scripture is called a *way* and a *path*, doubtless by reason of its entire certainty.

Come to the New Testament. Paul says in Rom. 1 that the gospel was promised 'by the prophets in the holy scriptures' (v. 2), and in the third chapter that the righteousness of faith was 'testified by the law and the prophets' (v. 21). But what sort of testifying is it, if it is obscure? Yet throughout all his epistles Paul depicts the gospel as a word of light, a gospel of clarity, and makes this point with great fulness in 2 Cor. 3 and 4, where he treats of the perspicuity of both Moses and Christ in a very exalted manner.

Peter says in 2 Pet. 1: 'We have a most sure word of prophecy; whereunto ye do well that ye take heed, as unto a light that shineth in a dark place' (v. 19). Here Peter makes the Word of God to be a bright lamp, all else being darkness. Should we then make obscurity and darkness out of the Word?

Christ repeatedly calls Himself 'the light of the world' (cf. John 8.12, 9.5) and John the Baptist 'a burning and a shining light' (John 5.35). This, doubtless, was not on account of the holiness of his life, but by reason of his word. So Paul calls the Thessalonians shining lights of the world, because, he says, 'you hold forth the word of life' (Phil. 2.15-16). For life without the word is unsure and dark.

And what are the apostles doing when they prove what they preach by the Scriptures? Is it that they want to hide their own darkness under greater darkness? Are they trying to prove what is better known by what is less well known? What is Christ doing when in John 5 he teaches the Jews to 'search the Scriptures,' because they testify of Him (v. 39)? Did he want to make them uncertain about faith in Himself? What were those mentioned in Acts 17 doing, who, after hearing Paul, read the Scriptures night and day to see 'whether those things were so' (v. 11)? Does not all this prove that the apostles, like Christ Himself, appealed to Scripture as the clearest witness to the truth of what they were saying? With what conscience, then, do we make them to be obscure?

Tell me, are these words of Scripture obscure or equivocal: 'God created the heavens and the earth' (Gen. 1.1): 'the Word was made flesh' (John 1.14): and all the other items which the whole world has received as articles of faith? Whence were they received? Surely, from the Scriptures! What do preachers to-day do? They expound and proclaim the Scriptures! But if the Scripture they proclaim is obscure, who will assure us that their proclamation is dependable? Shall there be a further new proclamation to assure us? But who will make that proclamation? (At this rate we shall go on *ad infinitum*!)

In a word: if Scripture is obscure or equivocal, why need it have been brought down to us by act of God? Surely we have enough obscurity and uncertainty within ourselves, without our obscurity and uncertainty and darkness being augmented from heaven! And how then shall the apostle's word stand: 'All Scripture is given by inspiration of God, and is profitable for doctrine, for reproof, for correction?' (2 Tim. 3.16). No, no, Paul, you are altogether unprofitable; such blessings as you ascribe to Scripture must be sought from the fathers, who have found acceptance down the long line of the ages, and from the see of Rome. You must revoke the judgment which you express when you write to Titus that a bishop should be mighty in sound doctrine, to exhort, and convince gainsayers, and stop the mouths of vain talkers and deceitful teachers (Tit. 1.9f.); for how shall he be mighty, when you leave him Scriptures that are obscure—arms of tow, and feeble straws for a sword? Christ, too, must needs revoke the words in which he falsely promises us: 'I will give you a mouth and wisdom which all your adversaries shall not be able to resist' (Luke 21.15). For they are bound to resist, when we fight them with mere uncertainties and obscurities! And why do you, Erasmus, draw up an outline of Christianity for us, if the Scriptures are obscure to you?

I am sure that I have already made myself burdensome, even to slow-witted readers, by dwelling so long and spending so much strength on a point that is as clear as can be. But I had to do it in order to overthrow that shameless blasphemy that the Scriptures are obscure; so that even you, my good Erasmus, might see what you are saying when you deny that Scripture is clear. In the same breath you ought to be telling me that all those saints whom you quote must needs be much less clear; for who gives us information about the light that was in them, if you make the Scriptures to be obscure? Those who deny the perfect clarity and plainness of the Scriptures leave us nothing but darkness.

Here you may say: all this is nothing to me. I do not say that the Scriptures are obscure at every point (who would be such a fool as to say that?), but just on this point, and on those like it. I reply: my remarks are not aimed at you only, but at all who hold such views. Against you particularly, I would say of the whole of Scripture that I do not allow any part of it to be called obscure. There stands within it the statement which we quoted from Peter, that the word of God is to us a lamp shining in a dark place. If part of the lamp does not shine, then it is a part of the dark place rather than of the lamp! When he enlightened us, Christ did not intend that part of His Word should be left obscure to us, for He commands us to mark the Word; and this command is pointless if the Word is not clear.

So if the doctrine of 'free-will' is obscure or ambiguous, then it is no concern of Christians, nor of the Scriptures, and should be left alone entirely and classed among the fables which Paul condemns in contentious Christians (cf. 1 Tim. 4.7). But if it is a matter of concern to Christians and to the Scriptures, then it ought to be clear, open and plain, just like all the other articles, which are perfectly plain. All the articles which Christians hold should be both fully certain to themselves, and also supported against opponents by such plain and clear Scriptures as to stop all their mouths, so that they can say nothing in reply. This was the burden of Christ's promise to us: 'I will give you a mouth and wisdom which all your adversaries shall not be able to resist.' But if our mouth is weak at this point, so that our adversaries can resist, His statement that no adversary should be able to resist our mouth is false. On this doctrine of 'free-will', therefore, either we shall have no adversaries (which will be the case if it is not our business), or, if it is our business, we shall have adversaries, certainly, but such as shall not be able to resist us.

However, this inability of our adversaries to resist (I deal with it, since it has come up here) does not mean that they are forced to abandon their view, or persuaded to acknowledge the truth, or to be silent. Who can force men against their will to believe, or confess their error, or be silent? 'What chatters more than an empty head?' says Augustine (*De Civ. Dei.* 5.26). What

is meant by their mouth being stopped is that they have nothing
to say in reply, and though they may say a great deal in reply,
yet the judgment of common sense is that they say nothing.
This is best demonstrated by examples.

When Christ in Matt. 22 silenced the Sadducees (vv. 23ff.),
by proving the resurrection of the dead with a Scripture quotation from Moses in Exod. 3 (' "I am the god of Abraham,"
etc. [Exod. 3.6]; He is not the God of the dead, but of the
living'), they were not able to resist or gainsay. But did they
therefore give up their view? How often did He confute the
Pharisees with the plaintest Scriptures and arguments, so that
the people could clearly see that they were worsted, and indeed
they knew it themselves? None the less, they continued to
oppose Him.

Stephen so spoke, Acts 7 tells us, that, on Luke's testimony
'they could not resist the spirit and wisdom with which he
spake' (Acts 6.10). But what did they do? Yield? No! Mad-
dened by mortification at being worsted, and by their own
inability to resist, they shut their ears and eyes and suborned
false witnesses against him (6.11f.). See how he confutes his
opponents as he stands before the council! Having listed God's
mercies from the beginning of the nation's life and proved that
God never commanded a temple to be built for Him (for that
was what he was on trial about; the dispute centred there), at
length he grants that there was a temple built under Solomon.
Then he takes up that point as follows: 'But the Most High
dwelleth not in temples made with hands.' To prove it, he
quotes from chapter 66 of the prophet Isaiah, 'What is the
house that ye build unto me?' (v. 1). Tell me, now, what could
they reply against so plain a Scripture? Yet they continued
unmoved in attachment to their own view. Whereupon he
attacks them directly, saying: 'Ye uncircumcised in heart and
ears, ye do always resist the Holy Ghost,' etc. He says that they
do resist, though they could not resist.

Come to our own day. John Hus preached against the Pope
from Matt. 16[1]: ' "The gates of hell shall not prevail against my
church" (v. 18). Is there any obscurity or ambiguity here? But
the gates of hell do prevail against the Pope and his men, for

---

[1] In his treatise, *De Ecclesia*, VII (1413).

they are notorious throughout the world for their open impiety and crimes. Is there anything obscure about that? Therefore the Pope and his men are not the church of which Christ speaks.' What could they gainsay here? How could they resist the mouth that Christ had given him? But they did resist, and persisted till they burnt him; so far were they from abandoning their views. Christ declares that this will happen when He says: 'Your *adversaries* shall not be able to resist.' They are adversaries, He says; so they will resist; else they would not be adversaries, but would become friends. Yet He says 'they shall not be able to resist.' What is this but to say that their actual resistance will show their inability to resist?

And if I too shall succeed in so confuting 'free-will' that my adversaries cannot resist, even though they persist in their views and, despite the protests of conscience, resist still, then I shall have done enough. For I know well enough by experience how reluctant we all are to admit defeat. As Quintilian says, there is none who would not rather appear to know than to learn. And this remains true, despite the proverbial refrain which all around us keep mouthing (more because it is in popular use, or rather misuse, than because it expresses their heart): 'I want to learn; I am ready to be taught and to follow the better when I am told it; I am man, and prone to err.' But under this mask, this fair semblance of humility, they may then confidently say: 'I am not satisfied. I do not grasp it. He does violence to the Scriptures. He asserts so obstinately'—taking it for granted, you see, that none will ever suspect such humble souls of obstinately resisting and vigorously assailing what they know to be true! And they take this line so that their failure to give in may have to be put down, not to ill-will, but to the obscurity and equivocation of our arguments! The Greek philosophers behaved in a similar way: rather than that one should admit defeat at the hands of another, they began to deny first principles, as Aristotle tells us. Yet all the time we cheerfully persuade ourselves and others that there are many good men in the world who will gladly embrace the truth if someone makes it plain; and that we must not suppose that so many scholars over so many centuries were all astray and ignorant. As if we did not know that the world is the kingdom of Satan, where, over and above the natural blindness engendered from our flesh, we are under the dominion of evil spirits, and are hardened in our very blindness, fast bound in a darkness that is no more human, but devilish!

(v) *That the blindness of man does not disprove the clarity of Scripture* (658-659)

'*But,*' you say, '*if Scripture is clear, why is it that men of superior ability throughout so many ages have been blind at this point?*'

I reply: They were thus blind for the praise and the glory of 'free-will', so that this highly-vaunted 'power by which a man can apply himself to things that concern eternal salvation' might be shown up for what it is—namely, a power which neither sees what it sees, nor hears what it hears, much less understands those things, or seeks after them. To it apply the words which Christ and the evangelists so often quote from Isaiah: 'Hearing ye shall hear and shall not understand, and seeing ye shall see and shall not perceive' (6.9). What is this but to say that 'free-will' (or, the human heart) is so bound by the power of Satan that, unless it be wondrously quickened by the Spirit of God, it cannot of itself see or hear things which strike upon ear and eye so manifestly that they could almost be touched by hand? So great is the misery and blindness of mankind! Thus, too, the very evangelists, when they wondered how it could be that the Jews were not won by the works and words of Christ, incontrovertible and undeniable as they were, answered themselves from that self-same passage of Scripture, which teaches that man, left to himself, seeing sees not and hearing hears not. What is more fantastic? 'The light shineth in darkness, and the darkness comprehendeth it not' (John 1.5). Who would believe it? Who ever heard of such a thing?—that light should shine in darkness, yet the darkness remain darkness, and not receive illumination!

Thus it is no wonder that in so many ages men of superior ability should be blind concerning the things of God. Such ignorance would be surprising on the human plane; but in the realm of divine things it would be more surprising if one or two were *not* blind! That all should be completely blind is no wonder at all. For what is mankind in the mass, without the Spirit, but the devil's kingdom, as I said, a disordered chaos of darkness? Hence Paul calls the demons 'rulers of this darkness' (Eph. 6.12), and tells us in 1 Cor. 1 that none of the princes of this world knew the wisdom of God (1 Cor. 2.8). What do you think is his opinion of the rest of men, when he tells us that the very princes of this world are slaves of darkness? And by 'princes' he means men of the first rank and the highest distinction—those whom you call men of superior ability! Why were all the Arians blind? Were there not among them men of superior ability? Why is Christ foolishness to the Gentiles? Are there not men of superior ability among the Gentiles? Why is He a stumbling-block to the Jews? Were there not men of superior ability among the Jews? 'God knoweth the thoughts of the wise, that they are vain,' says Paul (1 Cor. 3.20). He would not say 'of men,' as his text has it (cf. Ps. 94.11), but specifies the first and greatest among men, from whom we may form a judgment of the rest. But I hope to deal with this more fully later. Let it suffice for now to have laid down, by way of introduction, that the Scriptures are perfectly clear in their teaching, and that by their help such a defence of our position may be made that our adversaries cannot resist; and that what cannot be thus defended is not our business, and is of no concern to Christians. Any who cannot see the aforementioned clarity, and blindly stumble in the sunlight of Scripture, thereby reveal, if they are godless, how mighty is the dominion and power of Satan over the sons of men, which prevents them hearing and grasping the plainest words of God, and makes them like men whom an illusionist has mesmerised[1] into thinking that the sun is a cold cinder, or believing that a stone is gold. If they are godly, however, they are to be numbered among those of the elect who are led into a degree of error, in order that the power of God, without which we cannot see or do anything at all, may be displayed in us. For man's failure to grasp God's words does not spring from weakness of understanding, as you would suggest; indeed, there is nothing better adapted for grasping God's words than weakness of understanding, for it was for the weak and to the weak that Christ

1 *prestigio illusus.*

came, and to them that He sends His Word. No, the cause is the wickedness of Satan, who is enthroned and reigns over us in our weakness, and who himself resists the Word of God. If Satan did not do so, the whole world could be converted by a single word of God, heard once; there would be no need of more.

(vi) *Of the inconsistency o Erasmus in appealing to antiquity* (659-661)

Why need I enlarge? Why should I not end the discussion with this introduction, and bring in my verdict against you on the basis of your own words, according to Christ's dictum: 'By thy words thou shalt be justified, and by thy words thou shalt be condemned?' (Matt. 12.37). You say that Scripture is not clear on the matter on hand. Forthwith you suspend judgment and discuss the pro's and con's on each side—and you do nothing more all through your book! That is why you wished to call it a Diatribe (*discussion*) rather than an Apophasis (*denial*), or anything else, because your aim when you wrote it was to gather all the material without the intention of asserting anything. But if Scripture is not clear about it, why were your heroes so stupid and foolhardy in their blindness as to define and affirm 'free-will' as if they went on a basis of clear and certain Scripture teaching? I refer, of course, to your *great array of very learned men, unanimously acclaimed by many ages down to the present day, many of whom, over and above their admirable skill in the Holy Scriptures, are recommended by godliness of life, and some of whom bore witness by their blood to the doctrine of Christ which they defended by their writings.* Now, if you say this from your heart, then it is your fixed conviction that 'free-will' has had champions who were gifted with wonderful skill in the Holy Scriptures, and who even bore witness to 'free-will' by their blood. But if this is so, they surely possessed a Scripture that was clear; else, what becomes of their admirable skill in the Holy Scriptures? And what inconsiderate foolhardiness it would show, to shed one's blood over something obscure and uncertain! That befits the devil's martyrs rather than Christ's!

Now, do you just face and ponder this question: do you consider that more credit should be given to the judgments of all these scholars, orthodox divines, saints, martyrs, theologians ancient and modern, colleges, councils, bishops and supreme pontiffs, who were convinced that the Scriptures were clear and confirmed them both by their writings and by their blood; or to your own private judgment when you deny that the Scriptures are clear—you who, I dare say, never dropped a tear or uttered a sigh for the doctrine of Christ in your life! If you think they were right, why do you not follow them? If you think they were wrong, why do you cry them up with such a great fanfare of language, as if you wanted to drown me in the stormy deluge of your eloquence?—a deluge whose force is unloosed rather upon your own head, while my ark rides aloft to safety! In fact, you credit all these great men with a complete lack of sense and sobriety by describing them as experts upon Scripture, who asserted it by pen, and by life, and by death, while yet you maintain that Scripture is obscure and ambiguous! This is just to make them out to be wholly inexpert in their understanding and great fools in their asserting. Not even I, who as a private individual set little store by them, would have paid them so poor a compliment as do you, who stand up in public to sing their praises!

Here, then, I have you (as they say) on the horns of a dilemma.[1] One of your assertions *must* be false: either your verdict that they were men to be admired for their skill in the sacred writings, and for their life and martyrdom, or else your view that Scripture is not clear. And since you are more drawn in the latter direction, towards believing that the Scriptures are not clear (for you harp on this point all through your book), we are forced to conclude that it was to gratify pride, or to flatter, and not with any serious intent, that you spoke of these men as experts upon Scripture and martyrs of Christ; merely in order to throw dust in the eyes of an unlearned public, and to cause Luther trouble by burdening his case with empty expressions of spleen and contempt! But I maintain that in fact *neither* assertion is true; *both* are false. Firstly, I hold that the Scriptures are perfectly clear; secondly, I hold that the persons you mention, so far as they asserted 'free-will', were wholly inexpert in the sacred writings; but

[1] *cornuto . . . syllogismo.*

that they did not assert it by life or death, but only on paper, and that only when their mind was straying.

So I round off this little argument thus: By Scripture, as being obscure, nothing certain ever has been or could be defined concerning 'free-will'. I say this on your own testimony. By the lives of all men from the beginning of the world, nothing whatever has been disclosed that favours 'free-will'. That I proved above. And to teach something that is not laid down by a single word within the Scriptures, nor evidenced by a single fact outside the Scriptures, is appropriate for the 'true tales' of Lucian, but not for Christian doctrine! Except that Lucian, who seeks only to entertain with the sly humour of his comic narratives, deceives and injures nobody; but our adversaries of your party play the fool over a solemn matter that affects eternal salvation, and thereby ruin countless souls.

Thus I might finish this whole discussion about 'free-will', for even the testimony of my opponents makes for me and against themselves; and there is no stronger proof than the confession and testimony of the guilty party against himself! But since Paul instructs us to stop the mouths of vain talkers (cf. Tit. 1.11), let us advance upon the debate proper, handling the subject in the order in which the Diatribe proceeds. We shall *first* confute the arguments which it has brought forward for 'free-will'; *secondly*, we shall defend our own arguments, which it has attacked; *finally*, we shall do battle against 'free-will' for the grace of God.

IV

REVIEW OF ERASMUS' ARGUMENTS FOR 'FREE-WILL' (*W.A.* 661-699)

(i) *Of Erasmus' definition of 'free-will'* (661-666)

And, first, we will begin, as we should, from your actual definition. You define 'free-will' thus: '*Moreover, I conceive of "free-will" in this context as a power of the human will by which a man may apply himself to those things that lead to eternal salvation, or turn away from the same.*'

Cautiously, indeed, you here propound a bare definition, but give no account of any of its parts, as others normally do—perhaps because you feared a succession of shipwrecks! I am thus compelled to investigate the several parts myself. The thing defined, if closely examined, is undoubtedly of greater extent than the definition. This is the kind of definition that the Sophists call *vicious*[1]—that is, one in which the definition fails to cover the thing defined. For I showed above that 'free-will' belongs to none but God only. You are no doubt right in assigning to man a will of some sort, but to credit him with a will that is free in the things of God is too much. For all who hear mention of 'free-will' take it to mean, in its proper sense, a will that can and does do, God-ward, all that it pleases, restrained by no law and no command; for you would not call a slave, who acts at the beck of his lord, *free*. But in that case how much less are we right to call men or angels *free*; for they live under the complete mastery of God (not to mention sin and death), and cannot continue by their own strength for a moment. Here then, right at the outset, the definition of the term and the definition of the thing are at odds, for the term connotes one thing and what is really in mind is another. It would be more correct to call it 'vertible-will' or 'mutable-will.' In this way Augustine, and the Sophists after him, diminish the glory and force of the term 'free', qualifying it

---

[1] *vitiosam.*

with this limitation, which they call the 'vertibility' of 'free-will'. And it becomes us to speak in the same way, lest we befool men's hearts with swollen and vainglorious words; as Augustine also thinks. We should speak according to a definite rule, in sober and proper terms; for what is wanted in teaching is simplicity and logical correctness, not the high-flown figures of a rhetorical persuasive.

However, lest we should seem to delight in a war of words, let us allow you for the present this piece of abusage, serious and dangerous though it is: let 'free-will' be the same as 'vertible-will'. And let us also allow Erasmus to make 'free-will' to be 'a power of the *human* will' (as if the angels had no 'free-will'!); seeing that he proposes in this book to treat only of the 'free-will' of man. (Otherwise, the definition would be narrower than the thing defined at this point also.)

We come then to the parts of the definition, on which everything hinges. Some of them are clear enough; others shun the light, as if they had a guilty fear of something!—though nothing needs to be stated more clearly and precisely than a definition, for to define obscurely is simply to define nothing at all. The clear parts of the definition are these: 'a power of the human will' and 'by which a man can'; and 'to eternal salvation'. But the following are complete enigmas:[1] 'to apply'; and, 'to those things that lead'; and 'turn away'. What shall we divine that 'apply' means, and 'turn away'? And what are the 'things that lead to eternal salvation'? Where do they lurk? I see I am contending with a very Scotus or Heraclitus, and must spend my strength in a twofold task. First, I must find my adversary, by groping and feeling for him in pits and dark corners (a bold and hazardous enterprise); for unless I find him I shall fight in vain with phantoms and beat the air in the dark. Then, if I can bring him to light, I shall have to join battle with him on equal terms when I am already worn out with hunting for him. I suppose, then, that this 'power of the human will' means a power, or faculty, or disposition, or aptitude to will or not to will, to choose or reject, to approve or disapprove, and to perform all the other actions of the will. Now, what it means for

---

[1] *Andabatae:* gladiators whose helmets had no eyeholes and who therefore fought blind.

this same power to 'apply itself' or to 'turn away' I do not see, unless this refers to the actual willing or not willing, choosing or rejecting, approving or disapproving—that is, the very action of the will itself. So we must suppose that this power is something that comes between the will and its action, something by which the will itself elicits the act of willing or not willing, and by means of which the action of willing or not willing is elicited. Nothing else is imaginable or conceivable. If I mistake the meaning here, blame the author who gave the definition, not me who examine it; for it is rightly said in the legal world that the words of one who speaks obscurely when he could have spoken more plainly should be interpreted against himself. And here I do not want to hear anything about my friends the Moderns[1] and their subtleties; in the interests of teaching and understanding, we ought to state matters bluntly.[2]

As for those things 'that lead to eternal salvation', I suppose they are the words and works of God, which are offered to the human will so that it may apply itself to them or turn away from them. I take the 'words of God' to include both the law and the gospel: the law requires works, the gospel faith. There is nothing else that leads to the grace of God, or eternal salvation, but the word and work of God—grace, or the Spirit, being that very life to which the word and work of God lead us.

But this life, or salvation, belongs to the eternal order and is incomprehensible to human capacity, as Paul shows from Isaiah in 1 Cor. 2: 'Eye hath not seen nor ear heard, neither hath it entered into the heart of man to conceive, the things which God hath prepared for them that love him' (1 Cor. 2.9; Isa. 64.4). For it also is enumerated among the principal articles of our faith, when we say: 'and the life everlasting.' Paul tells us what 'free-will' avails with respect to this article in 1 Cor. 2: 'God' (he says) 'hath revealed (these things) unto us by his Spirit' (v. 10)—which means that, unless the Spirit revealed them, no man's heart would know anything about the matter; so impossible is it that man could ever apply himself to it or seek after it. Look at experience; see what the most distinguished

---

[1] *Modernos*: i.e. the exponents of the Nominalist *via moderna*.
[2] *crasse enim dicendum est.*

minds among the nations have thought of the future life and the resurrection. Is it not a fact that the more distinguished their minds were, the more ridiculous the resurrection and eternal life was to them? Or were not those philosophers and Greeks at Athens, who called Paul a 'babbler' and a 'setter forth of strange gods' when he taught these things (Acts 17.18), men of mind? Porcius Festus in Acts 24 (26.24) cried out that Paul was mad because of his preaching of eternal life. What of Pliny's yapping about these matters in his seventh book? What of Lucian, that great wit? Were these stupid men? To this day, it is true of most men that the greater their wit and learning, the more they deride this article, and that openly, thinking it a fable. For no man on earth, unless imbued with the Holy Ghost, ever in his heart knows of, or believes in, or longs for, eternal salvation, even if he harps upon it by tongue and pen. And may you and I be free from this leaven, dear Erasmus; so rare is a heart that believes in this article! Have I, now, the sense of this definition?

Erasmus informs us, then, that 'free-will' is a power of the human will which can of itself will and not will the word and work of God, by which it is to be led to those things that exceed its grasp and comprehension. If it can will and not will, it can also love and hate; and if it can love and hate, it can in measure keep the law and believe the gospel. For, if you can will and not will, it cannot be that you are not able by that will of yours to do some part of a work, even though another should prevent your being able to complete it. Now, since death, the cross, and all the evils of the world, are numbered among the works of God that lead to salvation, the human will will thus be able to will its own death and perdition. Yes, it can will all things when it can will the contents of the word and work of God! What can be anywhere below, above, within or without the word and work of God, except God Himself? But what is here left to grace and the Holy Ghost? This is plainly to ascribe divinity to 'free-will'! For to will the law and the gospel, not to will sin, and to will death, is possible to divine power alone, as Paul says in more places than one.

Which means that nobody since the Pelagians has written of 'free-will' more correctly than Erasmus! For I said above that 'free-will' is a divine term, and signifies a divine power. But no one to date, except the Pelagians, has ever assigned to it such power. The Sophists, whatever their views, certainly do not say anything like this! Why, Erasmus far outdoes the very Pelagians; for they ascribe this divinity to the whole of 'free-will', while Erasmus ascribes it to half only! The Pelagians posit two parts of 'free-will', a power of discernment and a power of choice, attributing the one to the reason and the other to the will; and the Sophists do the same. But Erasmus sets aside the power of discernment and exalts the power of choice alone. Thus he makes a lame 'half-free-will' into a God! What do you think he would have done had he set out to describe the whole of 'free-will'?

Not content with this, he outstrips the philosophers too. For it has never yet been settled among them whether a thing can move itself; on this point the Platonists and the Peripatetics disagree throughout the whole body of philosophy. But according to Erasmus 'free-will' not only moves itself by its own power, but 'applies itself' to the things that are eternal—that is, incomprehensible to itself! Here is a completely new and unheard-of person—a man whose definition of 'free-will' leaves philosophers, Pelagians, Sophists and all far and away behind! Nor does this satisfy him; he does not spare himself, but disagrees and crosses swords with himself more than with all the rest! For earlier on he had said that 'the human will is wholly ineffective without grace' (did he say it for a joke?); but here, when he gives a serious definition, he says that 'the human will has power by which it can effectively apply itself to those things that belong to eternal salvation'—that is, things that are incomparably beyond that power! So that at this point Erasmus outdoes even himself!

Do you see, my good Erasmus, that by this definition you betray (unwittingly, I think) that you know nothing at all of these matters, or at any rate that you write of them in a thoughtless, off-hand way, knowing neither what you say nor whereof you affirm? As I said above, you say less about, and assign more to, 'free-will' than all the rest; for you fail to give a complete account of 'free-will', and yet you ascribe to it all things. The Sophists, or, at any rate, their sire, Peter Lombard, give us a much more tolerable view. They say: " 'free-will' is a faculty of discerning, and then of choosing, good, if grace is with it, but evil only, if grace be wanting." Lombard clearly agrees with Augustine that " 'free-will' of its own power has no power but to fall, nor avails but to sin."[1] Accordingly, in his second book *Against Julian* (8.23) Augustine calls it a *slave* will rather than a *free* will.[2] But you make the power of 'free-will' to be equal in both directions: by its own power, without grace, it can (you tell us) both apply itself to good and turn itself from evil. You do not realise what a mighty power you are ascribing to it by the pronoun 'itself,' or 'its own self,' when you say: '*can* apply *itself*'; for you completely exclude the Holy Spirit and all His power as if superfluous and unnecessary. Your definition, therefore, ought to be condemned even by the Sophists; were they not in the blindness of their hatred so mad against me, they would fume rather against your book. But now, because you are attacking Luther, all that you say is holy and catholic, even though you speak against yourself and them! —so great is the patience of holy men!

Not that I say this because I approve of the Sophists' view of 'free-will', but because I think it more tolerable than that of Erasmus; for they approach nearer to the truth than he. Though they do not say, as I do, that 'free-will' is nothing at all, yet since they say that it can do nothing of itself without grace, (especially the Master of the Sentences[3]) they are at odds with Erasmus; indeed, they seem to be at odds with themselves, caught in the toils of a merely verbal debate, and more desirous of argument than of truth—just as Sophists should be! Suppose a Sophist of the best type were given me, with whom I could talk these things over privately in informal discussion, I should ask for his candid and unbiassed judgment like this: "If anyone should tell you that a thing was *free*, which of its own power could go only one way, that is, the bad way—it could indeed go the other way, that is, the good way, but not by its own power, only with the help of another—could you refrain from laughing, my friend?" For on these grounds I shall easily establish that a stone or a log has 'free-will', because it can go up and

---

[1] Lombard, *Sententiarum*, lib. II dist. 25.5; Augustine, *De Spiritu et Littera*, 3.5.
[2] *servum potius quam liberum arbitrium.*   [3] i.e. Peter Lombard.

down; though by its own power it can only go down, and can go up only with the help of another! And, as I said above, we shall end by overturning all usage of words and language and saying: 'All men are no man, and all things are nothing!'— referring one term to the thing as it is in itself, and the other to something extraneous that might come upon it or happen to it! It is in this way that, after long argument, the Sophists finally make 'free-will' free by accident,[1] in that it could at some point be set free by another. But we are inquiring about the thing as it is in itself, and the reality of 'free-will'. And if this is the question that is to be settled, nothing is left us but an empty term, 'free-will'—whether they will or no!

The Sophists are also defective in that they assign to 'free-will' the power of discerning good from evil. They leave no room for regeneration and the renewing of the Spirit, but devise an extraneous 'assistance' which comes to 'free-will' as from without; of which more later. For the moment, let us look at the arguments that are offered to inflate this empty little term.

(ii) *Ecclus. 15.14-17: an inconclusive testimony* (666-667)

First comes the passage from Ecclus. 15 (vv. 14-17): 'God from the beginning made man, and left him in the hand of his own counsel. He added also his commandments and his precepts, saying, If thou art willing to keep my commandments, and to keep continually the faith that pleaseth me, they shall preserve thee. He hath set before thee fire and water; and upon which thou wilt, stretch forth thine hand. Before man is life and death; and whichever pleaseth him shall be given unto him.'

Though I might with justice repudiate this book, yet for the present I receive it, so as not to lose time by entangling myself in a dispute about books received into the Jewish canon. You are somewhat biting and derisive yourself about that canon, when you compare the Proverbs of Solomon and the Love-song (as with a sneering innuendo you term it) to the two books of Esdras and Judith, and the History of Susanna and of the Dragon, and the book of Esther (though they have this last in their canon; in my opinion, however, it is less worthy to be held canonical than any of these). I would shortly reply in your own

[1] *per accidens.*

words: 'The Scripture is in this place obscure and ambiguous'; therefore, it proves nothing for sure. And since my part is that of denial, I demand that you produce a passage that declares in plain words what 'free-will' is, and what it can do. It will take you all eternity to do it.[1] In fact, you squander many fine words in an attempt to escape this necessity; you tip-toe along, citing your list of opinions about 'free-will'—almost making Pelagius into an Evangelical! Then you invent a fourfold grace, so that you may ascribe a sort of faith and charity even to the philosophers; and with it a threefold law, of nature, of works and of faith, so that you may roundly assert that the precepts of the philosophers agree with the precepts of the gospel; and then you take Psalm 4 (v. 6), 'The light of thy countenance is sealed upon us, O Lord,' which refers to the knowledge of the very countenance of God—that is to faith—and apply it to blinded reason! All this laid together compels a Christian to suspect that you are mocking and deriding the doctrines and religion of Christian people; for to ascribe such great ignorance to one who has surveyed all my writings as you have, and stored them up in memory with so much care, I find very difficult. But I am content to drop the hint; I will keep off that subject for the moment, till a more suitable occasion offers. Yet I beg you, my good Erasmus, not to tempt me so, like one of those who say: 'Who sees us?' (cf. Ps. 64.5?) It is not safe, with so weighty an issue at stake, to be perpetually trifling in every company with your verbal sleight-of-hand.[2] But back to the point.

(iii) *Of Erasmus' distinction of three views about 'free-will'* (667-671)

Out of one view about 'free-will' you devise three! The first, that of those who deny that man can will good without special grace, neither start, nor make progress, nor finish, etc. seems to you *'severe, but probable enough'*. You approve of it because it leaves man effort and endeavour, but does not leave him anything that he may ascribe to his own strength. The second, that of those who contend that 'free-will' avails for nothing but sinning, and that grace alone works good in us, etc., seems to you *'more severe'*; and the third, that of those who say

---

[1] *Hoc facietis forte ad Calendas graecas*, i.e. never.   [2] *verborum vertumnis*.

that 'free-will' is an empty term, and God works in us both good and evil, and all that comes to pass is of mere necessity, seems to you '*most severe*'. It is against these two last that you profess to be writing.

Do you know what you are saying, my dear Erasmus? You represent here three opinions, as if of three parties, simply because you fail to realise that it is the same thing in each case, stated by us same spokesmen of the selfsame party, but in different ways and different words. Let me instruct you, and show you the sleepy stupidity of your judgment.

How, I ask, does that definition of 'free-will' which you gave above square with this first view, which is '*probable enough*'? You said that 'free-will' is a power of the human will by which a man can apply himself to good; but here you say, and approve of its being said, that man without grace cannot will good. The definition affirms what the statement parallel to it denies! So there is found in your 'free-will' at the same moment a *yes* and a *no*, and in the same breath you say that we are both right and wrong, and that you yourself are both right and wrong, over one and the same doctrine and article! Do you think that to apply itself to what bears on eternal salvation (as your definition says that 'free-will' does) is not *good*? If there were enough good in 'free-will' for it to apply itself to good, it would have no need of grace! So the 'free-will' you define is one thing, and the 'free-will' you defend is another. Erasmus now has two 'free-wills', more than anyone else, and they are at loggerheads with each other!

But, leaving aside the 'free-will' which the definition invented, let us consider the opposite one which this view posits. You grant that without special grace man cannot will good (for we are not now discussing what God's grace can do, but what man can do without it); you grant, then, that 'free-will' cannot will good; and this is just to grant that it can *not* apply itself to what bears on eternal salvation—which was the burden of your definition! Furthermore: a little earlier, you say that *the human will after sin is so depraved that it has lost its freedom and is forced to serve sin, and cannot recall itself to a better state!* And if I am not mistaken, you make the Pelagians to have been of this mind. Now here, I think, no way of escape is open to Proteus; he is caught and held fast by his own plain words, namely, that the will has lost its liberty and is tied and bound in slavery to sin. O excellently 'free' will! which has lost its freedom and is declared by Erasmus himself to be the slave of sin! Yet when Luther said the same, *'nothing so absurd was ever heard of!'* *'nothing could be more useless than that this paradox should be broadcast!'*—and it was your bounden duty to write Diatribes against him!

Perhaps nobody will believe me when I say that Erasmus says these things. Let doubters read the Diatribe at this point; they will be surprised! Not that I am particularly surprised. A man who does not treat this question seriously and has no interest in the issue, whose mind is not on it and who finds it a boring and a chilling and a distasteful business, cannot help uttering absurdities and follies and contradictions all along the line; he argues his case like a man drunk or asleep, blurting out between snores 'Yes!' 'No!' as different voices sound upon his ears! This is why rhetoricians require passion in one who pleads a case. Much more does theology require passion, to make a man vigorous, and keen, and earnest, and prudent, and energetic!

If, now, 'free-will' without grace has lost its freedom, is forced to serve sin, and cannot will good, I should like to know what that effort and endeavour amount to which the first view, the 'probable' one, leaves it. It cannot be a good effort or endeavour, for 'free-will' cannot will good, as the view states and you grant. It remains, then, that it must be an evil effort and endeavour, which has lost its freedom and is forced to serve sin. Now what does *that* mean? Does this view leave man effort and endeavour, without leaving him anything that he may ascribe to his own strength? Who can form any conception of that? If effort and endeavour are left to the strength of 'free-will', why should they not be ascribed to the same? If they should not be ascribed to it, how are they left to it? Are then the effort and endeavour that go before grace left, not to 'free-will', but to that very grace that comes after, so that they are at the same time left and not left to one and the same 'free-will'? If these positions are not paradoxes, or freaks, rather, then what *are* freaks?

But maybe this is the dream of the Diatribe, that between these two things, 'ability to will good' and 'inability to will good', there may be a middle term, that is, 'willing' in the abstract,[1] without respect to good and evil; so that, by a logical finesse, we may now steer clear of the rocks and say that there is in man's will a certain *willing*; without grace it cannot indeed will good, but it does not forthwith will only evil; it is just *willing*, pure and simple, and may be directed either upwards by grace towards good, or downwards by sin towards evil. But what then becomes of your statement that *it has lost its freedom and is forced to serve sin*? Where then is that effort and endeavour that you left it? Where is its power to apply itself to that which pertains to eternal salvation? For that power of applying itself to salvation cannot be just *willing*, unless salvation itself is said to be *nothing*! Nor can that effort and endeavour be just *willing*; for effort must strive and aim for something (such as, good), and cannot be active or inactive with *nothing* as its end in view! In a word, wherever the Diatribe turns it cannot keep clear of inconsistencies and contradictions, nor avoid making that very 'free-will' which it defends as much a prisoner as it is itself. In trying to free the will it gets so entangled that it ends up bound, as 'free-will' is, in bonds indissoluble!

Moreover, it is a mere logical fancy that there is in man a middle term, *willing* as such; nor can those who assert it prove it. The notion sprang from ignorance of things and preoccupation with words. As though things always corresponded in fact to the verbal analysis of them! (The Sophists make endless errors over this.) The truth is rather as Christ puts it: 'He that is not with me is against me' (Matt. 12.30). He does not say: he that is not with Me is not against Me either, but is in an intermediate position! For if God is in us, Satan is out of us, and then it is present with us to will only good. But if God is not in us, Satan is, and then it is present with us to will only evil. Neither God nor Satan permits there to be in us mere *willing* in the abstract; but, as you rightly said, we have lost our freedom and are forced to serve sin—that is, we *will* sin and evil, we *speak* sin and evil, we *do* sin and evil.

See where truth, invincible and all-powerful, has driven the

---

[1] *absolutum velle.*

witless Diatribe! It has so made foolish its wisdom that when it intends to speak against me it is forced to speak for me against itself! This is just how 'free-will' does a good deed: in the very act of going against evil, it goes against good, and does evil more than ever! So that the Diatribe is in speech just what 'free-will' is in action! And the entire Diatribe is nothing but a noble act of 'free-will' condemning itself in its own defence, and defending itself by its own condemnation: that is, being doubly stupid while it wishes to look wise!

This, then, is what the first view comes to when compared with itself: it says that man cannot will anything good, but leaves him effort, which is not, however, his own!

Now let us compare this view with the two remaining. The second is the '*more severe*' one, which holds that 'free-will' avails for nothing but sin. This is certainly Augustine's opinion, which he expresses in many places, particularly in his book *Of the Spirit and the Letter*, in chapter four or five, if I am not mistaken (*De Spiritu et Littera*, 3.5), where he uses those very words. The third is the '*most severe*' view, that of Wycliffe and Luther: that 'free-will' is an empty term, and that everything we do is done of pure necessity. With these two views, we are told, the Diatribe is in conflict.

Here let me say this: perhaps I am not good enough at Latin or German to have succeeded in explaining the point; but I call God witness that by the words of the last two views I meant to say nothing, and wished nothing to be understood, but what is stated in the first view; nor do I think that Augustine intended anything but this, nor do I understand any other meaning from his words than what the first view affirms; so that the three views retailed by the Diatribe are to my mind nothing but the one view which I hold. For once it is granted and settled that 'free-will' has lost its freedom, and is bound in the service of sin, and can will no good, I can gather nothing from these words but that 'free-will' is an empty term whose reality is lost. A lost freedom, to my way of speaking, is no freedom at all, and to give the name of freedom to something that has no freedom is to apply to it a term that is empty of meaning. If I am wrong here, let him who can put me right. If this is obscure or ambiguous, let him who can clarify and confirm it. I for one cannot call lost health, health; and if I were to credit an invalid with health I should think I was applying to him just an empty term.

Away with such freaks of language! Who can endure the abuse of speech involved in our saying that man has 'free-will' while at the same time we maintain that he has lost his freedom, and is bound in the service of sin, and can will no good? These things are contrary to common sense, and utterly overthrow our use of language. The Diatribe is rather blameworthy for the sleepy way it burbles out its own words without regard to other men's. It does not, I repeat, weigh up what it means, and how far-reaching it is, to say that man has lost his freedom, and is forced to serve sin, and can will no good. Were it awake and on the look-out, it would see clearly that there is only one sentiment contained in the three views which it makes to be contrary and opposite. For if a man has lost his freedom, and is forced to serve sin, and cannot will good, what conclusion can more justly be drawn concerning him, than that he sins and wills evil *necessarily*? Even the Sophists by their syllogisms would conclude as much. Whereas the Diatribe, unhappily enough, declares war on the last two views and approves the first, which is precisely the same as the other two; thus once more (as usual) condemning itself and approving my sentiments at one and the same moment.

(iv) *Ecclus. 15.14-17 (contd.): man, as subject to the will of God, is not free* (671-672)

Now let us come to that passage in Ecclesiasticus, and compare with it that first view, the '*probable*' one! The view states that 'free-will' cannot will good. The passage in Ecclesiasticus is cited to prove that 'free-will' is something and can do something. So the view which should be proved by Ecclesiasticus asserts one thing, and Ecclesiasticus is quoted to prove another! —as if one who wished to prove that Christ was Messiah should quote a passage which proves that Pilate was governor of Syria, or something equally inappropriate! This is how 'free-will' is proved here (not to advert to my earlier point, that no clear and definite statement or proof is given of what 'free-will' is and what it can do). It is worth while to look through the whole passage. First it says: 'God made man at the beginning.' Here it speaks of man's creation; it says nothing as yet of either 'free-will' or commandments. Then it goes on: 'and left him in the hand of his own counsel.' What have we here? Is this where 'free-will' is erected? But there is no mention here of commandments, for the performance of which 'free-will' is required; we read nothing of this in the reference to man's creation. If anything is to be understood by 'the hand of his own counsel', what should rather be understood is the fact, recorded in Gen. 1 and 2, that man was made lord of all things so that he might freely rule them, as Moses says: 'Let us make man to have dominion over the fishes of the sea' (cf. Gen. 1.26). Nothing else can be evinced from the words. For there man certainly could act according to his own will, all these things having been put under his control. Furthermore, it calls this 'the counsel of man', as being a different thing from the counsel of God.

After this, having said that man was thus made and left in the hand of his own counsel, it proceeds: 'He added also his commandments and his precepts.' Added them to what? Obviously to that counsel and will of man, over and above the constitution of man's dominion over other things. By these commandments He took from man his dominion over one part of the created order (that is, the tree of knowledge of good and evil), and willed rather that he should *not* be free. Having added the commandments, the text then comes to the will of man towards God and the things of God. 'If thou art willing to keep the commandments, they shall preserve thee,' etc.

With the words, then, 'If thou art willing,' the discussion of 'free-will' begins. So we learn from Ecclesiasticus that man falls under two kingdoms. In the one, he is led by his own will and counsel, not by any precepts and commandments of God; that is, in the realm of things below him. Here he reigns and is lord, as being left in the hand of his own counsel. Not that God leaves him alone in the sense that He does not co-operate with him in all things; but in the sense that He has granted him a free use of things at his own will, and not hedged him in with any laws or commands. You could say by way of parallel that the gospel has left us in the hand of our own counsel, to use and have dominion over things as we will; whereas Moses and the Pope did not leave us to that counsel, but constrained us by laws and subjected us rather to their will. In the other kingdom, however, man is not left in the hand of his own counsel, but is directed and led by the will and counsel of God. As in his own kingdom he is led by his own will, and not by the precepts of another, so in the kingdom of God he is led by the precepts of another, and not by his own will. This is what Ecclesiasticus means when he says: 'He added also his commandments and his precepts, saying, If thou art willing,' etc.

If, now, this is sufficiently plain, I have demonstrated that this passage of Ecclesiasticus does not make for 'free-will', but against it, inasmuch as it subjects man to the precepts and will of God, and takes his 'free-will' from him. If it is not sufficiently plain, I have at least ensured that this passage cannot count in favour of 'free-will', inasmuch as it can be understood in a sense different from that of our opponents, that is, in my sense already stated, which is not absurd, but is extremely sound, and in harmony with the whole Scripture; whereas their sense goes against the whole Scripture, and is derived from this one passage only, against the tenor of the whole Scripture. I stand secure upon the good sense, and upon my denial of 'free-will', until they shall confirm their strained and forced affirmation of it!

So when Ecclesiasticus says, 'If thou art willing to keep the commandments, and to keep the faith that pleaseth me, they shall preserve thee,' I fail to see how 'free-will' can be proved from his words. 'If thou art willing' is a verb in the subjunctive mood, which asserts nothing. As the logicians say, a conditional statement asserts nothing indicatively—such statements as, 'if the devil be God, he is deservedly worshipped'; or, 'if an ass flies, an ass has wings'; or, 'if there be "free-will", grace is nothing'. And if Ecclesiasticus had wished to assert 'free-will', he ought to have spoken thus: 'man is able to keep God's commandments'; or, 'man has power to keep the commandments'.

(v) *That a command does not always imply ability to fulfil it* (673-674)

Here the Diatribe will retort: '*Ecclesiasticus, by saying "if thou art willing to keep", indicates that there is a will in man to keep or not to keep; otherwise, what is the sense of saying to him who has no will, "if thou wilt"? Is it not ridiculous to say to a blind man: "if thou art willing to see, thou wilt find a treasure"? or to a deaf man: "if thou art willing to hear, I will tell thee a good story"? That would be mocking their misery.'*

I reply: These are arguments of human reason, which is wont to pour out wisdom of this sort. Wherefore, I now have to dispute, not with Ecclesiasticus, but with human reason, concerning an inference; for reason, by her inferences and syllogisms, explains and pulls the Scriptures of God whichever way she likes. I shall enter this dispute readily and with confidence, for I know that all her gabblings are stupid and absurd, and especially so when she begins to make a show of her wisdom in holy things.

First then: if I ask how it is proved that the existence of 'free-will' in man is indicated and implied wherever the phrases 'if thou art willing', 'if thou shalt do', 'if thou shalt hear', are used, she will say, 'Because the nature of words and use of language among men seem to require it.' Therefore, she bases her judgment of things and words that are of God upon the customs and concerns of men; and what is more perverse than that, when the former are heavenly and the latter earthly? Thus in her stupidity she betrays herself as thinking of God only as of man.

But what if I prove that the nature of words and use of language, even among men, is not always such as to make it an act of mockery to say to the impotent, 'if thou art willing', 'if thou shalt do', 'if thou shalt hear'? How often do parents thus play with their children, bidding them come to them, or do this or that, only in order that it may appear how impotent they are, and that they may be compelled to call for the help of the parent's hand? How often does a faithful physician tell an obstinate patient to do or stop doing things that are impossible or injurious to him, so as to bring him by experience of himself to a knowledge of his disease or weakness, to which he cannot lead him by any other course? And what is more common and widespread than to use insulting and provoking language when we would show our enemies or friends what they can and cannot do? I merely mention these things to show reason how stupid she is to tack her inferences on to the Scriptures, and how blind she is not to see that they do not always hold good even in respect of the words and dealings of men. Let her see a thing occur once, and she jumps precipitately to the conclusion that it occurs as a general rule in all the statements of both God and men—generalising from a particular case, which is the way of her wisdom.

If, now, God, as a Father, deals with us as with His sons, with a view to showing us the impotence of which we are ignorant; or as a faithful physician, with a view to making known to us our disease; or if, to taunt His enemies, who proudly resist His counsel and the laws He has set forth (by which He achieves this end most effectively), He should say: 'do', 'hear', 'keep', or: 'if thou shalt hear', 'if thou art willing', 'if thou shalt do'; can it be fairly concluded from this that therefore we can do these things freely, or else God is mocking us? Why should not this conclusion follow rather: therefore, God is trying us, that by His law He may bring us to a know-ledge of our impotence, if we are His friends? or else, He is really and deservedly taunting and mocking us, if we are His proud enemies? For this, as Paul teaches, is the intent of divine legislation (cf. Rom. 3.20, 5.20; Gal. 3.19, 24). Human nature is blind, so that it does not know its own strength—or, rather, sickness; moreover, being proud, it thinks it knows and can do everything. God can cure this pride and ignorance by no readier remedy than the publication of His law. We shall say more of this in its proper place. Let it suffice here to have touched upon it so as to refute this inference of a carnal and stupid wisdom: ' "if thou art willing"'; therefore, thou canst will freely.' The Diatribe dreams that man is whole and sound (as to human view, in his own sphere, he is); hence it argues from the phrases: 'if thou art willing', 'if thou shalt do', 'If thou shalt hear', that man is being mocked, unless his will is free. But Scripture describes man as corrupted and led captive, and, furthermore, as proudly disdaining to notice, and failing to recognise, his own corruption and captivity; therefore, it uses these phrases to goad and rouse him, that he may know by sure experience how unable he is to do any of these things.

(vi) *That Erasmus' argument, if valid, would establish plenary ability* (674-676)

Now I shall attack the Diatribe directly. If you really think, O mistress Reason, that your inferences hold good ('"if thou art willing"; therefore, thou freely canst'), why do you not follow them yourself? For you say in the words of that 'probable view' that 'free-will' cannot will any good. By what consequence will *that* come out of the passage under discussion ('if thou art willing to keep . . .'), from which you say it follows that man can will and not will freely? Do bitter and sweet come out of the same spring? Do you not mock man more yourself here, when you say that he can *keep* what he can neither will nor desire? So, then, you yourself do not think in your heart that ' "if thou art willing"; therefore, thou freely canst' is a good inference, even though you contend so zealously for it—or else, it is not from your heart that you call the view which maintains man's inability to will good, 'probable'! Reason is thus so entrapped in the inferences and words of her own wisdom, that she does not know what she is saying or talking about. It is, however, entirely appropriate that 'free-will' should be defended with the sort of arguments that mutually devour and destroy each other; just as the Midianites destroyed each other by mutual massacre when they fought against Gideon and the people of God (Judges 7.22).

Indeed, I shall expostulate more fully with the wisdom of the Diatribe. Ecclesiasticus does not say: 'if thou shalt have a desire and endeavour to keep, which is not to be ascribed to your own strength' (which is the meaning you gather from his words); what he says is this: 'if thou wilt *keep* the commandments, they shall preserve thee.' Now, if I want to draw inferences in the style of your wisdom, I shall draw them thus: 'therefore, man is able to keep the commandments!' Thus, I shall not make a tiny little effort, or a tiny spark of endeavour, to be left in man, but I shall ascribe to him entire, plenary and abundant power to keep the commandments. Otherwise, Ecclesiasticus would be mocking men's misery, commanding them to 'keep' when he knows that they cannot 'keep'! It would not be enough for effort and endeavour to be present with man, nor could Ecclesiasticus escape suspicion of mockery, unless he meant that there is in man power to 'keep'!

Let us suppose that the effort and endeavour of 'free-will' really exist. What shall we say to those (the Pelagians, I mean) who, on the basis of this passage, denied grace altogether, and ascribed everything to 'free-will'? If the Diatribe's inference stands good, the Pelagians have clearly won the day; for Ecclesiasticus' words speak, not of 'desiring' or 'endeavouring', but of 'keeping.' If you deny the Pelagians their inference with respect to 'keeping', they in reply will much more rightly deny your inference with respect to 'endeavouring'. If you take from them the whole of 'free-will', they will take from you your remaining particle of it; for you cannot assert of a part what you deny to the whole. So whatever you say against the Pelagians, who on the basis of this passage ascribe everything to 'free-will', that I also will say, much more strongly, against the tiny little effort of your 'free-will'! And the Pelagians will agree with us to this extent, that, if their view cannot be proved from this passage, much less can any other be proved from it, since, if the argument is to be conducted by inferences, Ecclesiasticus makes for the Pelagians most strongly of all; for he speaks in plain terms of a total 'keeping': 'If thou wilt *keep* the commandments.' Yes, and he speaks of faith: 'If thou wilt keep the faith'; so that, by the same inference, it ought to be in our power to keep the faith too. But that, as Paul says, is a special and rare gift of God (cf. Eph. 2.8).

In a word: seeing that so many divergent and contrary opinions may be counted that favour 'free-will', and none of them omits to grasp at this passage of Ecclesiasticus in its own support, they are bound to hold that Ecclesiasticus diverges from and contradicts themselves in this one selfsame utterance. So they can prove nothing from him; though, if your inference is allowed, it makes in favour of the Pelagians alone, and against all others. Hence it also makes against the Diatribe, which at this point is stabbed with its own sword!

I affirm, as I said at first, that this passage of Ecclesiasticus favours none of those who assert 'free-will', but fights against them all. The inference: ' "If thou art willing"; therefore, thou canst,' is not admissible; it should be understood that by this statement, and by those like it, man is admonished of his own impotence, which he, in his ignorance and pride, would not recognise or be aware of without these Divine admonitions. Here I speak, not of the first man only, but of every man; though it does not much matter whether you understand what is said of the first man, or of any other man. For although the first man was not impotent, inasmuch as grace assisted him, yet God by this commandment shows him clearly enough how impotent he would be without grace. And if he, who had the Spirit, could not with his new will will a good newly proposed (that is, obedience), because the Spirit did not add that to him, what can we, without the Spirit, do about the good that we have lost? By the dreadful example of that first man, it was shown us, with a view to breaking down our pride, what our 'free-will' can do if it is left to itself, and is not continually moved and increased more and more by the Spirit of God. That first man could do nothing to secure an increase of the Spirit Whose first-fruits he had, but fell from these first-fruits of the Spirit; what then could we, who are fallen, do to secure the first-fruits of the Spirit that have been taken from us? Especially when Satan, who cast Adam down by temptation alone, at a time when he was not yet Adam's ruler, now reigns in us with complete power over us! No stronger argument could be brought against 'free-will' than this passage of Ecclesiasticus, taken in conjunction with the fall of Adam. But there is no room for that now; maybe an opportunity will offer elsewhere. Meanwhile, it is enough to have shown that, in this passage, which the advocates of 'free-will' regard as their principal authority, Ecclesiasticus says nothing at all in favour of 'free-will', and that this passage and others like it ('if thou art willing', 'if thou hear', 'if thou do') declare, not man's *ability*, but his *duty*.

(vii) *Gen. 4.7: obligation does not imply ability* (676)

Another passage is cited by our Diatribe from Gen. 4, where the Lord says to Cain: 'Under thee shall be the desire of sin, and thou shalt rule over it' (v. 7). '*Here it is shown,*' says the Diatribe, '*that the motions of the mind to evil can be overcome, and that they do not bring with them a necessity of sinning.*'

These words, 'the motions of the mind to evil can be over-come,' are ambiguous; but from the force of the sentiment, the inference drawn, and the subject-matter, they must mean that it is in the power of 'free-will' to overcome its motions to evil, and that these motions do not bring upon it any necessity to sin. Here again, what is excluded from that which is ascribed to 'free-will'? What need is there of the Spirit, or Christ, or God, if 'free-will' can overcome the motions of the mind to evil? Again, where is that 'probable view' which says that 'free-will' cannot even will good? Victory over evil is here ascribed to that which neither wills nor desires good! The thoughtlessness of our friend the Diatribe is exceedingly excessive!

Here is the matter in a nutshell: As I said, by statements of this sort, man is shown, not what he can do, but what he ought to do. Cain is therefore told that he ought to rule over his sin, and keep its desires under his control. But this he neither did nor could do, for the rule of another, Satan, already bore heavily upon him. It is well known that the Hebrews often use the future indicative for the imperative, as in Exod. 20: '*Thou shalt* have none other gods but me,' '*Thou shalt* not kill,' '*Thou shalt* not commit adultery' (vv. 3, 13-14); and there are count-less such cases. If these words were taken indicatively, as they stand, they would be promises of God; and, since He cannot lie, the result would be that no man would sin; and then it would be needless to give men commandments! So our translator would have rendered this passage more correctly as follows: 'Let its desire be under thee, and rule thou over it.' Similarly, it ought to be said concerning the woman: 'Be thou under thy husband, and let him rule over thee' (Gen. 3.16). That the words were not spoken to Cain in an indicative sense is proved by the fact that then they would have been a Divine promise; but they were not a promise, for the opposite of them ensued in Cain's conduct.

(viii) *Deut. 30.19, etc.: the law is designed to give knowledge of sin* (676-680)

The third passage is from Moses: 'I have set before thy face life and death; choose what is good,' etc. (Deut. 30.19). '*What could be more clearly stated?*' says the Diatribe; '*it leaves man freedom of choice.*' I reply: What could be more clear than that at this point you are blind? Where, pray, does it leave freedom of choice? In its use of the word 'choose'? Does it, then, come to pass that, as soon as Moses says 'choose', they do choose? In that case, there is once more no need of the Spirit. Since you so often repeat and stress the same things, it will be legitimate for me too to reiterate the same points the more often. If freedom of choice remains to us, why did the 'probable view' say that 'free-will' cannot will good? Can it choose without willing, or against its will?

But listen to the Diatribe's analogy: '*It would be ridiculous to say to a man standing where two roads met: "You see two roads; go by which you will," when only one of them was open.*' Here is the very thing that I said of the arguments of human reason: reason thinks that man is mocked by an impossible commandment, whereas I maintain that by this means man is admonished and awakened to see his own impotence. It is true that we stand where two roads meet, and only one of them is open—indeed, neither is open; and the law shows us how impossible is the one, that leading to good, unless God bestows His Spirit, and how broad and easy is the other, if God lets us go that way. Now, it would not be ridiculous but a serious and necessary matter, to say to a man standing where two roads met: 'go by which you will,' if he in spite of weakness wanted to think himself strong, or maintained that neither way was closed. So the words of the law are spoken, not to assert the power of the will, but to illuminate the blindness of reason, so that it may see that its own light is nothing, and the power of the will is nothing. 'By the law is knowledge of sin,' says Paul (Rom. 3.20). He does not say: *abolition*, or *avoidance*, of sin. The entire design and power of the law is just to give knowledge, and that of nothing but of sin; not to display or confer any power. This knowledge is not power, nor does it bring power; but it teaches and displays that there is here no power, and great weakness. What can 'knowledge of sin' be, but knowledge of our weakness and badness? He does not say: 'by the law comes knowledge of power or goodness'! All that the law does, on Paul's testimony, is to make sin known.

It is from this passage that I derive my answer to you: that by the words of the law man is admonished and taught, not what he can do, but what he ought to do; that is, that he may know his sin, not that he may believe that he has any strength. Wherefore, my good Erasmus, as often as you confront me with the words of the law, so often shall I confront you with the words of Paul: 'By the law is knowledge of sin'—not power of will! Gather together from the big concordances all the imperative words into one chaotic heap (not the words of promise, but the words of the law and its demand)—and I shall at once declare that they always show, not what men can do, or do do, but what they should do! Even grammarians and schoolboys at street corners know that nothing more is signified by verbs in the imperative mood than what ought to be done, and that what is done or can be done should be expressed by verbs in the indicative. How is it that you theologians are twice as stupid as schoolboys, in that as soon as you get hold of a single imperative verb you infer an indicative meaning, as though the moment a thing is commanded it is done, or can be done? But there's many a slip 'twixt the cup and the lip!—and things that you commanded and that were possible enough may yet not be done, so great a gulf is there between imperative and indicative statements in the simplest everyday matters! Yet in this business of keeping the law, which is as far out of our reach as heaven is from the earth and just as impossible of attainment, you make indicatives out of imperatives with such alacrity that the moment you hear the word of command: 'do', 'keep', 'choose', you will straightway have it that it has been kept, done, chosen or fulfilled, or that these things can be done by our own strength!

In the fourth place you cite from Deut. 3 (actually, 30) many similar references to choosing, turning away and keeping, such as: 'if thou shalt keep', 'if thou shalt turn away', 'if thou shalt choose'. '*All these words would be inappropriately spoken*' you say, '*were man's will not free for good.*' I reply: You, too, my good Diatribe, speak inappropriately enough when you deduce the freedom of the will from these words! You set out to prove mere endeavour and effort on the part of 'free-will'; you quote no passage that proves such endeavour; but you quote passages which, if your inference held good, would ascribe everything to 'free-will'! Let me here again distinguish words quoted from Scripture from the conclusion which the Diatribe tacks on to them. The words quoted are imperative, and tell us merely what ought to be done. Moses does not say: 'you have the power and strength to choose', but: 'choose', 'keep', 'do'; he is conveying commandments to perform, not describing man's ability. But the inference appended by the would-be-wise Diatribe runs thus: 'therefore, man can do these things, else the commandments would be given in vain.' To which we reply: Mistress Diatribe, you reason badly; you do not prove your inference; it is only to your own blind sleepy-headed self that it seems to be proven and to follow. However, the commandments are not given inappropriately or pointlessly; but in order that through them proud, blind man may learn the plague of his own impotence, should he try to do what is commanded.

Hence there is no force in your analogy when you remark: '*Otherwise it would be just like saying to a man who was so bound that he could only stretch out his arm to his left; "Behold; thou hast excellent wine on thy right, and poison on thy left; on which thou wilt, stretch forth thy hand."* ' I am sure that these analogies give you enormous satisfaction. But yet you fail to see that if the analogies stand, they prove much more than you proposed to prove; indeed, they prove what you deny and would have disproved— that 'free-will' can do all things! Throughout your treatment you forget that you said that 'free-will' can do nothing without grace, and you prove that 'free-will' can do all things without grace! Your inferences and analogies go to prove, either that 'free-will' can of itself perform what is stated and commanded, or else that the commandments are given pointlessly, absurdly and inappropriately. But these are just the old songs of the Pelagians, which even the Sophists confuted, and which you have yourself condemned! Meanwhile, this absentmindedness and bad memory of yours indicates how little you know or care about your subject. And what can be more disgraceful in a rhetorician than to be constantly discussing and arguing matters that are off the point at issue; indeed, to be always declaiming against himself and his own case?

So I conclude thus: The passages of Scripture which you cite are imperative; and they prove and establish nothing about the ability of man, but only lay down what is and is not to be done. Your inferences, or appendages, and your analogies, if they prove anything, prove that 'free-will' can do all things without grace. This you did not undertake to prove and, indeed, have denied. Consequently, 'proofs' of this sort are nothing but disproofs of the strongest kind.

Let me see if I can rouse the Diatribe from its lethargy. Suppose I argue thus: 'When Moses says: "Choose life, and keep the commandment", it is ridiculous for Moses to give such an injunction to man unless man is able to choose life and keep the commandment.' Have I by this reasoning proved that 'free-will' can do nothing good, or has in itself endeavour without strength of its own? On the contrary. I have proved, by a pretty forcible argument, *either* that man can choose life and keep the commandment, as enjoined, *or* that Moses is a ridiculous legislator. But who would dare to say that Moses was a ridiculous legislator? It follows, therefore, that man can do what is commanded! This is how the Diatribe argues throughout, contrary to its own stated aim, by which it undertook, not to argue in this manner, but to show that there is a certain endeavour on the part of 'free-will'. However, so far is it from proving that this is so, that it rarely mentions the matter throughout the entire sequence of its arguments; indeed, it rather proves the contrary, that it is all its own asserting and disputing that is absurd!

As for its being absurd that (according to the analogy introduced) a man whose right arm was bound should be ordered to stretch forth his hand to the right, when he could only reach out to his left—is it absurd, pray, that a man who has both arms bound, but who proudly maintains or ignorantly assumes that he is wholly competent in either direction, should be commanded to stretch forth his hand in one direction or the other, not in order to make fun of his captivity, but to disprove his false assumption of freedom and power, and to make him realise his ignorance of his own captivity and misery? The Diatribe constantly imagines a man who either can do what he is commanded, or at any rate knows that he cannot. But such a man is nowhere to be found. If there were such, then, in truth, either the commanding of impossibilities would be absurd, or the Spirit of Christ would be in vain. But the Scripture sets before us a man who is not only bound, wretched, captive, sick and dead, but who, through the operation of Satan his lord, adds to his other miseries that of blindness, so that he believes himself to be free, happy, possessed of liberty and ability, whole and alive. Satan knows that if men knew their own misery he could keep no man in his kingdom; God could not fail at once to pity and succour wretchedness that knew itself and cried to Him, for God is proclaimed with mighty praise throughout the Scripture as being near to the broken-hearted. Thus Isa. 61 bears witness that Christ was sent 'to preach the gospel to the poor, and to heal the broken-hearted'. Hence, the work of Satan is to hold men so that they do not recognise their wretchedness, but presume that they can do everything that is stated. But the work of Moses the lawgiver is the opposite of this—namely, through the law to lay open to man his own wretchedness, so that, by thus breaking him down, and confounding him in his self-knowledge, he may make him ready for grace, and send him to Christ to be saved. Therefore, the function performed by the law is nothing to laugh at, but is most emphatically serious and necessary.

Those who now understand this much easily understand also that the Diatribe effects nothing whatsoever by all its string of arguments. It collects from the Scriptures nothing but imperative statements, the meaning and design of which it does not understand; then, by the addition of inferences and carnal similitudes of its own, it mixes such a mighty mouthful that it asserts and proves more than it had intended, and argues against itself. So there is no need to run through individual items any further; they are all met by a single answer, for they all rest on a single argument. However, in order that the Diatribe may be overthrown by that very mass of matter with which it sought to overthrow me, I shall proceed to review some of them.

Isa. 1: 'If ye be willing and hearken to me, ye shall eat the good things of the land' (v. 19). Here the Diatribe considers that, *if there is no such thing as freedom of will, it would have been more fitting to say: 'whether I will or no'*. The answer to this is clear enough from what was said above. Moreover, what fitness would there be were it said: 'If *I* will, ye shall eat the good things of the land'? Does the Diatribe in its vast wisdom suppose that the good things of the land can be eaten against God's will? or that it is a rare new truth, that we receive good things only by the will of God?

So with the words of Isa. 21: 'If ye will inquire, inquire ye; return, come' (v. 12). '*What is the point of exhorting those who have no measure of power of their own?*' says the Diatribe. '*It is like saying to someone bound in chains: "Move over here."* ' On the contrary, I reply, what is the point of citing passages which in themselves prove nothing, and by the addition of your inference (that is, by the perversion of their sense), ascribe everything to 'free-will', when what had to be proved was a certain endeavour only, and one that might not be ascribed to 'free-will' at that?

The same may be said of the words of Isa. 45: 'Assemble yourselves and come' (v. 20); 'Turn unto me, and ye shall be saved' (v. 22); and Isa. 52: 'Awake, awake'; 'shake thyself from the dust'; 'loose the bands of thy neck' (vv. 1-2); and Jer. 15: 'If thou wilt turn, then will I turn thee; and if thou take forth the precious from the vile, thou shalt be as my mouth' (v. 19). Zechariah indicates more plainly still the endeavour of 'free-will' and the grace prepared for him who endeavours: 'Turn ye unto me, saith the Lord of hosts, and I will turn unto you, saith the Lord' (1.3).

(ix) *Of Erasmus' confusion of law and gospel in Zech. 1.3; Jer. 15.19; Ezek. 18.23, etc.* (680-684)

In these passages, our friend the Diatribe makes no distinction at all between the voices of the law and of the gospel; so blind and ignorant is it that it does not see what the law and the gospel are. Out of the whole of Isaiah it cites no word of the law save this one passage: 'If ye be willing' (Isa. 1.19); all the other passages quoted are gospel, by which the afflicted and broken-hearted are summoned to consolation by the word that offers grace. But the Diatribe makes of them words of the law! Pray tell me, what can a man do in the realm of theology and the sacred writings, if he has not even reached the point of knowing what the law and the gospel are, or, if he does know, scorns to observe the distinction? He is bound to mix up everything, heaven with hell and life with death, and will not take the slightest trouble to know about Christ. I shall instruct my friend the Diatribe at some length on this matter in what follows.

Look at the words of Jeremiah and Zechariah: 'If thou wilt turn, then will I turn thee', and: 'turn ye unto me, and I will turn unto you'. Does it follow from: 'turn ye' that therefore you can turn? Does it follow from: 'Love the Lord thy God with all thy heart' (Deut. 6.5) that therefore you can love with all your heart? What do arguments of this kind prove, but that 'free-will' does not need the grace of God, but can do all things by its own power? How much more proper is it to take the words as they stand! 'If thou wilt turn, then will I also turn thee'; that is: 'if thou wilt cease sinning, I also will cease punishing; and if thou shalt be converted and live well, I also will treat you well by turning away your captivity and woes.' But it does not follow from this that man is converted by his own power, nor do the words say so; they simply say: 'If thou wilt turn', telling man what he should do. When he knows it, and sees that he cannot do it, he will ask whence he may find ability to do it—unless the Diatribe's Leviathan (that is, its inferential appendage) intervenes to say: 'if man cannot turn by his own power, "turn ye" is said in vain!' Enough has been said of the nature and worth of this conclusion.

Only a person in a stupor or a daze could think that the words: 'turn ye', 'if thou wilt turn', and the like, establish the power of 'free-will', and yet not see that by parity of reasoning it is also established by this word: 'Thou shalt love the Lord thy God with all thine heart'. For the meaning of Him who commands and requires is parallel in each case. The love of God is required no less than our conversion and the keeping of all the commandments; for the love of God is our true conversion. Yet no one tries to prove 'free-will' from the command to love; all argue from the words: 'if thou wilt', 'if thou wilt hearken', 'turn ye', and the like. If then it does not follow from that word ('love the Lord thy God with all thy heart') that 'free-will' has any existence or ability, it is certain that it does not follow either from the words: 'if thou wilt', 'if thou wilt hear', 'turn ye', and the like, which either require less, or require it less peremptorily, than the words: 'Love God!' 'Love the Lord!' Therefore, all that is said against concluding in favour of 'free-will' from this word, 'love God', must also be said against concluding in favour of 'free-will' from any other words of command or requirement. If we suppose that the command to love shows us the tenor of the law and our duty only, but not our power of will or ability (inability, rather), then the same is shown by all other words of demand. It is an acknowledged fact that even the Schoolmen, with the exception of the Scotists and the Moderns, assert that man cannot love God with all his heart. That being so, he cannot perform any of the other precepts, for Christ assures us that they all hang on this one. Thus, even on the testimony of the Scholastic doctors, it remains sure that the words of the law do not prove the power of 'free-will', but show us the extent of our duty and our inability.

But our friend the Diatribe grows more stupid still; it not only infers from Zechariah's words ('Turn ye unto me') an indicative sense, but further exerts itself to prove from them that 'free-will' makes endeavours and that grace is prepared for it when it endeavours. Here, at long last, it mentions its cherished 'endeavour', and, by a novel piece of grammar, takes 'turn' to mean 'endeavour so to do'; so that the sense is: 'turn ye unto me' (that is, endeavour to turn), 'and I will turn unto you' (that is, I will endeavour to turn unto you). Thus it ends by attributing endeavour even to God! Perhaps it would have grace prepared for Him too on His endeavouring! For if 'turn' means 'endeavour' in one place, why not everywhere?

Again, it says that from the passage in Jer. 15 ('If thou take forth the precious from the vile') not only endeavour, but freedom of choice, is proved; which freedom it had previously declared to be lost, and turned into a necessity of serving sin! You see, then, that in handling the Scriptures the Diatribe employs 'free-will' with a vengeance, forcing statements of the same type to prove endeavour at one point, and freedom at another, just as it sees fit!

But away with these vanities. The word 'turn' is used in the Scriptures in two ways, the one legal, the other evangelical. In its legal use, it is an utterance of exaction and command, requiring, not endeavour, but a change in the whole life. Jeremiah frequently uses it in this sense, saying: 'Turn ye now every one from his evil way', and: 'Turn ye unto the Lord' (Jer. 25.5, 35.15, 4.1), where it is plain enough that he includes a requirement of all the commandments. In its evangelical sense, it is an utterance of divine consolation and promise, by which nothing is required of us, but the grace of God is offered to us. Such is this, in Ps. 15: 'When the Lord shall turn again the captivity of Zion' (Ps. 14.7, cf. 126.1); and this in Ps. 22: 'Turn again unto thy rest, O my soul' (Ps. 116.7, cf. 23.3). Zechariah has therefore set out in the shortest compass the proclamation of both law and grace. It is the whole sum of the law, when he says: 'Turn ye unto me'; and it is grace when he says: 'I will turn unto you.' Just as much as 'free-will' is proved from this word, 'Love the Lord,' or from any other word of a particular law, just so much is it proved from this word which summarizes the law: 'Turn ye.' It is the mark of a wise reader to notice which words in the Scripture are law and which are grace, so that he may not have everything muddled, like the filthy Sophists and this sleepy-headed Diatribe!

See how the Diatribe handles that famous passage in Ezek. 18: 'As I live, saith the Lord, I desire not the death of a sinner, but rather that he should turn from his wickedness and live' (v. 23). First, it says: '*The expressions: "shall turn away", "hath done", "hath committed", are repeated many times in this chapter with reference to both good and evil. Where then are they who deny that man can do anything?*' Pray, view this excellent inference! The Diatribes set out to prove that 'free-will' endeavours and desires, and proves instead that all is accomplished and everything fulfilled by 'free-will'! Where now, pray, are those who need grace and the Holy Spirit? For thus it reasons, saying: '*Ezekiel says, "If the wicked man shall turn away, and shall do righteousness and judgment, he shall live." Therefore the wicked man straightway does so, and can do so.*' Ezekiel is signifying what should be done, but the Diatribe understands that it is being done, and has been done! Thus once more it would teach us, by its novel grammar, that owing and having, command and performance, requirement and rendering, are identical.

Then it twists that sweetest voice of the gospel, 'I desire not the death of a sinner,' etc., like this: '*Does the righteous Lord deplore the death of his people which He Himself works in them? If He does not will our death, it must be laid to the charge of our own will if we perish. But what can you lay to the charge of him who can do no good or evil?*'

Pelagius sang this same tune long ago, when he assigned to 'free-will' not desire nor endeavour only, but complete power to do and fulfil all things. Your inferences, if they prove anything, prove this power, as I have said; so that they make with equal, indeed, with greater force against the Diatribe, which denies this power of 'free-will' and would establish endeavour only, than they do against us, who deny 'free-will' altogether. But we will say no more of the Diatribe's ignorance, and speak to the subject itself.

It is the voice of the gospel, the sweetest consolation to miserable sinners, when Ezekiel says: 'I desire not the death of a sinner, but rather that he should be converted and live.' The words are in all respects like these of Ps. 28: 'For His wrath is but for a moment, His will is rather life' (Ps. 30.6); and of Ps. 68: 'How sweet is Thy loving-kindness, O Lord' (Ps. 36.7); and: 'For I am merciful' (Jer. 3.12); and Christ's word in Matt. 11: 'Come unto me, all ye that labour, and I will refresh you' (v. 28); and the words of Exod. 20: 'I will show mercy unto many thousands to them that love me' (v. 6). And what is rather more than half the Holy Scripture, but mere promises of grace, by which mercy, life, peace and salvation are offered by God to men? And what do the words of promise mean but this: 'I desire not the death of a sinner'? Is not His saying: 'I am merciful', the same as if He were to say: 'I am not angry, I am unwilling to punish, I desire not your death, My will is to pardon, My will is to spare'? If those Divine promises did not stand firm, to raise up consciences tormented with a sense of sin and terrified by fear of death and judgment, what place would there be for pardon or for hope? What sinner would not sink in despair? But as 'free-will' is not proved by any of the other words of mercy or promise or comfort, so neither is it proved by this: 'I desire not the death of a sinner', etc.

But our friend the Diatribe, again making no distinction between words of law and words of promise, makes this passage of Ezekiel the voice of the law, and expounds it thus: '*I desire not the death of a sinner,*' that is, '*I desire not that he should sin mortally, or become a sinner guilty of death, but rather that he should be converted from sin, if he has committed any, and so live.*' If it did not thus expound it, the passage would be an irrelevance. But this is completely to overthrow and destroy this sweetest word of Ezekiel: 'I desire not the death'. If we in our blindness will read and understand the Scriptures thus, what wonder if they are obscure and ambiguous? God does not say: 'I desire not the sin of man', but: 'I desire not the death of a sinner'; clearly indicating that He is speaking of the punishment of sin, of which the sinner is sensible by reason of his sin—that is, of the fear of death. He is raising up and comforting the sinner as he lies under this torment and despair, in order that he might not break the bruised reed and quench the smoking flax, but create for him a hope of pardon and salvation, so that he might rather be converted (that is, by saving conversion from the penalty of death) and might live (that is, might be well, and rejoice with an untroubled conscience). For this also must be noted: that as the voice of the law is brought to bear only upon those who neither feel nor know their sins, as Paul says in Rom. 3 ('By the law is the knowledge of sin' [v. 20]), so the word of grace comes only to those who are distressed by a sense of sin and tempted to despair. Therefore, in all the words of the law you will find reference made to sin, as we are shown what we ought to do; and so, on the other hand, in all the words of promise you will find mention made of the evil under which sinners (those, at any rate, that are to be raised up) are labouring. So here, in the words: 'I desire not the death of a sinner', it plainly mentions 'death' and 'a sinner', both the evil that is felt and the man who feels it. But in the words: 'Love God with all thine heart', what is intimated is, not the evil that we feel, but the good that we ought to do, in order that we might know how unable we are to do that good.

Nothing, therefore, could be quoted in support of 'free-will' less appropriately than this passage of Ezekiel; indeed, it makes most strongly against 'free-will'. For it is here shown in what state 'free-will' is, and what its ability is in the matter of recognising sin and turning from it—that is, that it cannot but fall into a worse condition, and add to its sins despair and impenitence, unless God comes straightway to its help and calls it back and raises it up by the word of promise. The careful concern of God in promising grace to recall and raise up the sinner is itself a sufficiently great and trusty proof that 'free-will' of itself cannot but grow worse and, as Scripture says, 'go down to hell' (cf. Prov. 5.5)—unless you believe that God is the kind of trifler who pours out words of promise in such abundance, not from any need of them for our salvation, but just because He likes talking! Thus you see that not only do all the words of law stand against 'free-will', but also that all the words of promise utterly refute it—that is, that the whole Scripture fights against it!

Hence, you see, this word: 'I desire not the death of a sinner', is concerned only to proclaim and offer to the world the mercy of God. None receive it with joy and gratitude but those who are distressed and troubled at death, those in whom the law has already completed its work, that is, given knowledge of sin. Those that have not yet experienced the work of the law, who do not recognise their sin and have no sense of death, scorn the mercy promised by that word.

(x) *Of God preached and not preached, and of His revealed and secret will* (684-686)

As to why some are touched by the law and others not, so that some receive and others scorn the offer of grace, that is another question, which Ezekiel does not here discuss. He speaks of the published offer of God's mercy, not of the dreadful[1] hidden will of God, Who, according to His own counsel, ordains such persons as He wills to receive and partake of the mercy preached and offered. This will is not to be inquired into, but to be reverently adored, as by far the most awesome secret of the Divine Majesty. He has kept it to Himself and forbidden us to know it; and it is much more worthy of reverence than an infinite number of Corycian caverns!

When, now the Diatribe reasons thus: '*Does the righteous Lord deplore the death of His people which He Himself works in them? This seems too ridiculous*'—I reply, as I have already said: we

---

[1] *metuenda.*

must discuss God, or the will of God, preached, revealed, offered to us, and worshipped by us, in one way, and God not preached, nor revealed, nor offered to us, nor worshipped by us, in another way. Wherever God hides Himself, and wills to be unknown to us, there we have no concern. Here that sentiment: 'what is above us does not concern us', really holds good. Lest any should think that this distinction is my own, I am following Paul, who writes to the Thessalonians of Antichrist that 'he should exalt himself above all that is God preached and worshipped' (2 Thess. 2.4); clearly intimating that a man can be exalted above God as He is preached and worshipped, that is, above the word and worship of God, by which He is known to us and has dealings with us. But above God not worshipped and not preached, that is, God as He is in His own nature and Majesty, nothing can be exalted, but all things are under His powerful hand.

Now, God in His own nature and majesty is to be left alone; in this regard, we have nothing to do with Him, nor does He wish us to deal with Him. We have to do with Him as clothed and displayed in His Word, by which He presents Himself to us. That is His glory and beauty, in which the Psalmist proclaims Him to be clothed (cf. Ps. 21.5). I say that the righteous God does not deplore the death of His people which He Himself works in them, but He deplores the death which He finds in His people and desires to remove from them. God preached works to the end that sin and death may be taken away, and we may be saved. 'He sent His word and healed them' (Ps. 107.20). But God hidden in Majesty neither deplores nor takes away death, but works life, and death, and all in all; nor has He set bounds to Himself by His Word, but has kept Himself free over all things.

The Diatribe is deceived by its own ignorance in that it makes no distinction between God preached and God hidden, that is, between the Word of God and God Himself. God does many things which He does not show us in His Word, and He wills many things which He does not in His Word show us that He wills. Thus, He does not will the death of a sinner—that is, in His Word; but He wills it by His inscrutable will. At present, however, we must keep in view His Word and leave alone His inscrutable will; for it is by His Word, and not by His inscrutable will, that we must be guided. In any case, who can direct himself according to a will that is inscrutable and incomprehensible? It is enough simply to know that there is in God an inscrutable will; what, why, and within what limits It wills, it is wholly unlawful to inquire, or wish to know, or be concerned about, or touch upon; we may only fear and adore!

So it is right to say: 'If God does not desire our death, it must be laid to the charge of our own will if we perish'; this, I repeat, is right if you spoke of God preached. For He desires that all men should be saved, in that He comes to all by the word of salvation, and the fault is in the will which does not receive Him; as He says in Matt. 23: 'How often would I have gathered thy children together, and thou wouldst not!' (v. 37). But why the Majesty does not remove or change this fault of will in every man (for it is not in the power of man to do it), or why He lays this fault to the charge of the will, when man cannot avoid it, it is not lawful to ask; and though you should ask much, you would never find out; as Paul says in Rom. 11: 'Who art thou that repliest against God?' (Rom. 9.20).

(xi) *Deut. 30.11-14: obligation is no evidence for ability* (686-688)

After this the Diatribe argues: '*If it is not in the power of every man to keep what is commanded, all the exhortations in the Scriptures, and all the promises, threats, expostulations, reproofs, adjurations, blessings, curses and hosts of precepts, are of necessity useless.*'

The Diatribe is continually forgetting the question at issue, and dealing with matters foreign to its purpose; and it does not see that all these things make more strongly against itself than against us. From all these passages it proves freedom and ability to fulfil all things, as the very words of the inference which it draws declare; whereas, its intention was to establish *such a* '*free-will*' *as can will no good without grace, and an endeavour that may not be ascribed to one's own strength.* I do not see that such an endeavour is proved by any of these passages, which only demand duty. This I should have said too often already, were it not that it has to be repeated many times, because the Diatribe harps so often on the same wrong note, putting its readers off with a useless profusion of words.

Almost the last passage which it brings forward from the Old Testament is Moses' word in Deut. 30: 'This commandment which I command thee this day is not above thee, neither is it far off. It is not in heaven, that thou shouldst say, Who of us shall go up to heaven and bring it down to us, that we may hear it, and do it? But the word is very nigh unto thee, in thy mouth and in thy heart, that thou mayest do it.' The Diatribe claims that *this passage declares that what is commanded is not only set within us, but is like falling off a log*;[1] that is, it is easy, or at any rate not hard. Thank you for such vast erudition! If Moses so plainly declares that there is in us, not merely a power, but also an aptitude, for keeping all the commandments, why do I labour so hard? Why did I not straightway produce this passage, and assert 'free-will' before all the world? What need now of Christ? What need of the Spirit? We have now found a passage which stops the mouths of all; not only does it clearly assert the freedom of the will, but it clearly teaches also that keeping the commandments is easy! What a fool was Christ, Who shed His blood to purchase for us the Spirit, Whom we do not need, in order that we might be made able to keep the commandments with ease, when we are so already by nature! Yes, and now let the Diatribe itself recant its own words, where it said that 'free-will' can will no good without grace! Let it now say that 'free-will' has such power that it not only wills good, but keeps the greatest commandments, yes, all the commandments, with ease!

Pray see what a disaffected mind can do, how it cannot help giving itself away! Is there still need to refute the Diatribe? Who could refute it more effectively than it refutes itself? It is truly a beast that eats itself! How true it is that a liar should have a good memory!

I spoke of this place in Deuteronomy before; I shall now discuss it briefly, and without reference to Paul, who handles the passage powerfully in Rom. 10 (vv. 5ff.). You see that nothing at all, not a single syllable, is said here of ease or difficulty, or of the power or impotence of 'free-will' or man to keep or not keep the commandments; but those who would entangle Scripture in their own inferences and ideas render it

[1] *in proclivi esse.*

obscure and ambiguous to themselves, that so they may make of it what they please. If you cannot turn your eyes, at least turn your ears, or feel with your hands! Moses says: 'it is not above thee, neither is it far off, nor is it in heaven nor across the sea'. What does 'above thee' mean? and 'far off'? and 'in heaven'? and 'across the sea'? Will they introduce such obscurity into our grammar and our commonest words that we shall not be able to say anything with a sure meaning, just in order to make their point that the Scriptures are obscure? According to my grammar, these words signify neither the extent nor the degree of human power, but local distance. 'Above thee' does not refer to any power of the will, but to a place that is above us. In the same way, 'far off', 'in heaven', 'across the sea', do not refer to any power in man, but to a place at a distance above us, to the right, to the left, behind us or over against us. Someone may laugh at me for arguing at this elementary level,[1] setting before such great men a primer, as one would before schoolboys who did not know their ABC, and teaching them how to put syllables together; but what can I do, when I see them looking for darkness in such clear light, and aspiring to be blind? They list a vast sequence of ages, many wits, saints, martyrs and doctors; they flaunt this passage of Moses most overbearingly; yet they will not deign to look at the syllables, nor to rule their thoughts so far as to give a moment's consideration to the passage of which they boast! Let the Diatribe now come and tell us how it is possible for one ordinary person[2] to see what all these public figures, the chief men of all these ages, did not see! Even a schoolboy would conclude that this passage proves them to have been blind pretty often!

What then does Moses mean by these extremely plain and clear words, if not that he has excellently discharged his office as a faithful lawgiver, one who does everything necessary to ensure that men have the commandments set before them, and know them; and that therefore no place is left them for making excuse that they did not know the commandments, or did not possess them, or were obliged to seek them elsewhere; so that if they do not keep them, the fault is not in the law or the

---

[1] *crasse.*   [2] *privatus.*

law-giver, but in themselves. The law is with them, and the law-giver has taught them, so that there is left them no excuse on grounds of ignorance, but only the accusation of negligence and disobedience. 'It is not necessary,' he says, 'to fetch the laws from heaven, or from lands across the sea, or from far away, nor can you make the excuse that you never had them or heard them; you have them nigh unto you; you have heard God command them by my mouth, and you have known them in your hearts; you have received them as a subject for continual exposition in your midst by the Levites, as this word and book of mine bear witness; only this remains, that you should do them.' What, pray, is here attributed to 'free-will' save that the keeping of the laws which it has is required of it, and the excuse of ignorance and absence of the laws is taken from it?

These are the passages which the Diatribe quotes for 'free-will' from the Old Testament. Now that they are answered, nothing remains that is not equally answered, whether or not it should quote more, or intend to quote more; for it can quote nothing but imperative or hypothetical passages, or wishes,[1] by which is signified, not what we can do, or do do (as I have often repeated to the repetitive Diatribe), but what we ought to do, and what is required of us, so that our impotence may be made known to us, and the knowledge of sin may be given to us. Or else, if they prove anything, by the addition of inferences and similes invented by human reason they prove this: that 'free-will' has, not just some small degree of endeavour or desire, but full force and completely free power to do all things, without the grace of God and without the Holy Spirit. Thus, nothing is less proved by the whole of this discursive, repetitive and laboured discussion than that which had to be proved, that is, the *'probable view'* which describes 'free-will' as *so impotent that it cannot will any good without grace, but is forced into the service of sin; though it has endeavour, which yet may not be ascribed to its own strength.* A real freak!—it can do nothing in its own strength, and yet it has endeavour within its own strength; its constitution involves a very obvious contradiction!

[1] *optativa.*

(xii) *Matt. 23.37: man must not pry into the secret will of God* (688-690)

Now we come to the New Testament, where there is once more marshalled in defence of the wretched slavery of 'free-will' a host of imperative sentences; and all the auxiliaries of carnal reason, that is, inferences and similes, are gathered with them. It is like seeing in a picture or a dream the king of flies and his host, armed with lances of hay and shields of straw, opposing a real, proper array of human warriors. Such as the man-made dreams of the Diatribe as they oppose the armies of the Word of God!

The words of Matt. 23 come forth in front, the Achilles of the flies: 'O Jerusalem, Jerusalem, how often would I have gathered thy children together, and thou wouldst not' (v. 37). *'If all comes to pass by necessity,'* says the Diatribe, *'could not Jerusalem have justly answered the Lord, "Why dost thou weary thyself with useless tears? If thou didst not wish us to hearken to the prophets, why didst thou send them? Why dost thou lay to our charge that which came to pass at Thy will, and so by necessity in us?"'* So speaks the Diatribe. I reply: Granting for the moment that the Diatribe's inference and conclusion is good and true, what, I ask, does it prove? Does it prove that 'probable view' which says that 'free-will' cannot will good? Indeed, no, it proves that the will is free, whole and able to do all that the prophets said. But the Diatribe did not set out to prove such a will. Nay, let the Diatribe answer this question: If 'free-will' cannot will good, why is it laid to its charge that it did not hear the prophets, who taught good things, and whom therefore it could not hear by its own strength? Why does Christ weep over them with empty tears, as though they could have willed what He knew for certain that they could not will? Let the Diatribe free Christ from the charge of madness in the light of that *'probable view'*, and my view is at once set free from the Achilles of the flies. So this passage in Matthew either proves plenary 'free-will', or else it makes with equal force against the Diatribe and lays it low with its own weapon!

I say, as I said before, that we may not debate the secret will of Divine Majesty, and that the recklessness of man, who shows unabated perversity in leaving necessary matters for an

attempted assault on that will, should be withheld and restrained from employing itself in searching out those secrets of
Divine Majesty; for man cannot attain unto them, seeing that,
as Paul tells us (cf. 1 Tim. 6.16), they dwell in inaccessible
light. But let man occupy himself with God Incarnate, that is,
with Jesus crucified, in whom, as Paul says (cf. Col. 2.3), are
all the treasures of wisdom and knowledge (though hidden);
for by Him man has abundant instruction both in what he
should and in what he should not know.

Here, God Incarnate says: 'I would, and thou wouldst not.'
God Incarnate, I repeat, was sent for this purpose, to will, say,
do, suffer, and offer to all men, all that is necessary for salvation; albeit He offends many who, being abandoned or
hardened by God's secret will of Majesty, do not receive Him
thus willing, speaking, doing and offering. As John says: 'The
light shineth in darkness, and the darkness comprehendeth it
not' (John 1.5). And again: 'He came unto His own, and His
own received Him not' (v. 11). It belongs to the same God
Incarnate to weep, lament, and groan over the perdition
of the ungodly, though that will of Majesty purposely leaves
and reprobates some to perish. Nor is it for us to ask why
He does so, but to stand in awe of God, Who can do, and
wills to do, such things. I do not think anyone will raise the
quibbling objection that this will, of which it is said: 'How
often would I!', was displayed to the Jews even before God was
incarnate, inasmuch as they are accused of having slain the
prophets before Christ, and of resisting His will thereby. For it
is well known among Christians that all that was done through
the prophets was done in the name of the coming Christ, Who
had been promised, that he might become God Incarnate.
Thus all that has been offered to men through the ministry of
the Word from the beginning of the world may rightly be called
the will of Christ.

But here Reason, in her knowing and talkative way, will
say: 'This is a nice way out that you have invented—that,
whenever we are hard pressed by force of arguments, we run
back to that dreadful will of Majesty, and reduce our adversary
to silence when he becomes troublesome in the manner of the
astrologers, who by inventing their "epicycles" dodge all

questions about the movement of the entire heavens.' I reply: This is not my invention, but a command grounded on the Divine Scriptures. In Rom. 11, Paul says: 'Why then does God find fault? Who shall resist His will? O man, who art thou that contendest with God? Hath not the potter power?' and so on (Rom. 9.19, 21). And before him Isaiah said, in chapter 58: 'Yet they seek me daily, and desire to know my ways, as a nation that did righteousness: they ask of me the ordinances of justice, and desire to approach unto God' (v. 2). I think these words make it clear enough that it is not lawful for men to search into the will of Majesty. Furthermore, the subject is of such a kind that perverse men are most strongly provoked to seek after that dreadful will; here most of all, therefore, is the place to urge upon them silence and reverence. In other subjects, of which we can and are commanded to give an account, we do not do this. If, however, any do not yield to our admonition here, but persist in searching out the procedure of that will, we let him go on and, like the giants, fight with God; we watch to see what triumph he will gain, sure that he will in no way hinder our cause nor advance his own. For it will still continue unalterably fixed that either he will prove that 'free-will' can do all things, or else the Scriptures he quotes will fight against himself. Whichever happens, he lies vanquished and I stand victorious!

(xiii) *Matt. 19.17: the law indicates the impotence of man, and the saving power of God* (690-691)

A second passage is in Matt. 19: 'If thou wilt enter into life, keep the commandments' (v. 17). '*With what conscience could "if thou wilt" be said to him whose will is not free?*' says the Diatribe. To this I say: Is the will then free, according to this word of Christ? You wanted to prove that 'free-will' can will no good, and that without grace it necessarily serves sin. With what conscience, then, do you now make it wholly free? The same will be said of these words: 'if thou wilt be perfect'; 'if any man will come after me'; 'he that wills to save his life'; 'if ye love me'; 'if ye shall continue'. In sum, as I have said— let every occurrence of the conjunction 'if', and all imperative verbs, be collected together (so that we may help the Diatribe

M

along with a good number of words, at any rate!). '*All these precepts are useless,*' it tells us, '*if nothing is attributed to the human will. How ill does that conjunction "if" accord with mere necessity?*' I reply: If they are useless, it is your fault that they are useless and, indeed, amount to nothing; for one moment you assert that nothing is to be attributed to 'free-will', making 'free-will' unable to will good, and here, on the contrary, you make it able to will all good! Or is it that to your mind the same words are freezing and flaming at the same time, asserting and denying everything at once?

And I wonder why our author takes a delight in repeating the same thing so often, always forgetting his stated intention; unless perhaps it is that he lacks confidence in his case, and wants to overcome his opponent by the sheer bulk of his book, or to drain his strength with the wearisome labour of reading it! By what consequence, I ask, does it follow that will and power must forthwith be present whenever it says: 'If thou wilt', 'If any man will', 'If thou shalt'? Do we not very commonly indicate impotence and impossibility, rather, by means of such expressions? For instance: 'If you want to equal Vergil as a poet, my good Maevius, you must sing a different strain.' 'If you want to surpass Cicero, Scotus, you must replace your subtleties with the highest eloquence.' 'If you want to stand comparison with David, you must produce psalms like his.' Here are plainly intimated things that are impossible by our own powers, though they may all be done by the power of God. So it is in the Scriptures: by means of such expressions, we are shown what can be done in us by the power of God, and what we cannot do ourselves.

Moreover, if such language were used of things which it is utterly impossible to do, things which even God would never do, then the words might rightly be called 'useless' or 'absurd,' for they would be spoken in vain. But as it is, they are used, not only to show up the impotence of 'free-will', which can effect none of the things mentioned, but also to intimate that a time will come when all these things shall be done—but by a power not our own; that is, by the power of God. This follows, at all events, if we allow that such expressions contain any indication of what can and must be done; as if one should explain: 'If thou wilt keep the commandments' like this: 'if ever thou shalt have the will to keep the commandments (which you will have, not of yourself, but of God, who gives it to whom He will), then they also shall preserve thee.' Or, to put it more fully: These words, especially those that are hypothetical, seem also to be put as they are on account of the predestination of God, which is unknown to us, and they include it in their scope; as if they mean to say this: 'If thou art willing, if thou shalt be willing' (that is, if thou art such with God that He sees fit to give thee this will to keep the commandments) 'thou shalt be saved.' By means of this figure of speech, we are enabled to understand the twin truths, namely, that we can do nothing of ourselves, and that anything that we do God works in us. This would be my reply to those who are not content to have it said that these words show up our impotence only, and claim that they also prove some power and ability in us to do the things commanded. In this way, it would also become true that we can do none of the things commanded, and yet at the same time we can do them all; true, that is, if we ascribe our impotence to our own strength and our ability to the grace of God.

(xiv) *That the purpose of precepts under the New Testament is to guide the justified* (692-693)

In the third place, this thought moves the Diatribe: '*When mention is so often made of good and bad works,*' it says, '*I do not understand how there can be any place for mere necessity, for neither nature nor necessity has merit.*' I understand only this: that whereas the 'probable view' asserts 'mere necessity' when it says that 'free-will' can will no good, here the Diatribe actually assigns merit to that will! 'Free-will' has made such strides as the book grows and the Diatribe's argument advances that now it not only possesses endeavour and effort of its own (though by another's strength)—nay, it not only wills and does good—it also merits eternal life, according to Christ's words: 'Rejoice and be exceeding glad, for great is your reward in heaven' (Matt. 5.12). 'Your reward' means the reward of 'free-will' (for so the Diatribe understands this passage); so that Christ and the Spirit of God are nothing! What need of them is there, if we have good works and merit by 'free-will'? I say this so that we may see that it is no rare thing for men of superior intellect to be habitually blind in a matter that would be clear even to a dull and untrained mind; and that we may also see how weak is the argument from human authority in the things of God, where God's authority alone avails.

Here we must speak of two things: *first*, the commandments of the New Testament; *second*, merit. We shall deal with each in short compass, having spoken of them more fully elsewhere.

The New Testament, properly speaking, consists of promises and exhortations, just as the Old, properly speaking, consists of laws and threats. In the New Testament, the gospel is preached and this is just the word that offers the Spirit and grace for the remission of sins which was procured for us by Christ crucified. It is all entirely free, given by the mercy of God the Father alone as He shows His favour towards us, who are unworthy, and who deserve condemnation rather than anything else. Exhortations follows after this; and they are intended to stir up those who have obtained mercy and have been justified already, to be energetic in bringing forth the fruits of the Spirit and of the righteousness given them, to exercise themselves in love and good works, and boldly to bear the cross and all the other tribulations of this world. This is the whole sum of the New Testament. But the complete failure of the Diatribe to understand it is sufficiently declared by the fact that it does not know how to make any distinction between the Old and the New Testaments; for it sees nothing anywhere but laws and comments, by which men may be moulded in good manners. What rebirth, renewal, regeneration and the whole work of the Spirit are, it does not see at all. I am amazed and astounded that a man who has spent so much time in studying the sacred writings should be so utterly ignorant. This passage, then ('Rejoice and be exceeding glad, for great is your reward in heaven'), squares as well with 'free-will' as light agrees with darkness. Christ is there exhorting, not 'free-will', but the Apostles, who at that time not only were in grace, higher than 'free-will' can rise, and so were righteous; they were actually engaged in the ministry of the word, which is the highest point of grace; and Christ is there telling them to endure the tribulations of the world. But our present debate specifically concerns 'free-will' without grace; which is taught by laws and threats (the Old Testament) to know itself, that it might run to the promises offered in the New Testament.

(xv) *That the ground of reward under the New Testament is the promise of God, not the merit of man* (693-696)

As for merit, or the proposal of a reward, what is it but a kind of promise? But that promise does not prove that we can do anything; it proves only this, that if anyone does this or that, he shall then have a reward. And our question is, not what reward will be given, nor how it will be given, but, whether we can do the things for which the reward is given. That is what needed to be established. Is not this ridiculous logic: The prize is set before all in the race; therefore, all can run and obtain it? If Caesar conquers Turkey, he will gain the kingdom of Syria; therefore, Caesar can and does conquer Turkey! If 'free-will' rules sin, it shall be holy before the Lord; therefore, 'free-will' is holy before the Lord! Away with such excessive follies, such patent absurdities (though it is highly appropriate that 'free-will' should be *established* by such fine arguments as these!). Let us instead speak to this point: *necessity has neither merit nor reward*. If we speak of *necessity of compulsion*, it is true; but if we speak of *necessity of immutability*, it is false. Who would reward an unwilling workman, or ascribe merit to him? But for those who do good and evil willingly, even though they cannot alter their will by their own strength, reward and punishment follow *naturally* and *necessarily*; as it is written: 'thou shalt render unto every man according to his works' (cf. Ps. 62.12). *Natural* consequence is this: if you sink under water, you will be drowned; if you swim out of it, you will be saved. In a word: In the matter of merit and reward, we deal with either *worthiness* or *consequence*. If you have *worthiness* in view, there is no merit and no reward. If 'free-will' cannot will good by itself alone, but wills good by grace alone (for we are speaking of 'free-will' apart from grace, and inquiring into the proper power of each), who does not see that the good will, and merit, and reward, are of grace alone? And here again the Diatribe disagrees with itself; for it argues the freedom of the will from the fact of merit, and hereby comes under the same condemnation as do I, against whom it contends—that is, its claim that there are such things as merit, and reward, and freedom, wars against it no less than I do; seeing that it asserted earlier that 'free-will'.wills no good, and undertook to prove as much! If, on the other hand, you have *consequences* in view, there is nothing, good or evil, that has not its reward. And hence comes the mistake, that, in the matter of merits and rewards, we ponder unprofitable thoughts and questions about *worthiness* (which is non-existent) when we ought to be discussing *consequence* alone. Hell and the judgment of God await the wicked as a necessary consequence; though they do not themselves desire or conceive of such a reward for their sins, and indeed think it abominable and, as Peter says, rail against it (cf. 2 Pet 2.12). In the same way, a kingdom awaits the godly, though they themselves neither seek it nor think of it; for it was prepared for them by their Father, not only before they themselves existed, but before the foundation of the world (cf. Matt. 25.34). Indeed, should they do good works in order to obtain the kingdom, they never would obtain it, but would belong rather to the number of the ungodly, who with an evil, mercenary eye seek the things of self even in God. The sons of God, however, do good with a will free from self-concern,[1] seeking no reward, but the glory and will of God only, and ready to do good even if (though this is impossible) there was neither a kingdom nor a hell.

These things are, I think, sufficiently established by that single saying of Christ which I have just cited from Matt. 25: 'Come, ye blessed of My Father, receive the kingdom prepared for you from the foundation of the world' (v. 34). How do they *merit* what is already theirs, and was prepared for them before they were in existence? We could more accurately say that it is rather the kingdom of God that merits its possessors; so putting the merit where our opponents put the reward, and the reward where they put the merit. The kingdom is not in process of preparation, but was prepared before, and the sons of the kingdom do not prepare the kingdom, but are in process of being prepared themselves; that is, the kingdom merits the

---

[1] *gratuita.*

sons, not the sons the kingdom. So also hell rather merits and makes ready its sons; for Christ says: 'Depart, ye cursed, into eternal fire, prepared for the devil and his angels' (v. 41).

What then is the meaning of all those Scriptures which promise the kingdom and threaten hell? Why is the word 'reward' repeated so often in the Scriptures? 'There is a reward for thy work' (2 Chron. 15.7). 'I am thy exceeding great reward' (Gen. 15.1). Again: 'Who rendereth to every man according to his work' (cf. Job 34.11). And Paul says in Rom. 2: 'To those who by patient continuance in well-doing seek eternal life' (v. 7); and there are many similar statements. The answer is that what is established by all these passages is simply a *consequence of reward*, not in any way a *worthiness of merit*; inasmuch as those who do good do not do so in a servile, mercenary spirit, with a view to gaining eternal life—although they seek eternal life in the sense that they are in the way by which they will find and attain eternal life; so that their 'seeking' is an earnest striving and diligent endeavour after that which regularly follows upon a good life. The reason why the future consequences of a good and a bad life are declared in the Scriptures is that men might be instructed, disturbed, awakened and terrified. As 'by the law is the knowledge of sin,' and instruction concerning our impotence—by which, however, it is not implied that we ourselves can do anything; so by these promises and threats comes a warning of what follows upon the sin and impotence which the law has pointed out—but they do not ascribe any worthiness to our merit. Wherefore, as the words of the law serve their turn by instruction and illumination, to teach us both what we ought to do and what we cannot do, so the words of reward, signifying what is to be, serve their turn by exhorting and threatening, and animate, comfort and uphold the godly to press on, persevere and triumph in doing good and enduring evil, lest they should be wearied, or their spirit broken. So Paul exhorts his Corinthian converts, saying: 'Quit you like men, knowing that your labour is not in vain in the Lord' (cf. 1 Cor. 16.13, 15.58). So also God upholds Abraham, saying: 'I am thy exceeding great reward' (Gen. 15.1). It is just as if you were to comfort someone by intimating to him that his works certainly please God. This is a kind of consolation which Scripture often employs. And it is no small consolation to know that one pleases God, so that nothing untoward can follow, impossible though that may seem to be.

This is the intention of all that is said about our hope and expectation that the things which we hope for shall certainly be (though the godly do not hope merely on account of these things, nor do they seek such things for their own sake). So too by the words of threatening and future judgment the ungodly are terrified and cast down, so that they may cease and abstain from wickedness, and not become puffed up, and complacent, and vainglorious, in their sins.

If Reason should here wrinkle up her nose and say: 'Why does God will that these things be done by His words, when nothing is achieved by such words, and the will cannot turn itself in either direction? Why does He not do what He does without speaking a word, when He can do all things without a word? For a will that has heard His Word can do and does no more than before, if the inner moving of the Spirit is wanting; nor could it avail or do any less without the Word being spoken, if the Spirit was with it; for all depends on the power and operation of the Spirit' to this I shall say: It has pleased God not to give the Spirit without the Word, but through the Word; that He might have us as workers together with Him, we sounding forth without what He alone breathes within wheresoever He will. This He could do without the Word; but He will not. And who are we to inquire into the cause of the Divine will? It is enough for us to know that God so wills, and it becomes us to worship, love and adore His will, bridling the presumption of reason. Thus, he might feed us without bread; he has, indeed, given us power to feed without bread, as Matt. 4 tells us: 'Man is not fed by bread alone, but by the word of God' (v. 4); yet it has pleased Him to feed us by means of bread, by the provision of bread without, and by His Word within.

It stands sure, therefore, that merit is not proved from reward, not at any rate in the Scriptures; and also that 'free-will' is not proved from merit, much less such a 'free-will' as the Diatribe set out to prove, one which of itself can will no good! Even it you grant merit, and add to it your usual 'rational' similes and inferences, thus: 'in vain is it commanded, in vain is the reward promised, in vain are threats directed, if the will is not free'—all these arguments, I repeat, if they prove anything, prove this: that 'free-will' can do all things by itself! For if it cannot do all things by itself, it remains the 'rational' inference that therefore, precepts, promises and threats are given in vain. Thus, the Diatribe perpetually argues against itself in its argument against me. God alone by His Spirit works in us both merit and reward, but by His word without He intimates and declares them both to the whole world, so that His power and glory and our own impotence and vileness may be proclaimed even among the wicked, unbelieving and ignorant. But only the godly receive these things into their hearts and faithfully keep them; the rest despise them.

(xvi) *Matt. 7.16; Luke 23.34; John 1.12; Rom. 2.4: necessity does not destroy moral responsibility* (696-699)

It would be too wearisome to go over each imperative passage which the Diatribe enumerates from the New Testament, always tacking on its own inferences and arguing that what is said is 'purposeless', 'useless', 'absurd', 'nothing at all', unless the will is free. I have spent a long time saying, and am heartily sick of saying,[1] that such words effect nothing, and, if they prove anything, they prove a plenary 'free-will', which is precisely to overthrow the entire Diatribe; for it set out to prove a 'free-will' that can do no good and serves sin, and it actually proves a 'free-will' that can do all things! How ignorant and unmindful of itself it continually is!

So it is mere quibbling when it speaks as follows: ' "*By their fruits ye shall know them," saith the Lord* (Matt. 7.16). *He calls works "fruits", and calls them "ours"; but they are not ours, if all is carried on by necessity.*' Are not things which we did not produce ourselves, but received from others, spoken of as 'ours' in the most proper sense?[2] Why then should not works which God gave us by His Spirit be called ours? Shall we omit to call Christ ours, because we only received Him, and did not create Him? Again: if we create the things that are called ours, it follows that we created our eyes, we created our hands, we

---

[1] *usque ad multam nauseam.*   [2] *rectissime.*

created our feet for ourselves; unless our eyes, hands and feet are not to be called ours! Indeed, says Paul, what have we that we did not receive (cf. 1 Cor. 4.7)? Shall we then say, either that all this is not ours, or else that we created it all ourselves? Imagine, now, that our 'fruits' are called ours because we produce them—what place remains for grace, and the Spirit? Christ does not say: 'By their fruits, *of which a tiny element is their own*, ye shall know them'! It is rather these trivial objections that are *absurd*, and *superfluous*, and *useless*, yes, and stupid and detestable; for they defile and profane holy words of God.

A similarly trifling account is given of Christ's words on the cross: 'Father, forgive them, for they know not what they do' (Luke 23.34). Here, instead of the expected statement that should establish 'free-will', recourse is again had to inferences. '*With how much more justice*', says the Diatribe, '*might He have excused them, on the ground that they have no "free-will", and cannot do otherwise if they would?*' But this inference does not prove the 'free-will' which can will no good, which is what we are discussing; it proves the 'free-will' that can do all things, which nobody is discussing, and which everybody except the Pelagians denies! Now, when Christ openly states that 'they know not what they do', does He not thereby bear witness that they were unable to will good? For how can you will that which you do not know? You certainly cannot desire the unknown! What stronger statement can be made against 'free-will' than that it is such a nonentity that it not only cannot will good, but does not even know how much evil it is doing, and what good is? Is there *obscurity* in any single word of the statement: 'They know not what they do'? What is left in the Scriptures that cannot affirm 'free-will' at the Diatribe's prompting, when this word of Christ's, which is so clear and so entirely against it, is made to affirm it? One could as easily say that 'free-will' is affirmed by this: 'And the earth was without form and void' (Gen. 1.2), or: 'God rested on the seventh day' (Gen. 2.2), or the like! Then the Scriptures would in truth be obscure and ambiguous; they would, indeed, be at the same moment everything and nothing! But to dare to handle God's words in this way argues a mind that is notable for its contempt of both God and man, and deserves no forbearance whatsoever.

Again, the Diatribe takes these words from John 1: 'To them gave He power to become the sons of God' (v. 12), like this: *'How is power given them to become the sons of God, if there is no freedom of our will?'* This passage also is a hammer against 'free-will', as is almost the whole of John's gospel; yet it too is cited in favour of 'free-will'! Let us look at it, please! John is not speaking of any work of man, great or small, but of the actual renewal and transformation of the old man, who is a son of the devil, into the new man, who is a son of God. In this, man is simply *passive* (as the term is used); he *does* nothing, but the whole of him *becomes* something. John is speaking of this becoming: He says that we become the sons of God, by a power divinely given us—not by any power of 'free-will' inherent in us! Our friend the Diatribe, however, concludes from these words that 'free-will' has so much power that it makes us the sons of God; otherwise, it is ready to aver that John's words are absurd and useless! But who ever so exalted 'free-will' as to credit it with the power of making the sons of God?—especially a 'free-will' that cannot will good, such as the Diatribe has presupposed! This may be dismissed along with the rest of these oft-repeated inferences, which, if they prove anything, prove just what the Diatribe denies—namely, that 'free-will' can do everything!

John means this: The coming of Christ into the world through the gospel, by which grace is offered without works being required, creates for all men the truly splendid opportunity of being sons of God, if they will believe. But this willing and believing on His name is something of which 'free-will' had no previous knowledge or conception—so much the less can it do it by its own strength! How could reason conceive that faith in Jesus as Son of God and Son of Man was necessary, when even at this day it can neither grasp nor believe, though the whole creation should cry aloud, that there is a person who is both God and man! Indeed, it rather finds offence in such a statement, as Paul tells us in 1 Cor. 1 (cf. vv. 17-31)—so impossible is it that it should be either willing or able to believe it! So John is preaching, not the virtues of 'free-will,' but the riches of the kingdom of God, which are offered to the world by the gospel; and at the same time he intimates how few there are that receive it, just because 'free-will' opposes it. The power of 'free-will' amounts to this: because Satan rules over it, it rejects even grace, and the Spirit Who fulfils the law—so excellently do its own 'endeavour' and 'effort' avail to fulfil the law!

We shall show more fully at a later stage what a thunderbolt this passage of John is against 'free-will'. However, I am not a little astonished that the Diatribe should cite in favour of 'free-will' passages which are so clear, and so forcible against it. But its stupidity is such that it makes no distinction at all between the words of promise and of law; with supreme foolishness, it establishes 'free-will' from words of law, and confirms it, far more ludicrously still, by words of promise! But this absurdity is easily explained if account is taken of the proud and disaffected frame of mind in which the Diatribe disputes: it is not at all concerned whether grace stands or falls, whether 'free-will' lies vanquished or sits on the throne, if only it can oblige the tyrants by prejudicing our case with empty words!

After this we come to Paul, the most determined adversary of 'free-will'; and even he is forced to set up 'free-will', in Rom. 2: 'Or despisest thou the riches of His goodness and patience and long-suffering, not knowing that the goodness of God leadeth thee to repentance?' (v. 4). 'How can a charge of despising the commandment be brought,' says the Diatribe, 'where there is no free will? How does God invite to repentance, if He is the author of impenitence? How is condemnation just, when it is the judge who compels to evil-doing?' I reply: The Diatribe may see to these questions itself. What are they to us? The Diatribe stated in that 'probable view' that 'free-will' cannot will good and is compelled of necessity to serve sin. How, then, can the despising of the commandment be charged upon it, if it cannot will good, and there is in it no freedom, but a necessary bondage to sin? How does God invite it to repentance when He Himself prevents its repentance by abandoning it, or not giving grace to it, when it cannot will good of itself? How is condemnation just, when the Judge, by withdrawing His aid, compels the ungodly to be left in his wickedness, since of his own power he can do nothing else? All these questions recoil on the Diatribe's own head; or else, if they prove anything, they prove, as I said, that 'free-will' can do all things, which the Diatribe and everybody else denies! Its own rational inferences trouble the Diatribe throughout all the statements of Scripture; for it seems to the Diatribe absurd and useless to enforce and exact in such peremptory words when there is nobody who can comply. But the design of the Apostle in these threatenings is to bring the proud and ungodly to knowledge of themselves and of their impotence, so that, having humbled them by the knowledge of their sin, he might prepare them for grace.

What need is there to review one by one all the passage cited from Paul? For the Diatribe collects only imperative and conditional statements, or words in which Paul exhorts Christians to the fruits of faith; and then, by tacking on its inferences, it proceeds to envisage a 'free-will' whose power is so great that it can without grace do all that Paul commands in his exhortations. Christians, however, are made to act, not by 'free-will', but by the Spirit of God, as Rom. 8 tells us (v. 14); and to be made to act is not to act, but to be impelled, as a saw or an axe is made to act by a carpenter.

Lest any should at this point doubt that Luther said such foolish things, the Diatribe recites his own words—which, indeed, I acknowledge; for I confess that Wycliffe's tenet ('all things come to pass by necessity') was falsely condemned by the Council—or, rather, the Cabal and Conspiracy—of Constance. Indeed, the Diatribe itself maintains the same as I do when it asserts that 'free-will' by its own strength can will no good, and necessarily serves sin—even though it lays this down in the course of proving the exact opposite!

Suffice it to have said this much in reply to the first part of the Diatribe, where it sought to establish 'free-will'. Now let us consider the later part, where it attempts to refute my arguments—those, that is, by which 'free-will' is abolished. Here you shall see what the smoke of man can do against the thunder and lightning of God!

V

REVIEW OF ERASMUS' TREATMENT OF TEXTS THAT DENY 'FREE-WILL'—(i) (*W.A.* 699-733)

(i) *Of Erasmus' evaluation of the texts in question* (699-700)

THE Diatribe has cited countless Scripture passages in support of 'free-will'; they look an exceedingly dreadful army! Hereby it has sought to inspire courage in the confessors, and martyrs, and all the saints, male and female, that 'free-will' boasts, and to strike fear and trembling into all who sin against 'free-will' by denying it. Its first move after this is to depict the opponents of 'free-will' as a contemptible handful, and actually to make out that only two passages, '*more plausible than the rest*', stand on their side.[1] (It is ready for the kill, you see, and for that only, and does not expect it to involve any great trouble.) One passage is from Exod. 9: 'The Lord hardened the heart of Pharaoh' (v. 12); the other is from Mal. 1; 'Jacob have I loved, Esau have I hated' (vv. 2-3). Paul explains both at length in Romans (cf. Rom. 9.11ff.), but in the course of a discussion which strikes the Diatribe as remarkably unpleasing and unprofitable. Did not the Holy Ghost know a little rhetoric, there would be some risk that He would break down before such a skilfully acted display of contempt, and despair of His cause, and yield the palm to 'free-will' before battle begins! I, however, lowly reserve[2] though I am, will take occasion by these two passages to display the hosts on our side—although, when the fortune of battle is such that one can put ten thousand to flight, such hosts are not needed; for if one passage

---

[1] '*Now it is time to review some Scripture texts on the other side, which seems to take away "free-will" completely. Several such confront us in the pages of Holy Writ, but two among them are outstanding and more plausible than the rest. Paul deals with both of these in such a way that at first sight he seems to attribute nothing at all either to our own works or to the strength of "free-will".*'

[2] *succenturiatus.*

overthrows 'free-will', its own countless hordes will profit it nothing.

(ii) *That figures of speech may not be postulated in Scripture without adequate reason* (700-703)

Here, now, the Diatribe invents a new technique for evading the force of the clearest passages: that is, it will have it that in the clearest and simplest passages there is a 'figure'.[1] As before, when speaking in defence of 'free-will', it evaded the force of all the imperative and subjunctive passages in the law by tacking on inferences and devising similes, so now, when it comes to speak against me, it wrests all the words of Divine promise and declaration at its own pleasure by discovering in them a 'figure.' Everywhere it is a real Proteus for elusiveness! Yes, and it demands with great *hauteur* that we should sanction this manoeuvre, on the grounds that we too in tight corners have a habit of finding 'figures' in order to get away, like this: 'Upon which thou wilt, stretch forth thy hand' (Ecclus. 15.17): that is, grace shall stretch forth thine hand upon which it wills; 'Make you a new heart' (Ezek. 18.31): that is, grace shall make you a new heart; and the like. It seems to the Diatribe unfair that it should be permissible for Luther to propound such forced and twisted explanations, if it is not much more permissible to follow the explanations of the most reputable doctors.

You see, now, that the conflict here concerns not the text itself, nor yet implications and similes, but 'figures' and 'explanations'. When shall we ever have a plain straightforward text, free from 'figures' and 'implications', for or against 'free-will'? Does Scripture contain no such texts anywhere? Shall the 'free-will' question remain in everlasting doubt, as one which no clear text settles, but which wrangling men agitate by means of mere 'implications' and 'figures' introduced by themselves, as a reed is tossed by the winds?

Rather let this be our conviction: that no 'implication' or 'figure' may be allowed to exist in any passage of Scripture unless such be required by some obvious feature of the words

[1] *tropum.*

and the absurdity of their plain sense, as offending against an article of faith. Everywhere we should stick to just the simple, natural meaning of the words, as yielded by the rules of grammar and the habits of speech that God has created among men; for if anyone may devise 'implications' and 'figures' in Scripture at his own pleasure, what will all Scripture be but a reed shaken with the wind, and a sort of chameleon?[1] There would then be no article of faith about which anything could be settled and proved for certain, without your being able to raise objections by means of some 'figure'. All 'figures' should rather be avoided, as being the quickest poison, when Scripture itself does not absolutely require them.

See what became of that famous figurer[2] Origen in his expositions of Scripture! What just occasion did he give his critic Porphyry to say: 'those who defend Origen seem to set little store by Jerome!' What became of the Arians in respect of the figure by which they made Christ to be 'God *nominally*'? What has befallen the new prophets of our own day in respect of Christ's words, 'This is my body'? One finds a figure in the pronoun 'this', another in the verb 'is', and a third in the noun 'body'! I have noticed that all heresies and errors in handling the Scriptures have come, not from the simplicity of the words, (as almost all the world tells us), but from not regarding the simplicity of the words, and from hankering after figures and implications that come out of men's own heads.

Look at this example: 'Upon whichever thou wilt, stretch forth thine hand.' As far as I recall, I never treated these words by giving this forced explanation of them, 'grace shall stretch forth thine hand upon which it wills'; nor did I ever say that 'Make you a new heart' means: 'grace shall make you a new heart', or anything like it—albeit the Diatribe traduces me in print[3] to this effect;[4] but the Diatribe is so swollen and self-deceived with its figures and implications that it does not see what it is saying about anything! What I said was this: that the words 'stretch forth thine hand', taken simply as they stand, without bringing in figures and implications, just mean that the

---

[1] *vertumnus aliquis.*   [2] *tropologo.*   [3] *publico libello.*

[4] In his *Hyperaspistes*, Erasmus acknowledges that the author of this exegesis was actually Carlstadt, debating 'free-will' with Eck in the Leipzig disputation.

stretching forth of our hand is required of us; so that here we are told what we ought to do, according to the nature of an imperative verb as fixed by the grammarians and the common use of language. But the Diatribe disregards this simple meaning of the phrase, violently drags in implications and figures, and interprets thus: 'Stretch forth thine hand' means: 'you can stretch forth your hand by your own power'; 'Make you a new heart' means: 'You can make a new heart'; 'Believe on Christ' means: 'you can believe'. It treats imperative and indicative statements as meaning the same thing, and if this is not granted it is ready to make out that Scripture is absurd and futile. And when these 'explanations', which no grammarian could tolerate, occur in theologians, they may not be called violent or arbitrary; they are *'the views of the most reputable and time-honoured doctors'*!

The Diatribe is easily able to sanction and pursue figures at this point, for it is indifferent as to whether what is said is sure or unsure. Indeed, it aims to have all things unsure, for it advises that the doctrines concerning 'free-will' should be left alone and not investigated. Hence it would be satisfied with any way of warding off statements by which it felt itself embarrassed. But for me what is in hand is a serious matter; I want to be as sure about the truth as I can, in order to settle men's consciences; and I must act far differently. I say, then, that for me it is not enough for you to say: there *may* be a figure; my question is, whether there *need* be, and *must* be a figure; and if you do not prove that there must necessarily be a figure there, you achieve nothing. Here stands God's word: 'I will harden the heart of Pharaoh' (Exod. 4.21). You may say that it should, or could, be taken as meaning: 'I will permit it to be hardened'. I hear you tell me that it could be so taken, and that this figure is frequently used in common speech, thus: 'I ruined you, in that I did not at once correct you when you went wrong.' But there is no place here for such a 'proof'. We are not enquiring whether this figure is in use; we are not enquiring whether one *could* employ it to explain this passage in Paul; our question is, whether we may with safety and certainty suppose that we are correct in invoking it to explain this passage, and whether Paul meant to use it here. We do not want to know how a strange

N

reader might use it, but whether Paul himself, the writer, used it. What will you do for a conscience that raises this question: 'Look, the Divine Author says: "I will harden the heart of Pharaoh". The meaning of the word "harden" is plain and well known. But a human reader tells me that "harden" here means: "give an occasion of hardening, by not correcting the sinner at once". On what authority, and to what purpose, and by what need, is the natural meaning of the passage thus distorted? What if the reader is astray in his explanation? How is it proved that his distortion of the words in this passage is correct? It is both dangerous and impious to wrest the Word of God without authority and without need.' Will you counsel this poor burdened soul by saying: 'Origen thought so and so'? or 'Abandon such inquiries, for they are idle and superfluous'? His answer will be that this advice should have been given to Moses and Paul before they wrote, and also to God himself; why do they unsettle us with writings that are superfluous and idle?

This wretched refuge of 'figures' is therefore no help to the Diatribe. Our Proteus must here be held fast and made to give us full information about the 'figure' in this passage, and that either by very clear Scriptures or by indubitable miracles. We give no credit to its own mere opinion, even if the scholarship of all ages supports it; but we continue to insist that there can be no figure here; the Word of God must be taken in its plain meaning, as the words stand. For it is not left to our discretion (as the Diatribe persuades itself) to fashion and refashion the words of God as we please; else nothing is left in the entire Scripture that will not revert to the philosophical position of Anaxagoras: 'anything may come out of anything'! In that case, I may say: 'God created the heavens and the earth'—that is, He set them in place, but did not make them out of nothing. Or this: 'He created the heavens and the earth'—that is, the angels and the devils, or the righteous and the wicked! Who pray, would not at this rate be a theologian as soon as he opened the Book?

Let this, then, be fixed and settled: if the Diatribe cannot prove that there is a figure in these passages which it seeks to overthrow, then it is bound to grant me that the words must be taken as they stand, even though it should prove that the same figure is commonly found in all parts of Scripture and on all men's lips. And by this principle all my arguments, which the Diatribe sought to refute, are once for all safeguarded, and its refutation is found to achieve nothing, to have no force and to be nothing whatsoever!

(iii) *Of Erasmus' explanation of the hardening of Pharaoh* (703-709)

So when Moses' words, 'I will harden the heart of Pharaoh', are interpreted as meaning: 'My long-suffering, by which I bear with the sinner, and which leads others to repentance, shall make Pharaoh more obstinate in wickedness'—it is prettily said, but there is no proof that it is right. And I am not content with a mere statement; I want proof.

In the same way, Paul's words: 'He hath mercy on whom he will have mercy, and whom he will he hardeneth' (Rom. 9.18), are plausibly explained as meaning that God hardens when He does not straightway punish the sinner, and He has mercy when He forthwith invites him to repentance by afflicting him. But how is this interpretation proved?

The same goes for Isaiah's words: "Why hast thou made us to err from thy ways and hardened our hearts from thy fear?' (Isa. 63.17). Granted, Jerome derives from Origen the explanation that He is said to 'make to err' in that He does not at once recall from error. But who gives us assurance that the explanation of Origen and Jerome is right? Furthermore, we agreed not to base arguments on the authority of any teacher whatsoever, but only on that of Scripture. What a crew of Origens and Jeromes does the Diatribe set against me!—but it has forgotten our agreement! In any case, among all the ecclesiastical writers there are scarcely any who have handled the words of God in a more absurd and clumsy fashion than Origen and Jerome.

To put it in a word: the result of your exegetical license is that by your new, unheard-of grammar everything is thrown topsy-turvy. When God says: 'I will harden the heart of Pharaoh', you change the persons, and take it thus: 'Pharaoh hardens himself by my long-suffering'! 'God hardens our hearts' means: 'we harden ourselves while God postpones punishment'.

'Thou, Lord, hast made us to err' means: 'we have made our-selves to err while Thou dost omit to punish us'. So, too, for God to 'have mercy' no longer means that He gives grace, or shows pity, or remits sin, or justifies, or delivers from evil, but that, on the contrary, He brings evil upon one in punish-ment!

Your 'figures' will ultimately bring you to the point of saying that God had mercy on the children of Israel when He sent them to Assyria and Babylon, because there He punished the sinners and invited them to repentance by means of afflictions; but when He brought them back again and set them free, He did not then show mercy towards them, but hardened them; that is, He gave them an occasion of hardening by His own long-suffering and mercy. So, too, His sending Christ the Saviour into the world will not be called God's mercy, but God's hardening, because by this act of mercy He gave men an occasion of hardening. But His destroying Jerusalem and scattering the Jews, even to this day, will be an act of mercy on them, because by punishing those who sin He invites them to repentance! Furthermore, His carrying the saints into heaven at the day of judgment will be an act, not of mercy, but of hardening, because by His goodness He will give them an occasion of abusing that goodness! But He will be showing mercy to the wicked whom He thrusts down to hell, because He is punishing the sinners! Pray tell me, who ever heard of such acts of Divine mercy and wrath as these?

Granted, good men are made better by both the long-suffer-ing and the severity of God; yet, when we speak of both good and bad together, these 'figures', running as they do completely counter to our habits of speech, will make wrath out of God's mercy, and mercy out of His wrath; for they call it the wrath of God when He does good, and His mercy when He afflicts. But if God ought to be said to harden when He does good and to have mercy when He afflicts and punishes, why is He said to have hardened Pharaoh more than the children of Israel, or for that matter the whole world? Did He not do good to the children of Israel? Does He not do good to all the world? Does He not bear with the wicked? Does He not send rain on the evil and on the good? Why is He said to have had mercy on the children of Israel more than on Pharaoh? Did He not afflict the children of Israel in Egypt and in the desert? Granted, some abuse, and only some make a right response to, the goodness and the wrath of God; but you define 'harden' as 'show indulgence to the wicked by long-suffering and goodness', and 'show mercy' not as 'show indulgence', but as 'visit and punish'; which means that, so far as God is concerned, by continual goodness He does nothing but harden, and by continual punishment He shows nothing but mercy!

This is far and away your prettiest thought—that God is said to harden when by His long-suffering He shows indulgence to sinners, but to show mercy when He visits and afflicts, and invites them to repentance by His severity. Tell me, what did God leave undone in afflicting and punishing Pharaoh, and calling him to repentance? Are not ten plagues recorded in that narrative? If your definition stands, that showing mercy means straightway punishing and calling the sinner, God certainly showed mercy to Pharaoh! Why then does God say, not: 'I will have mercy on Pharaoh,' but: 'I will harden the heart of Pharaoh'? In the very act of showing mercy to Pharaoh (that is, of afflicting and punishing him—your equation!) He says, 'I will harden him'—that is, I will bear with him and do him good (your equation again!). What more outrageous statement could be heard? Where now are your figures? And Origen? And Jerome? And the *most reputable doctors, whom only Luther has the audacity to contradict?* But the carnal thoughtlessness of a man who trifles with God's words and does not take them seriously makes it inevitable that he should talk like this.

Moses' actual text, therefore, proves incontrovertibly that your 'figures' are worthless fancies at this point, and that by the words: 'I will harden the heart of Pharaoh' is meant something distinct from, and more far-reaching than, *doing good*, or *afflicting and punishing*. For we cannot deny that both of these were tried on Pharaoh most carefully and energetically! What acts of wrath and punishment could be more prompt and pressing than his being assailed with so many signs of plagues that Moses himself bears record that the like had never been? Even Pharaoh himself was roused by them more than once, as if to repent; though he was not thoroughly aroused and did not continue. What acts of long-suffering and well-doing could be more bountiful than God's taking away the plagues so readily, remitting Pharaoh's sin so often, restoring good and removing evil so many times? Yet neither course availed, and still God said: 'I will harden the heart of Pharaoh!' You see, then, that, even were it granted that your brand of 'hardening' and 'mercy' (that is, as represented by the figure in your gloss) was in fact employed, and may be seen exemplified, in the fullest measure in dealing with Pharaoh, yet a 'hardening' still remains; and that 'hardening' of which Moses speaks must needs differ from that of which you dream.

However, seeing that I am fighting with fabricators and the fancies that haunt them, let me give rein to my own fancy and imagine the impossible—that the figure of which the Diatribe dreams really is found in this passage. Then I will see how the Diatribe can help being forced to declare that all things come to pass by the will of God alone, and by necessity as far as we are concerned; and how it can clear God of being Himself the author and cause of our hardening. If it is true that God is said to harden when He bears with long-suffering and does not at once punish, yet both the following positions still stand firm:—

First, man serves sin of necessity nevertheless. Since it is granted that 'free-will' cannot will good (and that is the kind of 'free-will' that the Diatribe undertook to prove), then the goodness of a long-suffering God does not make it any better, but necessarily makes it worse, unless in God's mercy the Spirit is joined to it; so that all things still take place by necessity as far as we are concerned.

Second, God appears to be just as merciless in bearing with us in His long-suffering as He is thought to appear when we proclaim that He deliberately hardens according to His own inscrutable will. For since He sees that 'free-will' cannot will good, but grows worse as in long-suffering He bears with it, He appears in this very long-suffering to show the greatest cruelty, and to find delight in our misery. He could remedy it, if He will, and could cease to bear with it, if He willed; indeed, He could not bear with it unless He did will. Who shall compel Him against His will? Now, if that will, without which nothing comes to pass, stands firm, and if it is further granted that 'free-will' can will no good, all that is said to clear God and throw the blame on 'free-will' is said in vain; for 'free-will' always speaks thus: 'I cannot, and God will not: what can I do? Suppose He shows mercy by afflicting me; I gain nothing by it, but must needs grow worse, unless He gives me His Spirit. But this He does not give; and He would give it, if He so willed; so it is certain that He wills not to give.'

The analogies cited completely miss the point. The Diatribe says: '*As by the same sun mud is hardened and wax melted; as after the same rain tilled ground bears fruit, and untilled ground thorns; so by the same long-suffering of God some are hardened and others converted.*' But we are not now dividing 'free-will' into two different natures, one like mud, the other like wax; one like tilled ground, the other like untilled ground. We are speaking of that one 'free-will' which is equally impotent in all men, and is like mud and untilled ground only, inasmuch as it cannot will good. As mud grows ever harder, and untilled ground ever thornier, so 'free-will' always grows worse, as well under the hardening sun of long-suffering as under the softening shower of rain. Now, if 'free-will' has the same character[1], the same impotence, in all men, no reason can be given why it should attain to grace in one and not in another, if no more be proclaimed than the long-suffering forbearance of God and the merciful chastisement of God; for it has been laid down already that 'free-will' in all men has the same character—total inability to will good.

On your view, God will elect nobody, and no place for election will be left; all that is left is freedom of will to heed or defy the long-suffering and wrath of God. But if God is thus robbed of His power and wisdom in election, what will He be but just that idol, Chance, under whose sway all things happen at random? Eventually, we shall come to this: that men may be saved and damned without God's knowledge! For He will not have marked out by sure election those that should be saved and those that should be damned; He will merely have set before all men His general long-suffering, which forbears and hardens, together with His chastening and punishing mercy,

---

[1] *definitionis.*

and left it to them to choose whether they would be saved or damned, while He Himself, perchance, goes off, as Homer says, to an Ethiopian banquet![1]

Aristotle also depicts for us a God of this kind, that is, one who is asleep, and who leaves it for anyone to use or abuse His long-suffering and chastisement at will. Nor can reason come to any other conclusion about God than the Diatribe does here. As she herself snores over and makes light of the things of God, so she thinks of God as snoring over them too, not using His wisdom, will and presence to elect, separate and inspire, but entrusting to men the tiresome business of heeding or defying His long-suffering and anger! This is what we come to when we seek to measure God and make excuses for Him by human reason, not reverencing the secrets of His majesty, but peering and probing into them; with the result that we are overwhelmed by the glory of them and instead of a single excuse we vomit out a thousand blasphemies! We forget ourselves, and gabble like lunatics, speaking against both God and ourselves, while all the time we were intending, in the greatness of our wisdom, to plead both God's cause and our own!

Here you see what the figure in the Diatribe's gloss will make of God; and you further see how well the Diatribe accords with itself. Before, by a single definition it made 'free-will' to be precisely the same in all men; now, as its argument proceeds, it forgets its definition, and makes one 'free-will' to be 'tilled' and another 'untilled', according to the difference of men's works and manners. Thus it makes two distinct 'free-wills', one doing good, the other not. And this is by its own strength before grace; that strength by which, according to the foregoing definition, 'free-will' can will no good! Thus it is that, by not ascribing the will and power of hardening, showing mercy, and doing all things, to the will of God alone, we ascribe to 'free-will' itself power to do all things without grace; when yet we have denied that it can do any good thing without grace!

So the similes of the sun and the rain are worthless. The Christian will use them more properly if he calls the gospel the sun and the rain, as Ps. 18 (Ps. 19.4-5) does, and Heb. 10 (Heb. 6.7), and makes the tilled ground to be the elect and the

[1] *Od.* I.22ff.

untilled the reprobate; since the former are made better by the
Word, while the latter are offended and made worse. Apart
from grace, 'free-will' by itself is Satan's kingdom in all men.

Let us look into the reasons for inventing this figure in this
passage. *'It seems absurd'* (says the Diatribe) *'that God Who is not
just but good, should be said to have hardened the heart of a man so that
by means of his iniquity God should show His power.'* So it has
recourse to Origen, who admits that the occasion of hardening
was God-given but throws the blame back on Pharaoh, and
who has also pointed out that God said: 'For this purpose have
I *raised thee up'*, and did not say: 'for this purpose have I *made
thee'*. *'Pharaoh would not have been wicked had God made him what he
was, for "God beheld all His works, and they were very good"'* (Gen.
1.31). Thus the Diatribe.

So one of the main reasons why the words of Moses and Paul
are not taken in their plain sense is their 'absurdity'. But
against what article of faith does that 'absurdity' transgress?
And who is offended by it? It is human reason that is offended;
which, though it is blind, deaf, senseless, godless, and sacrilegious, in its dealing with all God's words and works, is at this
point brought in as judge of God's words and works! On these
same grounds you will deny all the articles of the faith, for it is
the highest absurdity by far—foolishness to the Gentiles and a
stumbling-block to the Jews, as Paul says (cf. 1 Cor. 1.23)—
that God should be man, a virgin's son, crucified, sitting at the
Father's right hand. It is, I repeat, *absurd* to believe such things!
So let us invent some figures with the Manichaeans, and say that
he is not truly man, but a phantom who passed through the
virgin like a ray of light through glass, and then fell, and so was
crucified! This would be a fine way for us to handle the
Scriptures!

But the figures are still no help; the 'absurdity' is not escaped.
It remains absurd to reason's judgment that God, Who is just
and good, should require of 'free-will' impossibilities; and that,
though 'free-will' cannot will good and serves sin of necessity,
He should yet lay sin to its charge; and that, by not giving the
Spirit, He should act so severely and mercilessly as to harden,
or allow to be hardened. Reason will insist that these are not the
acts of a good and merciful God. They are too far beyond her

grasp; and she cannot bring herself to *believe* that the God Who acts and judges thus is good; she wants to shut out faith, and to see, and feel, and understand, how it is that He is good and not cruel. She would certainly understand, were it said of God that He hardens none and damns none, but has mercy on all and saves all, so that hell is destroyed, and the fear of death may be put away, and no future punishment need be dreaded! It is along this line that reason storms and contends, in order to clear God of blame, and to vindicate His justice and goodness! But faith and the Spirit judge otherwise, believing that God is good even though he should destroy all men. And what do we gain by wearying ourselves with these speculations, so as to throw back upon 'free-will' the blame for man's hardening? Let all the 'free-will' in the world do all it can with all its strength; it will never give rise to a single instance of ability to avoid being hardened if God does not give the Spirit, or of meriting mercy if it is left to its own strength. What difference does it make whether it is 'hardened' or 'deserves hardening', if hardening necessarily supervenes as long as there remains in it that impotence which, as the Diatribe itself informs us, disables 'free-will' from willing good? Seeing, now, that these figures do not remove the 'absurdity', or, if they do, only at the cost of introducing greater absurdities, by assigning all things to 'free-will', away with such unprofitable and misleading figures, and let us cleave to the pure and simple Word of God!

Your observation that what God made was very good, and that God did not say: 'for this purpose have I made thee', but: 'for this purpose have I raised thee up', raises a further issue. *Firstly*, I would remark that the first words you quote refer to the time before the fall of man, when what God had made was very good. But the immediate sequel, in the third chapter, tells how man became evil, and was abandoned by God and left to himself. Of that one man, thus corrupt, all men were born ungodly, Pharaoh included; as Paul says: 'We were all by nature the children of wrath, even as others' (Eph. 2.3). So God created Pharaoh ungodly, that is, of an ungodly and corrupt seed; as it says in the Proverbs of Solomon: 'The Lord hath made all things for Himself, yea, even the ungodly for the day of evil' (Prov. 16.4). It does not follow that, because God made the ungodly, he is therefore not ungodly! How can he fail to be ungodly, coming of an ungodly seed? It is as Ps. 50 says: 'Behold, I was conceived in sin' (Ps. 51.5); and as Job says: 'Who can make a clean thing (when it is conceived) out of an unclean (seed)?' (Job 14.4). Though God does not make sin, yet He does not cease to form and multiply our nature, from which the Spirit has been withdrawn and which sin has impaired. He is like a carpenter who makes statues out of warped wood. As is the nature, so are men made; for God creates and forms them out of that nature. *Secondly*, this must be said: if you want the words 'they were very good' to be understood of God's works after the fall, you will notice that the words were spoken with reference, not to us, but to God. It does not say: '*Man* saw what God had made, and it was very good.' Many things seem, and are, very good to God which seem, and are, very bad to us. Thus, afflictions, sorrows, errors, hell, and all God's best works are in the world's eyes very bad, and damnable. What is better than Christ and the gospel? But what is there that the world abominates more? How things that are bad for us are good in the sight of God is known only to God and to those who see with God's eyes, that is, who have the Spirit. But there is as yet no need of such subtle argumentation; for the time being, the preceding answer is sufficient.

(iv) *Of God's method of working evil in man* (709-710)

Perhaps it will here be asked, by what means God is said to work evil in us, as (for instance) in hardening us, giving us up to our desires, causing us to err, and so on?

We should in any case be content with the words of God, and simply believe what they say; for the works of God are wholly indescribable. However, to humour reason (that is, human folly), I do not mind aping its stupidity and foolishness and seeing if I can make any impression on it by my own broken words on this subject.

In the first place even reason and the Diatribe allow that Gods works all in all, and that without Him nothing is effected nor effective; for He is omnipotent, and effective action belongs to His omnipotence, as Paul tells the Ephesians (cf. Eph. 1.11).

Now, Satan and man, being fallen and abandoned by God, cannot will good (that is, things that please God, or that God wills), but are ever turned in the direction of their own desires, so that they cannot but seek their own. This will and nature of theirs, thus turned from God, cannot be *nothing*, nor are Satan and ungodly man *nothing*; nor have they a nature and will that is *nothing*, though they certainly have a nature that is corrupt and turned from God. So that which we call the remnant of nature in the ungodly and in Satan, as being a creature and a work of God, is no less subject to Divine omnipotence and action than all the rest of God's creatures and works. Since God moves and works all in all, He moves and works of necessity even in Satan and the ungodly. But He works according to what they are, and what He finds them to be: which means, since they are evil and perverted[1] themselves, that when they are impelled to action by this movement of Divine omnipotence they do only that which is perverted and evil. It is like a man riding a horse with only three, or two, good feet; his riding corresponds with what the horse is, which means that the horse goes badly. But what can the rider do? He is riding this horse in company with sound horses; this one goes badly, though the rest go well; and so it is bound to be, unless the horse is healed.

Here you see that when God works in and by evil men, evil deeds result; yet God, though He does evil by means of evil men, cannot act evilly Himself, for He is good, and cannot do evil; but He uses evil instruments, which cannot escape the impulse and movement of His power. The fault which accounts for evil being done when God moves to action lies in these instruments, which God does not allow to be idle. In the same way a carpenter would cut badly with a saw-toothed axe. Hence it is that the ungodly man cannot but err and sin always, because under the impulse of Divine power he is not allowed to be idle, but wills, desires and acts according to his nature.

This is sure and certain, if we believe that God is omnipotent; as it is also certain that the ungodly man is a creature of God, but one which, being perverted and left to itself without the Spirit of God, cannot will or do good. God's omnipotence makes it impossible for the ungodly man to escape the action upon

[1] *aversi.*

him of the movement of God; of necessity he is subject to it, and obeys it; but his corruption, his turning of himself from God, makes it impossible for him to be moved and made to act well. God cannot suspend His omnipotence on account of man's perversion, and the ungodly man cannot alter his perversion. As a result he sins and errs incessantly and inevitably until he is set right by the Spirit of God. In all this Satan continues to reign in peace; under this movement of Divine omnipotence he keeps his palace undisturbed.

(v) *Of God's method of hardening man* (710-711)

There follows upon this the business of hardening, which proceeds thus: As we have said, the ungodly man, like Satan his prince, is wholly turned to self and to his own. He does not seek God, nor care for the things of God: he seeks his own riches, and glory, and works, and wisdom, and power, and sovereignty in everything, and wants to enjoy it in peace. If anyone stands in his way, or wants to detract from any of these things, he is moved with the same perverted desire[1] that leads him to seek them, and is outraged and furious with his opponent. He can no more restrain his fury than he can stop his self-seeking, and he can no more stop his self-seeking than he can stop existing— for he is still a creature of God; though a spoiled one.

This is precisely the rage which the world shows against the gospel of God. By the gospel there comes that stronger One, to vanquish him who keeps his palace in peace; and He condemns those desires of glory, wealth, wisdom, righteousness of one's own, and all the things in which the world trusts. This very galling of the ungodly, as God says and does to them the reverse of what they wanted, is the hardening and embittering of them. As of themselves they are turned away from God by the very corruption of their nature, so their antipathy greatly increases and they grow far worse as their course away from God meets with opposition or reversal. Thus, when God purposed to deprive ungodly Pharaoh of his kingdom, he galled and hardened him, and brought bitterness to his heart, by falling upon him through the word of Moses, who seemed about

[1] *aversione.*

to take away his kingdom and deliver the people from under his dominion. He did not give Pharaoh the Spirit within, but allowed his own ungodly corruption, under Satan's sway, to blaze with anger, to swell with pride, to boil with rage and to advance along the path of scornful recklessness.

Let none think, when God is said to harden or work evil in us (for hardening is working evil) that he does it by, as it were, creating fresh evil in us, as you might imagine an ill-disposed innkeeper, a bad man himself, pouring and mixing poison into a vessel that was not bad, while the vessel itself does nothing, but is merely the recipient, or passive vehicle, of the mixer's own ill-will. When men hear us say that God works both good and evil in us, and that we are subject to God's working by mere passive necessity, they seem to imagine a man who is in himself good, and not evil, having an evil work wrought in him by God; for they do not sufficiently bear in mind how incessantly active God is in all his creatures, allowing none of them to keep holiday. He who would understand these matters, however, should think thus: God works evil in us (that is, by means of us) not through God's own fault, but by reason of our own defect. We being evil by nature, and God being good, when He impels us to act by His own acting upon us according to the nature of His omnipotence, good though He is in Himself, He cannot but do evil by our evil instrumentality; although, according to His wisdom, He makes good use of this evil for His own glory and for our salvation.

Thus God, finding Satan's will evil, not creating it so (it became so by Satan's sinning and God's withdrawing), carries it along by His own operation and moves it where He wills; although Satan's will does not cease to be evil in virtue of this movement of God.

David spoke in this way of Shimei, in the second book of Kings: 'Let him curse, for God hath bidden him to curse David' (2 Sam. 16.10). How could God bid anyone to curse, an act so virulent and evil? There was nowhere any external precept to that effect. But David keeps in view the fact that God omnipotent speaks and it is done: that is, He works all things by His own eternal word. In this case, therefore, the Divine action and omnipotence impel Shimei's already evil will (which was hot against David before), and all his members with it; confronts him at an appropriate moment, when David deserves such blasphemy; and the good God Himself, by means of an evil blaspheming instrument, commands this blasphemy (that is, speaks and effects it through His word, which is just the impelling force of His acting).

(vi) *Of the hardening of Pharaoh* (711-714)

Thus God hardens Pharaoh: He presents to the ungodly, evil will of Pharaoh His own word and work, which Pharaoh's will hates, by reason of its own inbred fault and natural corruption. God does not alter that will within by His Spirit, but goes on presenting and bringing pressure to bear; and Pharaoh, having in mind his own strength, wealth and power, trusts to them by this same fault of his nature. So it comes to pass that, being inflated and uplifted by the idea of his own greatness, and growing vaingloriously scornful of lowly Moses and of the unostentatious word of God, he becomes hardened; and then grows more and more irked and annoyed, the more Moses presses and threatens him. His evil will would not have been moved or hardened of itself, but as the omnipotent Agent makes it act (as He does the rest of His creatures) by means of His own inescapable movement, it needs must actively will something. As soon as God presents to it from without something that naturally irritates and offends it, Pharaoh cannot escape being hardened, even as he cannot escape the acting of Divine omnipotence and the perversion and villainy of his own will. So God's hardening of Pharaoh is wrought thus: God presents from without to his villainous heart that which by nature he hates; at the same time, He continues by omnipotent action to move within him the evil will which He finds there. Pharaoh, by reason of the villainy of his will, cannot but hate what opposes him, and trust to his own strength; and he grows so obstinate that he will not listen nor reflect, but is swept along in the grip of Satan like a raging madman.

If I have gained your assent to these things, I have won this point. I have shattered the figures and glosses of men, and taken the words of God in their simple sense; and now there is no necessity to make excuses for God, nor to accuse him of unrighteousness. When He says: 'I will harden the heart of Pharaoh', He uses the words in their simple meaning. It is as if he said: 'I will cause the heart of Pharaoh to be hardened'; or 'it shall be hardened by My operation and action'. We have heard how it was to be done; thus: 'By my ordinary movement within I will so move his evil will that he shall go on in his present headstrong course of willing; I will not cease to move it, nor can I. From without, I will present to him My word and work; and his evil fury shall hurl itself against it; for he, being evil, cannot but will evil as I move him by the power of omnipotence.' Thus God with full certainty knew, and with full certainty declared, that Pharaoh should be hardened; for He knew with full certainty that Pharaoh's will could neither resist the movement of omnipotence, nor put away its own villainy, nor bow to Moses, the adversary set before him. While his will remained evil, Pharaoh must necessarily grow worse, more hardened and more proud; in his headstrong course, he would hurl himself against that which he would not have and which he despised, for he was confident of his power. So here you see that these very words confirm that 'free-will' can do nothing but evil, inasmuch as God, Who does not make mistakes through ignorance nor speak lies in iniquity, thus surely promises the hardening of Pharaoh; for well He knew that an evil will can only will evil, and that when good is presented as opposing it, it cannot but wax worse.

It now remains for someone to ask: Why then does God not cease from that movement of omnipotence by which the will of the ungodly is moved to go on being evil, and to grow worse? The answer is: this is to desire that for the sake of the ungodly God should cease to be God; for you are desiring that His power and activity should cease—that is, that He should cease to be good, lest the ungodly should grow worse!

Why then does He not alter those evil wills which He moves? This question touches on the secrets of His Majesty, where 'His judgments are past finding out' (cf. Rom. 11.33). It is not for us to inquire into these mysteries, but to adore them. If flesh and blood take offence here, and grumble, well, let them grumble; they will achieve nothing; grumbling will not change God!

And however many of the ungodly stumble and depart, the elect will remain (cf. John 6.60ff.).

The same reply should be given to those who ask: Why did God let Adam fall, and why did He create us all tainted with the same sin, when He might have kept Adam safe, and might have created us of other material, or of seed that had first been cleansed? God is He for Whose will no cause or ground[1] may be laid down as its rule and standard; for nothing is on a level with it or above it, but it is itself the rule for all things. If any rule or standard, or cause or ground, existed for it, it could no longer be the will of God. What God wills is not right because He ought, or was bound, so to will; on the contrary, what takes place must be right, because He so wills it. Causes and grounds are laid down for the will of the creature, but not for the will of the Creator—unless you set another Creator over him!

By these arguments, the figure-mongering Diatribe and its figure with it are, I think, adequately confuted. However, let us go to the text itself to see what agreement there is between it and the figure. It is the way of all who parry arguments with figures to hold the text in sovereign contempt, and to concern themselves merely with picking out a word, torturing it with their figures, and nailing it to the cross of their own chosen meaning, in utter disregard of the surrounding context, of what comes before and after, and of the author's aim and intention. So it is here. Without stopping to see the point and purpose of Moses' words, the Diatribe tears from the text the phrase: 'I will harden', which it finds objectionable, and makes of it what it pleases, without a thought as to how it may be re-inserted and fitted back so as to square with the body of the passage. This is the reason why those learned and time-honoured friends of yours have found Scripture insufficiently clear. No wonder! The sun itself could not shine if assailed by such devices as theirs!

I demonstrated above, that it is not right to say that Pharaoh was hardened because a long-suffering God bore with him and he was not punished at once; for in fact he was chastised with all the plagues. That I here pass by. But now—if 'harden' means

[1] *ratio.*

'bear with Divine long-suffering and not punish at once', what need was there for God to promise so often, at the time when the signs were occurring, that he would harden the heart of Pharaoh? For already, before those signs and that hardening took place, God had in long-suffering borne with Pharaoh, and omitted to punish him, while Pharaoh, puffed up with his success and his power, was inflicting great woe upon the children of Israel! Do you see, now, that your figure completely misses the point of this passage? It would apply indiscriminately to all who sin while Divine long-suffering bears with them. In this sense, we shall say that all men are hardened, for there is none that does not sin, and none would sin did not Divine long-suffering bear with him! This hardening of Pharaoh is therefore something distinct, over and above the general forbearance of Divine long-suffering.

Moses' concern is to proclaim, not so much the villainy of Pharaoh as the veracity and mercy of God, lest the children of Israel should distrust the promises of God whereby He undertook to set them free. Since this was a tremendous task, He forewarns them of its difficulty, so that, knowing that it was all foretold and would be duly carried out by the executive action of Him Who had promised, they might not be shaken in their faith. It is as if He had said: 'I will certainly deliver you, but you will find it hard to believe, because Pharaoh will so resist and delay the deliverance. But trust nevertheless; for by My operation all his delaying shall only result in My performing more and greater miracles to confirm you in your faith and to display My powers, so that henceforth you may have more faith in Me in all other matters.'

Christ acts in the same way when at the last supper He promises His disciples a kingdom. He foretells abundance of difficulties—His own death, and their many tribulations—so that, when it came to pass, they might from then on have much more faith.

Moses plainly shows us that this is the meaning when he says: 'But Pharaoh shall not let you go, that many wonders may be wrought in Egypt' (Exod. 3.19-20); and again: 'For this cause have I raised thee up, for to show in thee my power; and that my name may be declared throughout all the earth'

(9.16). Here you see that Pharaoh was hardened to resist God and to delay redemption in order that occasion might be given for many signs and a display of the power of God, so that He might be declared and believed on throughout all the earth. What does this mean, but that all these things were said and done to strengthen faith and to comfort the weak, that henceforth they might without hesitation believe in God as true, faithful, mighty and merciful? It is as if He were speaking in the most soothing strains to little children, saying: 'Do not be terrified at Pharaoh's stubbornness, for I work that very stubbornness Myself, and I Who deliver you have it under My control. I shall simply make use of it to work many signs and to declare My majesty, so as to help your faith.'

This is why Moses generally repeats after each plague: 'And the heart of Pharaoh was hardened, so that he would not let the people go; as the Lord had spoken' (Exod. 7.13, 22; 8.15; 9.12). What was the point of: 'As the Lord had spoken', but that the Lord might appear true, as having foretold that Pharaoh should be hardened? Had there been in Pharaoh any power to turn, or freedom of will that might have gone either way, God could not with such certainty have foretold his hardening. But as it is, He who neither deceives nor is deceived guarantees it; which means that it is completely certain, and necessary, that Pharaoh's hardening will come to pass. And it would not be so, were not that hardening wholly beyond the strength of man, and in the power of God alone, in the manner that I spoke of above: that is, God was certain that He would not suspend the ordinary operation of omnipotence in Pharaoh, or on Pharaoh's account—indeed, He could not omit it; and He was equally certain that the will of Pharaoh, being naturally evil and perverse, could not consent to the word and work of God which opposed it; hence, while by the omnipotence of God the energy of willing was preserved to Pharaoh within, and the word and work that opposed him was set before him without, nothing could happen in Pharaoh but the offending and hardening of his heart. If God had suspended the action of His omnipotence in Pharaoh when He set before him the word of Moses which opposed him, and if the will of Pharaoh might be supposed to have acted alone by its own power, then there could perhaps have been a place for debating which way it had power to turn. But as it is, since he is impelled and made to act by his own willing, no violence is done to his will; for it is not under unwilling constraint, but by an operation of God consonant with its nature it is impelled to will naturally, according to what it is (that is, evil). Therefore, it could not but turn upon one word, and thus become hardened. Thus we see that this passage makes most forcibly against 'free-will,' on this account that God, who promises, cannot lie; and, if He cannot lie, then Pharaoh cannot but be hardened.

(vii) *Rom. 9.15ff.: proof that Paul teaches the necessitating fore-*
knowledge of God (714-718)

Now let us look at Paul, who takes up this text from Moses in Rom. 9 (v. 17). How wretchedly is the Diatribe tormented by that passage! It adopts every conceivable posture to avoid losing 'free-will'. At one moment, it says: '*there is a necessity of consequence, but not of the thing consequent.*' At another: '*there is a will of appointment, or of sign, which can be resisted, and a will of purpose,*[1] *which cannot.*' At another: '*the passages cited from Paul have no force, they do not speak about man's salvation.*' In one place, '*the foreknowledge of God imposes necessity*'; in another place, it does not. In another, '*grace goes before the will to make it will, and then attends it as it proceeds and brings it to a happy issue.*' At one stage, '*the first cause does all things itself*'; elsewhere, '*it acts by second causes, being itself inactive.*' Its sole achievement by this and by similar jugglings with words is to fill up time, and momentarily to whisk the real issue out of sight, and to drag the discussion away in another direction. It thinks we are as thickheaded and dimwitted, or as little interested in this subject, as it is itself! As little children in fear, or at play, cover their eyes with their hands and think that because they see nobody, nobody sees them, so the Diatribe, which cannot bear the bright beams, nay, the lightning-flashes, of the clearest words, uses every means to pretend that it does not see what the facts are, in hope of persuading us that our eyes are covered also and that we cannot see them either. All these manœuvres, however, are signs of a

---

[1] *ordinatam, seu voluntatem signi . . . voluntatem placiti.*

mind under conviction, recklessly resisting invincible truth. The fancy about necessity of *consequence* and of *the thing consequent*[1] was refuted earlier. Let the Diatribe invent and go on inventing, let it quibble and quibble again—if God foreknew that Judas would be a traitor, Judas became a traitor of necessity, and it was not in the power of Judas or of any creature to act differently, or to change his will, from that which God had foreseen. It is true that Judas acted willingly, and not under compulsion, but his willing was the work of God, brought into being by His omnipotence, like everything else. It is a principle of clear, unassailable truth that God does not lie or make mistakes. There are no obscure or ambiguous words here, even though all the most learned men of all ages should be so blind as to think and affirm the contrary. However much you may boggle, yet your conscience, and everybody's conscience, is convinced, and bound to confess, that, if God is not mistaken in what He foreknows, then what He foreknows must necessarily come to pass. Otherwise, who could believe His promises, and who would fear His threatenings, if what He promised or threatened did not necessarily ensue? How can He promise or threaten, if His foreknowledge deceives Him, or can be obstructed by our instability? The supremely clear light of certain truth stops all mouths, ends all questions and gives victory over all the subtleties of evasion.

We know that *man's* foreknowledge is fallible. We know that an eclipse does not occur because it is forecast, but is forecast because it is going to occur. But what relevance has that foreknowledge for us? We are discussing the foreknowledge of *God*! And if you do not allow that the thing which God foreknows is necessarily brought to pass, you take away faith and the fear of God, you undermine all the Divine promises and threatenings, and so you deny Deity itself!

Even the Diatribe, after holding out for a long time and trying everything, is at last pressed so hard by the force of

---

[1] '*Those who discuss this matter with scholastic subtlety accept* necessity of consequence, *but reject* necessity of the thing consequent. (*These are the terms in which they regularly express their view.*) *They admit that it follows of necessity that Judas will betray the Lord, if God has so willed from eternity by His own efficacious will: but they say that it does not follow that Judas was bound of necessity to betray him simply because he undertook that unholy task of his own wicked will.*'

truth that it subscribes to my own sentiments, saying: '*The question about the will and predestination of God is rather difficult. For God wills what He foreknows. This is the meaning of what Paul subjoins: who resists His will, if He has mercy on whom He will and hardens whom He will. For if there was a king who could bring about whatever he chose, and none could resist him, he would be said to do whatever he willed. Thus, since the will of God is the principle cause of all that comes to pass, it seems to impose necessity on our will.*' So speaks the Diatribe.

Thank God for sound sense in the Diatribe at last! Where is 'free-will' now? But the eel slips away again; suddenly it says: '*However, Paul does not explain this point: he just rebukes the disputer: "Who art thou, O man, that repliest against God?"*' (v. 20).

A fine way out! Is this the way to handle the sacred text, thus to lay down the law on your own authority, out of your own head, without Scripture and without miracles—yes, and to pervert the clearest words of God? Does not Paul explain that point? What then does he do? 'He rebukes the disputer,' says the Diatribe. And is not that rebuke the completest explanation? What was your inquiry about the will of God? Was it not, whether it imposes necessity on our will? Paul is replying that it is so: 'He has mercy on whom he will have mercy, and whom he will he hardeneth. It is not of him that willeth, nor of him that runneth, but of God that showeth mercy' (vv. 15.16, 18). Not content with having given this explanation, he goes on to introduce those who in the name of 'free-will' grumble against it, and rattle on to the effect that there is then no merit, and we are damned through no fault of our own, and the like; and he silences their grumbling and displeasure, saying: 'Thou sayest to me then, Why doth He yet find fault? for who shall resist His will?' (v. 19). Do you see to whom he addresses himself? To those who, when they hear that the will of God brings necessity upon us, blasphemously complain, and say: 'Why doth He yet find fault?' That is, 'Why does God thus press, urge, exact and so find fault? Why does He accuse? Why does He reprove? As though we men could do what he requires, if we would! He has no just cause for His complaint; let Him rather accuse His own will; there let Him find fault, and press His demands! "For who shall resist His will?" Who can obtain mercy when that is not His will? Who can be softened, if He wills to harden? It is not in our power to change His will, much less to resist it when it wills our hardening; by that will we are compelled to be hardened, willy-nilly!'

If Paul had not explained this point, and definitely assured us that necessity is imposed upon us by the foreknowledge of God, what need was there to introduce these objectors, who complain that His will cannot be resisted? Who would object or take offence, if he did not think that this necessity had been enunciated? The words in which Paul speaks of resisting the will of God are not obscure; and is there anything ambiguous about what 'resisting' is, or what he is talking about when he speaks of the will of God? Let myriads of the most reputable doctors be blind, and fancy that the Scriptures are *not quite clear*, and tremble at the difficulty of the question; we have here the plainest words, and this is what they say: 'He hath mercy on whom He will have mercy, and whom He will He hardeneth' and: 'Thou sayest to me then, Why doth He yet find fault? Who shall resist His will?' The question is not difficult; indeed, nothing is more straightforward, even by common sense, than that the following inference is sure, well-founded and true: If God foreknows a thing, it necessarily happens (assuming that the Scriptural position that God neither errs nor makes mistakes, is premised). It would certainly be a hard question, I allow—indeed, an insoluble one—if you sought to establish *both* the foreknowledge of God *and* the freedom of man together; for what is harder, yes, more impossible, than maintaining that contraries and contradictories do not clash? that the same number may be both nine and ten at the same time? There is no difficulty attaching to my point; the difficulty is sought out and brought in from outside, just as ambiguity and obscurity in the Scriptures are sought out and brought in by doing violence to the text!

The apostle, therefore, is bridling the ungodly who take offence at his plain speaking, telling them they should realise that the Divine will is fulfilled by what to us is necessity, and that it is definitely established that no freedom or 'free-will' is left them, but all things depend on the will of God alone. And he bridles them by commanding them to be silent, and to revere the majesty of God's power and will, against which we have no rights, but which has full rights against us to do what It pleases. No injustice is done to us, for God owes us nothing, He has received nothing from us, and He has promised us nothing but what He pleased and willed. So this is the time and place to adore, not your 'Corycian caverns', but the true Majesty in its awful, wondrous, incomprehensible judgments, and to say: Thy will be done, as in heaven, so in earth (Luke 11.2). We are nowhere more recklessly irreverent than when we trespass upon and argue about these inscrutable mysteries of judgments. We pretend all the while that we are showing incredible reverence, in that we are searching the Holy Scriptures, which God told us to search. But them we do not search; whereas, in the place where He forbade us to search, there we do nothing but search, with endless audacity, not to say blasphemy! Is it not an audacious way of searching, to try and harmonize the wholly free foreknowledge of God with our own freedom, and to be ready to deny the foreknowledge of God if it does not allow us freedom and if it imposes necessity on us, to say with the blasphemous complainers: 'Why doth He yet find fault? For who shall resist His will? Where is the God Whose nature is kindness itself? Where is He that willeth not the death of a sinner? Has He created us merely to delight Himself in men's torments?'—and the like; which sentiments the damned in hell will be howling out to all eternity!

(viii) *That natural reason must admit that Divine freedom implies human necessity* (718-719)

Natural reason herself is forced to confess that the living and true God must be One who by His own liberty imposes necessity on us. He would be a ludicrous Deity—idol, rather—if His foreknowledge of the future were unreliable and could be falsified by events; for even the Gentiles ascribed to their gods 'fate inevitable'! He would be equally ludicrous if He could not and did not do all things, or if anything were done without Him. But if the foreknowledge and omnipotence of God are conceded, it naturally follows by irrefutable logic that we were not made by ourselves, nor live by ourselves, nor do anything by ourselves, but by His omnipotence. Seeing that He foreknew that we should be what we are, and now makes us such, and moves and governs us as such, how, pray, can it be pretended that it is open to us to become something other than that which He foreknew and is now bringing about? So the foreknowledge and omnipotence of God are diametrically opposed to our 'freewill'. Either God makes mistakes in His foreknowledge, and errors in His action (which is impossible), or else we act, and are caused to act, according to His foreknowledge and action. And by the omnipotence of God I mean, not the power by which He omits to do many things that He could do, but the active power by which He mightily works all in all. It is in this sense that Scripture calls Him omnipotent. This omnipotence and foreknowledge of God, I repeat, utterly destroy the doctrine of 'free-will'. Nor can the obscurity of Scripture, or the difficulty of the subject, be invoked against this conclusion. The words are entirely clear; boys know them; the point is plain and simple, and is established even by the natural verdict of common sense; so your list, however long, of ages, times and persons that wrote and taught otherwise, goes for nothing.

Doubtless it gives the greatest possible offence to common sense or natural reason, that God, Who is proclaimed as being full of mercy and goodness, and so on, should of His own mere will abandon, harden and damn men, as though He delighted in the sins and great eternal torments of such poor wretches. It seems an iniquitous, cruel, intolerable thought to think of God; and it is this that has been a stumbling block to so many great men down the ages. And who would not stumble at it? I have stumbled at it myself more than once, down to the deepest pit of despair, so that I wished I had never been made a man. (That was before I knew how health-giving that despair was, and how close to grace.) This is why so much toil and trouble has been devoted to clearing the goodness of God, and throwing the blame on man's will. It is at this point that distinctions have been invented between God's will of appointment and His absolute will, between necessity of consequence and of the thing consequent, and many more such. But nothing has been achieved by means of them beyond imposing upon the unlearned by empty verbiage and 'opposition of science falsely so called' (cf. 1 Tim. 6.20). None the less, the arrow of conviction has remained, fastened deep in the hearts of learned and unlearned alike, whenever they have made a serious approach to the matter, so that they are aware that, if the foreknowledge and omnipotence of God are admitted, then we must be under necessity.

Natural reason itself, which finds this necessity offensive and labours so hard to get rid of it, would be forced by the conviction of its own judgment to concede this much, even if no Scripture existed. For all men find the following convictions written in their hearts, and acknowledge and acquiesce in them (albeit unwillingly) when they hear them propounded: *first*, that God is omnipotent, not only in power but also in action (as I said), and would be a ludicrous God were it not so; *second*, that He knows and foreknows all things, and can neither err nor be deceived. These two points being allowed by the hearts and minds of all men, they are at once compelled by irrefutable logic to admit that we were not made by our own will, but by necessity, and accordingly that we do not do anything by right of 'free-will', but according to what God foreknew and works by His infallible and immutable counsel and power. Wherefore, it is also found written in the hearts of all men that there is no such thing as 'free-will'; though that conviction is obscured by much arguing against it and by the great authority of all those persons who down many ages have taught otherwise. In the same way, every other law is written in our hearts (we have Paul's word for this [cf. Rom. 2.15]), and is acknowledged when it is correctly propounded, but is obscured when ungodly teachers mishandle it and other views fill its place.

(ix) *Rom. 9.15ff. (contd.)* (719-720)

Now I return to Paul. If in Rom. 9 he does not explain this point, and clearly state that we are under necessity by virtue of the foreknowledge and will of God, why need he have introduced the analogy of the potter, who makes of the selfsame clay one vessel to honour and another to dishonour; and yet the thing formed does not say to him that formed it: 'Why hast thou made me thus?' (cf. 9.20-21). He is speaking of men, comparing them to clay and God to a potter. The comparison is surely pointless—inappropriate, indeed, and futile—if he does not think that our freedom is nil. Yes, and in that case Paul's whole argument in defence of grace is futile! The entire Epistle is concerned to show that we can do nothing, not even when we seem to do well. Paul says as much when he tells us that Israel did not reach righteousness by following after righteousness, whereas the Gentiles reached it by not following after it (vv. 30-31). (I shall discuss that passage at greater length when I bring my own resources to bear.) But the Diatribe turns a blind eye to the whole content and design of Paul's argument, and comforts itself by detaching and corrupting isolated words. Nor is it helped by Paul's subsequent exhortation in Rom. 11: 'Thou standest by faith; be not high-minded'; and: 'They also, if they shall believe, shall be graffed in', etc. (vv. 20, 23). Paul there says nothing about the strength of man, but puts down verbs in the imperative and subjunctive, the significance of which has been sufficiently stated already. And he himself at that point forestalls the braggarts of 'free-will' by saying, not that *they* are able to believe, but that 'God is able to graff them in'.

In short, the Diatribe proceeds so tardily and hesitantly in its treatment of these passages of Paul, that its conscience seems to be at odds with its words. Just where it ought to go on and prove its point, it nearly always breaks off and says: '*But enough of this*'; '*I shall not now proceed with this*'; '*this is not my present concern*'; 'they *would say*'; and much more of the same sort. It leaves the matter half-way, so that you do not know whether it would be thought to be speaking for 'free-will', or merely using empty verbiage to evade Paul's meaning! Seeing that it has no serious interest in the issue, this is quite in character. But it is not for me to be thus cold and distant, walking on tip-toe, moved as a reed by every wind that blows; my task is to *assert*, with precision, and consistency, and warmth, and give solid, skilful, substantial proof for my teaching.

(x) *That necessity does not involve compulsion: the case of Judas:* (720-722)

See how successfully the Diatribe retains freedom alongside necessity when it says: '*Not all necessity excludes "free-will". Thus, God the Father begets a Son of necessity; yet He begets Him willingly and freely, for He is not forced to do so.*' Are we now discussing compulsion and force? Have I not put on record in many books that I am talking about *necessity of immutability*? I know that the Father begets willingly, and that Judas betrayed Christ willingly. My point is that this act of will in Judas was certainly and infallibly bound to take place, if God foreknew it. That is to say (if my meaning is not yet grasped), I distinguish two necessities: one I call *necessity of force*,[1] referring to action; the other I call *necessity of infallibility*,[1] referring to time. Let him who hears me understand that I am speaking of the latter, not the former; that is, I am not discussing whether Judas became a traitor willingly or unwillingly, but whether it was infallibly bound to come to pass that Judas should willingly betray Christ at a time predetermined by God.

See what the Diatribe says about this: '*In respect of the infallible foreknowledge of God, Judas was necessarily bound to become a traitor; nonetheless, Judas was able to change his will*'. Do you understand, my good Diatribe, what you are saying? To say nothing of the point proved above, that the will can only will evil, how could Judas change his will while God's infallible foreknowledge stands? Could he change God's foreknowledge and make it fallible? Here the Diatribe gives up, abandons its position, throws down its arms and leaves the field, relegating the discussion to the realm of scholastic subtleties about necessity of consequence and of the thing consequent, and professing itself unwilling to pursue such nice points.

Wisely done indeed! First you lead our subject into the midst of the *mêlée*; now, when there is most need of a champion to plead its cause, you turn your back, and leave the task of definition and reply to others. You should have followed this plan at the beginning, and held back from writing altogether! 'He who ne'er knew the training-field should shun the battle's

---

[1] *necessitatem violentam: necessitatem infallibilem.*

brunt!'[1] It was not expected of Erasmus that he would remove the difficulty of knowing how God surely foreknows all things while yet all that we do is done contingently; that difficulty was in the world long before the Diatribe; but it was expected that he would attempt a definition and a reply. But he avails himself of a rhetorical device for changing the subject,[2] and tries to drag with him us, who know nothing of rhetoric—as though we were here dealing with something of no significance, and it was all a matter of mere logical subtleties!—and thus he races strongly away from the battlefield, wearing the crowns of warrior and bard together![3]

Not so, brother! No rhetoric can cheat an honest conscience. The arrow of conscience is proof against all the forces and figures of eloquence. I shall not allow our rhetorician thus to dissimulate and change the subject. There is no room now for this manœuvre. We are now facing up to the central issue in our debate, the point on which everything hinges. Here 'free-will' either expires or will triumph altogether. And you, seeing the risk, yes, the certainty of victory going against 'free-will', pretend to see nothing here but logical subtleties! Is this the part of a faithful theologian? Does the issue seriously concern you? You leave your hearers in suspense, and the argument in a confused and tantalized condition, and you would be thought nevertheless to have given honourable satisfaction, and to have won the day! Your craft and cunning may gain forbearance in secular matters, but in a theological discussion, where plain straightforward truth is required, for the salvation of souls, it is supremely objectionable and intolerable.

The Sophists also felt the insuperable, irresistible force of this argument; that is why they devised the distinction between necessity of *consequence* and of *the thing consequent*. But I showed above how unavailing that fancy is. They themselves fail to observe what they are saying, and how much they are admitting against themselves. For if you grant necessity of consequence, 'free-will' lies vanquished and slain, and neither necessity nor contingency in respect of the thing consequent can help it. What does it matter to me that 'free-will' is not under compulsion, but does what it does willingly? It is enough for me

[1] Horace, *Ars Poet.* 379.   [2] *Rhetorica transitione.*   [3] *hedera coronatus et lauro.*

that you grant that its willing performance of what it does will come to pass necessarily, and that if God has thus foreknown it, then it cannot be otherwise. If God foreknew, either that Judas would be a traitor, or else that he would alter his purpose of being a traitor, whichever God foreknew will necessarily come to pass; otherwise God will be mistaken in His foreknowledge and prediction, and that is impossible. Necessity of consequence ensures that if God foreknows a thing, it necessarily takes place. This means that 'free-will' does not exist. Necessity of consequence is not obscure or ambiguous, and the doctors of all ages, blind though they may be, are yet compelled to acknowledge it, it is so palpably clear and certain. But the necessity of the thing consequent, with which they console themselves, is a mere phantom, diametrically opposed to necessity of consequence. For instance: it is necessity of consequence if I say, 'God foreknows that Judas will be a traitor; therefore, it will certainly and infallibly come to pass that Judas will be a traitor.' Against this necessity of consequence you console yourself thus: 'Because Judas can alter his purpose of being a traitor, therefore there is no necessity of the thing consequent.' How, I ask you, will these two positions agree: 'Judas can will not to betray', and: 'Judas must necessarily will to betray'? Are they not directly opposed and contradictory? He will not be compelled, you say, to betray against his will. What of that? You were speaking of the *necessity* of the thing consequent, and saying that it does not follow from necessity of consequence; you said nothing of the *compulsion* of the thing consequent. The point to which you were supposed to speak was the necessity of the thing consequent, and you propound an example concerning the compulsion of the thing consequent! I raise one question, you answer another! This comes of the sleepy-headedness which makes you overlook the futility of this fabrication about the necessity of the thing consequent.

(xi) *Mal. 1.2-3: rightly quoted by Paul to prove the sovereignty of God in grace* (722-727)

So much for the first passage, which dealt with the hardening of Pharaoh (it has in fact involved all the passages, and a great part of our own invincible resources). Let us now look at the second, concerning Jacob and Esau, of whom, while yet unborn, it was said: 'the elder shall serve the younger' (Rom. 9.12).

The Diatribe parries this passage by saying that, '*rightly understood, it does not bear on man's salvation; for God may will that a man should be a servant and a pauper, willy-nilly, without his being rejected from eternal salvation.*'

See, I pray you, what abundance of by-ways and bolt-holes a slippery mind will seek out in its flight from truth! Yet it does not escape. Suppose it is true that this passage does not relate to man's salvation (I will discuss that later) are we to imagine that there is no point at all in Paul's citation of it? Shall we represent Paul as making a fool and a laughing-stock of himself in so serious a discussion? That is the way of Jerome, who dares to say in more places than one, superciliously enough, and sacrilegiously too, that 'things have a force in Paul which they do not possess in their own places'. This is just to say that when Paul lays the foundations of Christian doctrine, he does nothing but corrupt the Divine Scriptures, and delude the souls of the faithful, with an idea conceived in his own brain, and violently thrust into those Scriptures! So this is the respect due to the Holy Spirit in Paul, that holy, elect instrument of God! And whereas Jerome should be read with discernment, and this remark of his counted among the numerous impieties which he wrote (so dull and sleepy-headed was he in understanding the Scriptures), the Diatribe drags him in without any discernment; it does not see fit to soften his words with any kind of gloss, but takes him as an unerring oracle for judging of, and modifying, the Divine Scriptures. So do we take the impious words of men as our rules and measures for the Scripture of God. And yet we wonder that it should grow obscure and ambiguous, and that so many fathers should be blind about it, when they work on this impious and sacrilegious principle!

So let him be anathema, who says that 'things have a force in Paul which they do not possess in their own places'! It is merely said; it is not proved; and it is said by people who understand neither Paul nor the passages cited by him, but are misled by taking his words in their own sense—that is, in an impious sense. However true it might be that this passage in Gen. 25 (vv. 21-23) should be understood of temporal servitude only (in fact, it is not true), Paul nonetheless quotes it rightly and effectively when he uses it to prove that it was not of the merits of Jacob or Esau, but 'OF HIM THAT CALLETH' that it was said to Sara:[1] 'the elder shall serve the younger.' Paul is discussing whether they attained to what was spoken of them by the power or merits of 'free-will'; and he proves that they did not, but that Jacob attained what Esau did not attain solely by the grace of 'Him that calleth'. This he demonstrates by the incontrovertible statements of Scripture, that they were not yet born, and had done no good or evil. The weight of the matter rests on this demonstration; this was the point at issue. But the Diatribe, with its fine rhetoric, studiedly overlooks all this, and passes it by; it does not discuss merit at all (which is what it undertook to do, and what Paul's theme requires), but raises objections about temporal servitude—as if *that* had any relevance! Its sole aim here is to avoid appearing to be overthrown by Paul's mighty words! For what could it find to growl out against Paul in behalf of 'free-will'? How did 'free-will' help Jacob, or harm Easu, when before either was born or had done anything it was already determined by the foreknowledge and predestination of God what the portion of each should be—that is, that the one should serve and the other rule? The rewards were decided before the workers set to work, or were even born! This is the point that the Diatribe should have met. Paul is insisting that at that time they had done neither good nor evil, and yet by Divine decision the one was ordained a slave, and the other his lord. The question here is not, whether that servitude bears on salvation, but, by what desert was it imposed on him who had not deserved it? It is very irksome contending with these depraved efforts to wrest and parry Scripture.

Furthermore, proof is derived from the text itself that Moses is not dealing with temporal servitude only, and that Paul is perfectly right in understanding it of eternal salvation. (This is not altogether relevant, but I will not suffer Paul to be besmirched by the slanders of the sacrilegious.) The oracle in Moses is as follows: 'Two peoples shall be separated from thy

---

[1] Actually, Rebecca.

bowels, and the one people shall be stronger than the other people; and the elder shall serve the younger' (Gen. 25.23). Here two peoples are clearly distinguished. One, though younger, is received into the gracious favour of God, that he might overcome the elder—not by his own strength, but through the favour of God; for how could the younger overcome the elder, unless God were with him? Now, since the younger was to be the people of God; it is not only an external lordship and servitude that is there being treated of, but everything that belongs to the people of God—that is, the blessing, word, Spirit and promise of Christ, and the eternal kingdom; as Scripture confirms more fully later when it describes Jacob's blessing and his reception of the promises of the kingdom (cf. Gen. 27.27ff.). All this Paul briefly intimates when he says: 'The elder shall serve the younger', referring us back to Moses, who deals with the matter more fully. So you may say in reply to the sacrilegious judgment of Jerome and the Diatribe that all the passages that Paul quotes have *more* force in their own places than they have in his writings!—which is true, not merely of Paul, but of all the Apostles. They all quote the Scriptures as witnesses and assertors of what they themselves are saying; and it would be ludicrous indeed to cite as a testimony something that testifies nothing and is not to the point! Even if there are among philosophers foolish men who prove what is unknown by what is less known or irrelevant, with what conscience can we attribute such behaviour to our chief guides and authorities in Christian doctrine, on which the salvation of our souls depends?— especially when they are teaching the fundamentals of faith! But such behaviour is quite in keeping for those who have no serious interest in the Divine Scriptures!

As for the passage of Malachi which Paul appends, 'Jacob have I loved, but Esau have I hated' (1.2-3), the Diatribe contrives three distinct methods of wresting it. The first is this: '*If you press the literal sense, God does not love as we love, nor does He hate anyone, for passions of this kind do not overtake God.*'

What do I hear? Do we now inquire *how* God loves and hates, and not rather *why* He loves and hates? The question is, through what merit on our part does He love and hate? We know well enough that God does not love and hate as we do for we love and hate inconstantly, but He loves and hates according to His eternal and immutable nature. Thus it is that unexpected incidents and passions do not overtake God. And it is just this that compels the conclusion that there is no such thing as 'free-will': namely, the fact that the love and hate of God towards men is immutable and eternal, existing, not merely before there was any merit or work of 'free-will', but before the world was made; and that all things take place in us of necessity, according as He has from eternity loved or not loved. So not only the fact of God's love, but even the manner of His loving, imposes necessity on us. You see how much its evasions profit the Diatribe; the more it strives to get away from the truth, the more it everywhere crashes into it—so unsuccessfully does it struggle against it!

Suppose your figure holds good, that the love of God means the effect of His love, and the hatred of God the effect of His hatred: do these effects take place without, and apart from, the will of God? Will you here say that God does not will as we do, and the impulse to will does not overtake him? If these effects take place, they do not take place but at God's will. Now, God either loves or hates what He wills. Tell me, then, by what desert is Jacob loved and Esau hated before they were born and began to work? Paul therefore stands vindicated as quoting Malachi most aptly to support the statement of Moses—that is, that God called Jacob before he was born, because He loved him, and that He was not loved by Jacob first, nor influenced by any desert on Jacob's part. Thus the case of Jacob and Esau shows what power our 'free-will' has!

The second contrivance is this: '*Malachi does not seem to be speaking of the hatred by which we are damned for eternity, but of temporal affliction: for those who wished to restore Edom are reproved.*' This also is said in order to cast aspersions on Paul, as though he did violence to the Scriptures. So utterly lacking are we in reverence for the majesty of the Holy Ghost, if only we can establish our own cause! But we will bear with this slander for a moment and see what it achieves. '*Malachi speaks of temporal affliction.*' What if he does? What does it matter? Paul proves from Malachi that this affliction was laid on Esau without reference to desert, by reason of God's hatred alone, and thence concludes that 'free-will' is non-existent. This is the point that is being urged against you, to which you should have directed your reply. I debate merit, and you discuss the reward; and that in such a way that you fail to avoid what you wanted to avoid; indeed, in your discussion of the reward you recognise merit as a fact. But you pretend not to see that. Tell me, then, what caused God to love Jacob and hate Esau when they were not yet born?

In any case, to say that Malachi speaks only of temporal affliction is false. He is not talking about the destruction of Edom; you pervert the prophet's entire sense by this contrivance of yours. The prophet shows what he means clearly enough, in the plainest words. He is upbraiding the Israelites for their ingratitude, because when God had loved them, they in return neither loved Him as their Father nor feared Him as their Lord (cf. Mal. 1.2-6). That God had loved them he proves both from Scripture and from the work of God: that is, though Jacob and Esau were brothers, as Moses records in Gen. 25, God loved Jacob and chose him before he was born, as was said a littler earlier, but He so hated Esau that He removed his place of abode into the desert. Moreover, God so continued and persisted in that hatred that when He brought Jacob back from captivity and restored him, He did not permit the Edomites to be restored, and when they said that they intended to build He threatened them with destruction. If these are not the contents of the prophet's plain text, let the whole world prove me a liar! So it is not the audacity of the Edomites that is here reproved, but, as I said, the ingratitude of the sons of Jacob, who fail to see what God has bestowed on them, and what He has taken from their brothers the Edomites, for no other reason than His hatred of the one and His love for the other.

How, now, will it hold good that the prophet is speaking of temporal affliction, when he himself testifies in clear terms that he is speaking of two peoples, born of two patriarchs, one taken to be a people and saved, the other abandoned and at last destroyed? This act of taking as a people, and of not taking as a people, affects not merely temporal prosperity and adversity, but all things; for our God is the God of all things, not of temporal things only. And God will not consent to be your God and to have you worship him with half a shoulder, or a lame leg (cf. Mal. 1.13), but with all your heart and strength, that He may be your God both here and hereafter, in all matters, on all occasions, at all times and in all your works.

The third contrivance is this: '*Taking the words in a figurative sense, God neither loves all Gentiles, nor hates all Jews, but some of each. The effect of this figurative interpretation is that this testimony is of no avail to prove necessity, but avails merely to beat down the arrogance of the Jews.*' Having made this way out, the Diatribe proceeds to escape down it, saying: '*God is said to hate men before they are born, because He foreknows that what they will do will merit hatred. Thus, the hatred and love of God do not at all militate against "free-will".*' Finally, it concludes: '*the Jews were cut off from the olive tree according to the desert of their unbelief, and the Gentiles grafted in according to the desert of their faith; we have that on Paul's authority; and he holds out hope to those that were cut off of being grafted in again, and calls for fear in those that were grafted in, lest they be cut off.*'

I'll be hanged if the Diatribe itself knows what it is talking about! Perhaps we have here the rhetorical trick of obscuring your meaning when danger is at hand, lest you be trapped in your words! I do not see in this passage the figurative language of which the Diatribe groundlessly dreams. So it is no wonder if Malachi's testimony is not of force against 'free-will' in its figurative sense; there is no such sense! Moreover, our dispute is not about the cutting off and grafting in, of which Paul speaks in his exhortation. I know that men are grafted in by faith and cut off by unbelief, and that they must be exhorted to believe, lest they be cut off. But it does not hence follow, nor does this prove, that they can believe or disbelieve by the power of 'free-will', which is the point that we are discussing. We are not arguing as to who are believers and who not, who are Jews and who are Gentiles, or what consequence ensues for believers and for unbelievers. That is the province of the preacher.[1] Our question is, *by what merit or work* do they arrive at the faith by which they are grafted in, or the unbelief by which they are cut off? It is this that is the concern of the theologian.[2] Describe this merit to me! Paul teaches that faith and unbelief come to us by no

---

[1] *exhortatorem.*   [2] *doctorem.*

work of our own, but through the love and hatred of God. When faith has come to men, he exhorts them to persevere, lest they be cut off. But exhortation establishes only what we ought to do, and not what we can do.

I am forced to hold on to my adversary with this multitude of words, lest he should leave the matter in hand and wander away from the discussion of it. In fact, to keep him to the point is to vanquish him, so clear and incontrovertible are these words. That is why almost his sole aim is to veer away from them, hurry himself out of sight, and take up something other than his stated theme.

(xii) *Of the potter and the clay* (727-729)

The third passage which the Diatribe takes up is from Isa. 45: 'Shall the clay say to him that fashioneth it, What makest thou?' (v. 9); and with it, Jer. 18: 'Behold, as the clay is in the potter's hand, so are ye in Mine hand' (v. 6). Here it says once more: '*These passages have more force in Paul than they have in the prophets from which they are taken; for in the prophets they refer to temporal affliction, but Paul uses them with reference to eternal election and reprobation*'—so insinuating ignorance or irresponsibility on Paul's part.

Before we see how the Diatribe proves that neither passage excludes 'free-will', I shall first make the following observation: Paul does not appear to have taken this passage from the prophets, nor does the Diatribe prove that he did. It is Paul's habit when he quotes to mention the name of the writer, or to declare that he is taking something from the Scriptures; but here he does neither. It is therefore nearer the truth to say that Paul, at the prompting of his own spirit, uses in connexion with his argument this commonplace simile, which others employ in other connexions. He does the same with the simile 'a little leaven leaveneth the whole lump', which in 1 Cor. 5 (v. 6) he applies to corrupt morals, and elsewhere to those who corrupt the Word of God (Gal. 5.9). (So too Christ speaks of the 'leaven' of Herod and of the Pharisees, Mark 8.15.) However true it may be, then, that the prophets are speaking of temporal affliction (I shall not discuss that here, lest I be taken up and distracted with irrelevant issues unduly often), Paul by his own spirit uses this simile against 'free-will'. As for your observation that freedom of will is not destroyed by our being as clay in the hand of an afflicting God, I do not know what point it has, nor why the Diatribe insists on it; for there is no doubt that afflictions come from God against our will, and impose on us the necessity of bearing them, willy-nilly, nor is it in our power to avert them; true though it is that we are encouraged to bear them *willingly*.[1]

It is worth listening to the Diatribe's subtle demonstration of how it is that Paul's discourse does not exclude 'free-will' by its use of this simile. It brings forward two absurdities, one derived from the Scriptures, the other from reason. From the Scriptures it gathers the following:

Paul says in 2 Tim. 2 that 'in a great house there are vessels of gold and silver, wood and earth, some to honour and some to dishonour'. He then at once adds: 'If a man therefore purge himself from these, he shall be a vessel unto honour', etc. (vv. 20-1). Hereupon the Diatribe agues thus: '*What could be more ridiculous than to say to an earthenware chamber-pot, If thou shalt purify thyself, thou shalt be a vessel unto honour? Yet this may rightly be said to the rational "pot", which can, when admonished, conform itself to the will of the Lord.*' On these grounds it would have us gather that the simile is not at every point applicable and that its force has been completely evaded.

I reply (not to quibble on the matter) that Paul does not say: 'if a man shall purify himself from his own filth', but: 'from these', that is, from the vessels unto dishonour; so that the sense is, if a man shall remain separate, and not mix with ungodly teachers, he shall be a vessel unto honour. Let us even grant that this passage of Paul is exactly as the Diatribe would have it—that is, that the comparison here does not make its point; how will the Diatribe then prove that Paul intends the same meaning in the passage in Rom. 9 which we are discussing? Is it sufficient merely to cite a second passage, with no regard as to whether it is making the same or a different point? There is, as I have often shown, no easier or commoner failing in dealing with the Scriptures than to bring together diverse passages as

[1] *voluntarie.*

if they were alike. Thus the likeness of the passages, of which the proud Diatribe makes so much, is less conclusive than the likeness of our simile, which it would refute! However, not to be quarrelsome, let us grant that both passages of Paul have the same meaning; and let us also grant (what is unquestionably true) that a simile is not always applicable at every point (for otherwise it would not be a simile, nor a metaphor, but the thing itself; as the proverb says, a simile halts, it does not always run on four feet!) Yet the Diatribe still errs and goes wrong in that it neglects the purpose of the simile, which should be our main concern, and catches contentiously at the words of it instead. 'Knowledge of meaning must be sought from the reasons for speaking,' says Hilary; it is not afforded by the terminology alone. So it is here: the force of a simile depends upon its purpose. Why then does the Diatribe ignore the point for the sake of which Paul uses this simile, and catch at what he says without reference to the intent of the simile? I mean that his words 'If a man purge himself from these', are in the category of exhortation, whereas his words: 'In a great house, there are vessels of gold', etc., are in the category of doctrine. From the entire context surrounding Paul's words and statement, you can see that the point which he is making concerns the different characters and uses of vessels. So his meaning is this: 'When so many depart from the faith, there is no comfort for us but our certainty that the foundation of God standeth sure, having this seal, The Lord knoweth them that are His. And let everyone that calleth upon the name of the Lord depart from iniquity' (2 Tim. 2.19). The intent and force of the simile are limited to this one point, that the Lord knows his own. The simile then follows—that there are different vessels, some to honour and some to dishonour. By this is proved the doctrine that it is not the vessels themselves, but their master, who prepares them for their intended use. This is the meaning of Paul's statement in Rom. 9 that 'the potter has power', etc. Thus, Paul's simile holds good, and proves most effectively that there is no such thing as freedom of will in God's sight. After this follows the exhortation: 'If a man purge himself from these', etc. The force of these words may be sufficiently known from what was said above. It does not follow from them that therefore a man can purge himself. If, indeed, they proved anything, they would prove that 'free-will' can purge itself without grace; for it does not say: 'if grace purge a man', but: 'if a man purge himself'. But we have said enough and to spare about imperative and hypothetical language. The terms, however, in which the simile is propounded are not hypothetical, but affirmative, thus: the elect and the reprobate *are* as *are* vessels unto honour and unto dishonour. In a word, if your evasion stands, Paul's entire argument falls to the ground. It is pointless for him to introduce persons grumbling against the Divine potter, if it appears that the fault is not in the potter, but in the vessels; for who would grumble if he were to hear of the damnation of one that merited damnation?

(xiii) *Of the righteousness of God in justifying and condemning sinners* (729-731)

The Diatribe gathers its second absurdity from Mistress Reason—'human' reason, so-called: to wit, that on my view blame must attach, not to the vessel, but to the potter, especially in view of the fact that He is a potter who creates this clay as well as moulds it. '*Here*' (says the Diatribe) '*the vessel is cast into eternal fire, a fate which it in no way deserved, except that it was not under its own control.*' Nowhere does the Diatribe more openly betray itself than here. You hear it saying (in different words, admittedly, but with identical meaning) just what Paul makes the ungodly say: 'Why doth He find fault? Who shall resist His will?' This is what Reason cannot receive nor bear. This is what offended so many men of outstanding ability, men who have won acceptance down so many ages. At this point, they demand that God should act according to man's idea of right,[1] and do what seems proper to themselves—or else that He should cease to be God! 'The secrets of His majesty,' they say, 'shall not profit him; let him render a reason why He is God, or why He wills and does that which has no appearance of justice in it. It is like asking a cobbler or a belt-maker to take the seat of judgement.' Flesh does not deign to give God glory to the extent of believing Him to be just and good when He speaks and acts

[1] *iure humano.*

above and beyond the definitions of Justinian's Code, or the fifth book of Aristotle's Ethics! No, let the Majesty that created all things give way before a worthless fragment of His own creation! Let the boot be on the other foot,[1] and the Corycian cavern fear those that look into it! So it is 'absurd' to condemn one who cannot avoid deserving damnation. And because of this 'absurdity' it must be false that God has mercy on whom He will have mercy, and hardens whom He will. He must be brought to order! Rules must be laid down for Him, and He is not to damn any but those who have deserved it by *our* reckoning! In this way, Paul and his simile are satisfactorily answered; so Paul must presumably recall it, and allow that it has no force, and remodel it; because the Potter in question (this is the Diatribe's explanation) makes the vessel unto dishonour on the grounds of merit preceding, just as He rejected some of the Jews by reason of unbelief, and received Gentiles by reason of their faith. But if God works in such a way as to regard merit, why do objectors grumble and complain? Why do they say: 'Why doth He find fault? Who resists His will?' Why need Paul restrain them? For who is surprised, let alone shocked or inclined to object, if one is damned who deserved it? Moreover, what becomes of the power of the Potter to make what vessel He will, if He is controlled by merits and rules, and is not allowed to make as He would, but is required to make as He should? Respect for merit militates against power and freedom for Him to make what He will; as is proved by the case of 'good man of the house' who, when the workmen grumbled and demanded their rights, replied by asserting his freedom of will in dealing with his own goods (cf. Matt. 20.15). It is these considerations that preclude the validity of the Diatribe's gloss.

Suppose we imagine that God ought to be a God who regards merit in those that are to be damned. Must we not equally maintain and allow that He should also regard merit in those that are to be saved? If we want to follow Reason, it is as unjust to reward the undeserving as to punish the undeserving. So let us conclude that God ought to justify on the grounds of merit preceding; or else we shall be declaring Him to be

---

[1] *versa vice.*

unjust. One who delights in evil and wicked men, and who invites and crowns their impiety with rewards! But then woe to us poor wretches with such a God! For who shall be saved?

Behold, therefore, the wickedness of the human heart! When God saves the undeserving without merit, yes, and justifies the ungodly, with all their great demerit, man's heart does not accuse God of iniquity, nor demand to know why He wills to do so, although by its own reckoning such action is most unprincipled; but because what God does is in its own interest, and welcome, it considers it just and good. But when He damns the undeserving, because this is against its interest, it finds the action iniquitous and intolerable; and here man's heart protests, and grumbles, blasphemes. So you see that the Diatribe and its friends do not judge in this matter according to equity, but according to their passionate regard for their own interest. If the Diatribe regarded equity, it would expostulate as much with God for His crowning of the unworthy as it does with Him for the damnation of the undeserving; and, conversely, it would praise and extol God in the same measure for damning and undeserving as it does when He saves the unworthy. The impropriety is the same in each case, if you regard our own judgment. Would it not have been equally improper to praise Cain for his murder and make him a king, while innocent Abel was cast into prison or executed?

Now, since Reason praises God when He saves the unworthy but finds fault with Him when He damns the undeserving, it stands convicted of not praising God as God, but as One who serves its own convenience—that is, what it looks for and praises in God is self, and the things of self, and not God and the things of God. But if a God who crowns the undeserving pleases you, you ought not be be displeased when He damns the undeserving! If He is just in the one case, He cannot but be just in the other. In the one case, He pours out grace and mercy upon the unworthy; in the other, He pours out wrath and severity upon the undeserving; in both He trangresses the bounds of equity in man's sight, yet is just and true in His own sight. *How* it is just for Him to crown the unworthy is incomprehensible now; but we shall see it when we reach the place where He will be no more an object of faith, but we shall with open face behold Him. So, too, it is at present incomprehensible how it is just for Him to damn the undeserving; yet faith will continue to believe that it is so, till the Son of Man shall be revealed.

(xiv) *That Paul attributes the salvation of man to God alone* (731-733)

The Diatribe, however, takes violent offence at this simile of the potter and the clay, and is not a little resentful at being so pestered with it. At last it comes down to this: it brings forward various passages from Scripture, of which some seem to attribute all to man, and others all to grace, and peevishly insists that *the Scriptures on both sides must be understood according to a 'sound explanation', not taken in their plain sense.* Otherwise, if we press against it our simile, it is ready in return to press against us its hypothetical and imperative passages, and especially Paul's words: 'If a man purge himself from these'. Here it makes out that Paul will be contradicting himself and assigning all to man, unless a 'sound explanation' is forthcoming. And if such an explanation is allowed here, to leave room for grace, why should not the simile of the potter also admit of an explanation that will leave room for 'free-will'?

I reply: It makes no difference to me whether you take the passages in their simple sense, in a double sense or in a hundredfold sense. I say this: that nothing is achieved by this 'sound explanation', and it fails to prove what you want. What should be proved is that 'free-will' can will no good. But this passage ('if a man purify himself from these') is a hypothetical statement, and proves nothing of any kind; Paul is merely exhorting. If you tack on the Diatribe's inference, and say: 'he exhorts in vain if man cannot purge himself,' it is then proved that 'free-will' can do everything without grace. And thus the Diatribe refutes itself.

I still wait, therefore, for some passage of Scripture to show me that your explanation is right. I give no credence to those who devise it out of their own head. I deny that any passage is found that attributes all to man. I also deny that Paul contradicts himself when he says: 'If a man purge himself from these'; I maintain that the contradiction in Paul is as fictitious as the 'explanation' which it extorts is artificial, and that neither is proved. I certainly admit that, if we may augment the Scriptures with the Diatribe's inferences and additions (as, for instance, by saying: 'if we cannot do what is commanded, the command is given in vain'), then in truth Paul clashes with himself, and so does the entire Scripture; for in that case Scripture would be different from what it was, and would actually prove that 'free-will' can do all things. And then what wonder if its statements elsewhere, that God alone does all things, are also found to clash? Scripture thus augmented makes not only against us, but also against the Diatribe itself, which laid it down that 'free-will' can will no good. So let the Diatribe first disentangle itself and tell us how these two assertions that it makes agree with Paul: one, 'Free-will can will no good', and the other: ' "If a man purge himself from these" implies that man can purge himself, or else it is said to no purpose'! You see, now, that the Diatribe, harassed and worsted by the simile of the potter, is concerned only to evade it, without a thought as to how much harm its explanation does to the cause it has in hand, and how it is confuting and ridiculing itself.

I, as I said, have never espoused an 'explanation', nor did I ever say that 'stretch forth thine hand' means: 'grace shall stretch it forth'. All this the Diatribe fabricates about me, to suit its own case. What I said was that there is no conflict in the words of Scripture, and no need of an 'explanation' to 'cut the knot'. The protagonists of 'free-will' create difficulties where none exist, and dream contradictions for themselves. For instance: there is no conflict between: 'If a man purge himself', and: 'God worketh all in all' (1 Cor. 12.6); nor is it necessary to cut the knot by saying that God does something and man does something. The former statement is hypothetical, and neither affirms nor denies any work or power in man, but simply lays down what work and power there should be in man. There is nothing figurative here, nothing that needs 'explanation'; the words are straightforward and the sense is straightforward, provided that you do not add inferences and corrupt meanings in the manner of the Diatribe. If you do, the sense will not be sound, but that will be the fault of its corruptor, not its own fault. The latter text, 'God worketh all in all', is an indicative statement, declaring that all works and all power are in God. How then do these two passages conflict, when the one does not deal at all with the power of man, and the other attributes all things to God? Do they not rather harmonize perfectly? But the Diatribe is so ruinously sunk in, choked with, and stifled by, this notion of its own carnal fancy, that it is pointless to command impossibilities, that it cannot control itself; but whenever it hears an imperative or hypothetical statement it straightway tacks on its own indicative inferences: 'something is commanded, therefore we can do it, else the command is stupid!'

From this it breaks out into bragging of victory everywhere, as though it considered that its inferences were established upon the very thought of them, as God's authority is! It proceeds complacently to declare that in some places in Scripture all is assigned to man; so there is a clash here, and an 'explanation' is needed! It does not see that this whole idea is a figment of its own brain, confirmed by not a jot of Scripture anywhere; and is, moreover, of such a kind that, were it allowed, it would confute no one more strongly than the Diatribe itself; for, if it proves anything, it proves that 'free-will' can do all things—the very opposite of what the Diatribe undertook to establish!

So too it constantly repeats: '*If man does nothing, there is no room for merit; and where there is no room for merit there will be no room for punishments or rewards.*' Here once more it fails to see that by these carnal arguments it confutes itself more strongly than us. What do its inferences prove, but that total[1] merit is within the power of 'free-will'? Where now will there be room for grace? Moreover, if 'free-will' merits a 'tiny bit', and grace the rest, why does 'free-will' receive the total[1] reward? Or shall we suppose that it receives only a tiny reward? If there is room for merit so that there may be room for reward, the merit ought to be as great as the reward. But why do I waste words and time on a thing of naught? Though all that the Diatribe devises should stand, and merit be partly the work of man and partly the work of God, no account can be given of the nature of this work, its character and its magnitude; so that the argument is about a will-o'-the-wisp.[2] As it is, seeing that the Diatribe cannot prove any of what it asserts, neither the

[1] *totum.*   [2] *de lana caprina.*

contradiction nor the 'explanation', nor point to a passage that attributes all to man (all these ideas being mere phantoms of its own imagination), Paul's simile of the potter and the clay stands unassailably secure, as proving that it is not our own 'free-will' that decides what sort of vessels we are formed to be. Paul's exhortations, 'If a man purge himself from these' and the like, are patterns according to which we ought to be formed, but not witnesses to any work or desire on our part.

Suffice it to have said this much about the passages that deal with the hardening of Pharaoh, with Esau, and with the potter.

VI

REVIEW OF ERASMUS' TREATMENT OF TEXTS THAT DENY 'FREE-WILL'—(ii) (*W.A.* 733-756)

(i) *Gen. 6.3: the meaning of 'flesh'* (733-736)

AT last the Diatribe comes to the passages cited by Luther against 'free-will', purposing to refute them also. The first is in Gen. 6: 'My Spirit shall not always remain in man, seeing that he is flesh' (v. 3). This passage it confutes in a number of ways. First, it says that 'flesh' here does not signify ungodly lust, but weakness. Then it adds to the text of Moses, telling us that *his words refer not to the whole human race, but to the men of that age*, so that he might equally have said: *'in those particular men'*. It further adds that *the words do not refer to all the men of that age, for Noah is excepted*. Finally, it affirms, on Jerome's authority, that *in Hebrew these words signify something different; namely, the mercy, not the severity of God.*[1] (Perhaps it wants to persuade us that, since the words refer, not to Noah, but to the wicked, it was not the mercy, but the severity of God that was Noah's portion, and the mercy, not the severity of God that was the portion of the ungodly!)

Away with these fooleries of the Diatribe, which everywhere evince that it regards the Scriptures as fables! I do not care what nonsense Jerome talks here; it is certain that he proves nothing. In any case, we are discussing the meaning of Scripture, not the meaning of Jerome. Suppose a corrupter of Scripture pretends that 'the Spirit of God' means His indignation: I tell him that a two-fold proof is needed, and that he lacks both items of it. First, he can produce no single passage of Scripture in which 'the Spirit of God' may be taken to mean His indignation; on the contrary, kindness and gentleness are everywhere ascribed to the Spirit. Then, should he succeed in

---

[1] '*Jerome, in his Hebrew Questions, points out that the reading in Hebrew differs from ours, thus: "My Spirit shall not judge these men for ever, because they are flesh." The words speak not of the severity of God, but of His mercy.*'

proving that somewhere 'the Spirit of God' may be taken to mean God's indignation, he still cannot prove forthwith as a necessary consequence that it ought to be so taken here. So he may pretend that 'flesh' is here used to mean infirmity; but he is as deficient as ever in proof. When Paul calls the Corinthians 'carnal,' he refers, not to weakness, but to corruption; for he accuses them of sectarianism and party spirit, which is not weakness or incapacity to receive more solid doctrine, but the old leaven of wickedness, which he commands them to purge out (cf. 1 Cor. 3.1-3, 5.7).

Let us look at the Hebrew.

'My Spirit shall not always judge in man; for he is flesh.' These are the exact words of Moses; and if we would clear our dreams out of the way, the words as they stand are, I think, plain and clear enough. That they are the words of an angry God is sufficiently shown by what comes before and after, including the resultant flood. The reason for their being uttered was that the sons of men married wives out of mere carnal lust, and oppressed the earth with violence to such an extent that they compelled God in anger to hasten the flood, scarcely withholding it for a hundred and twenty years, when otherwise He would never have brought it on them at all (cf. Gen. 6.1-2). Read and mark Moses, and you will see clearly that this is his meaning.

But what wonder is it that the Scriptures are obscure to you, or that you can establish from them a will that is not only free, but divine, if you are allowed to play with them as you do, as if you were making patchwork out of them![1] This, I suppose, is what you mean by 'cutting the knots', and settling questions by means of an 'explanation'! Jerome and his friend Origen filled the world with that kind of nonsense; they were the inventors of this pestilent practice of paying no heed to the simple sense of Scripture.

It is enough for me that this passage proves that Divine authority called men 'flesh', and 'flesh' to such a degree that the Spirit of God could not continue among them, but was at a set time to be withdrawn from them. What God means by saying

---

[1] *ac si Virgilicentonas in illis quaeras?* 'Virgilicentonae' were poems made up of words and phrases extracted from Vergil.

that His Spirit should not always judge among men, He at once explains, by specifying a hundred and twenty years as the period during which He would still continue to judge. He sets this 'Spirit' over against 'flesh' to show that men, as being flesh, do not receive the Spirit, and that He, as being spirit, cannot approve of 'flesh'; so that the Spirit is to be recalled after a hundred and twenty years. So you should understand this passage of Moses thus: 'My Spirit, which is in Noah and other holy men, rebukes the ungodly through the word that these men preach and through their godly lives' (for to 'judge among men' is to go among them in the office of the Word, to reprove, rebuke, and beseech them, in season and out of season); 'but it is done in vain; for the ungodly are blinded and hardened by the flesh, and grow worse the more they are judged.' This happens whenever the word of God comes into the world; the more men are instructed, the worse they grow. That is the reason why the wrath is hastened, as the flood also was hastened at that time; for now men not only sin, but also despise grace, and it is as Christ says: 'Light is come, and men hate the light' (cf. John 3.19).

Now, since, on God's own testimony, men are 'flesh', they can savour of nothing but the flesh; therefore 'free-will' can avail only to sin. And if, while the Spirit of God is calling and teaching among them, they go from bad to worse, what could they do when left to themselves, without the Spirit of God?

Your observation that Moses is speaking of the men of that age is not to the point at all. The same is true of all men, for all are 'flesh'; as Christ says, 'That which is born of the flesh is flesh' (John 3.6). How grave a defect this is, He Himself there teaches, when He says: 'Except a man be born again, he cannot enter the kingdom of God' (v. 5). Let the Christian know, therefore, that Origen, Jerome and all their followers go disastrously astray when they say that 'flesh' in these passages is not used to mean 'corrupt affection'. The words of I Cor. 3, 'For ye are yet carnal' (v. 3), refer to ungodliness: Paul means that there are still ungodly ones among them, although they are justified by the Spirit, and, moreover, that the godly are themselves 'carnal' insofar as they savour of carnal things. In a word, you will notice in the Scriptures that wherever 'flesh' is mentioned in contradistinction to 'spirit', there you may regularly understand by 'flesh' all that is contrary to the Spirit as here: 'the flesh profiteth nothing' (John 6.63); whereas if it is mentioned on its own, you may know that there it means the physical state and nature, as here: 'They twain shall be one flesh' (Matt. 19.5); 'My flesh is meat indeed' (John 6.55); 'The word was made flesh' (John 1.14). In these passages you could change the Hebrew mode of expression and for 'flesh' say 'body'; for Hebrew expresses by the use of the one term, 'flesh', what we express by using two words, 'flesh' and 'body'. I could wish that this distinction of terms was preserved in our translation of the whole canon of Scripture.

Thus, I think, my passage from Gen. 6 still stands strong against 'free-will'; for 'flesh' is proved to be that which Paul tells us in Rom. 8 (v. 7) cannot be subject to God, as we shall see when we come to that passage. And the Diatribe itself says that 'free-will' can will no good thing!

(ii) *Gen. 8.21 and 6.5: The corruption of mankind* (736)

A second passage is in Gen. 8: 'The thought and imagination of man's heart is inclined to evil from his youth' (v. 21). Gen. 6 is similar (v. 5): 'Every imagination of man's heart is intent on evil continually.' This it evades as follows: '*The proneness to evil which is present in most does not wholly take away their freedom of will.*' Does God, pray, speak here of '*most*', and not rather of '*all*'? Here, after the flood, God is, as it were, repenting: He promises to the men who remained and who were to come that He would no more bring a flood upon the earth 'for man's sake', and subjoins as his reason the fact that man is prone to evil. It is as if He should say: 'If man's wickedness had to be kept in view, I would have to continue the flood for ever. But I will not henceforth keep in view what they deserve,' etc. Thus you see that both before and after the flood God declares that men are evil; so that there is nothing in the Diatribe's reference to '*most*'.

A further point is this: proneness, or inclination, to evil seem to the Diatribe to be a matter of little moment, as though it were in our power to correct or restrain it; whereas Scripture means by that proneness the constant bent and energy of the will to evil. Why does the Diatribe not consult the Hebrew here? Moses says nothing about 'proneness'! (I say this so that you may have no grounds for carping). The Hebrew of Gen. 6 runs thus: *chol ietzer mahescheboth libbo rak ra chol haiom*: that is, 'Every imagination of the thought of the heart is only evil every day.' He does not say that it is 'intent on' or 'prone to' evil, but that it is wholly evil, and that nothing but evil is thought of or imagined by man throughout his life. The nature of his wickedness is described as not doing, and not being able to do, any differently; for it is itself evil, and Christ assures us that an evil tree can bring forth only evil fruit (cf. Matt. 7.17-18). The Diatribe smartly retorts: '*Why was time given for repentance, if no part of repentance depends on our will, but all is wrought by necessity?*' I reply: You may say the same of all the commandments of God—'Why does He command, if all things come to pass by necessity?' He commands in order to instruct and admonish men as to their duty, that they may be humbled by knowing their wickedness, and so arrive at grace; as has been fully stated.

So this passage still stands unconquered against the freedom of will.

(iii) *Isa. 40.1-2: man under the law can only sin* (736-739)

The third passage is in Isa. 40: 'She hath received at the Lord's hand double for all her sins' (v. 2). '*Jerome*,' says the Diatribe, '*interprets this of Divine vengeance, not of grace given in return for evil deeds.*' 'Jerome says so,' I am told; 'therefore it is true!' I discuss Isaiah who discourses in the plainest words, and Jerome is cast in my teeth; a man (to put it at its mildest) of no judgment or carefulness. Where is the pledge we made with each other, that we would go by the Scriptures themselves, and not by human commentaries upon them? The Evangelists tell us that this whole chapter of Isaiah speaks of the remission of sins which the gospel proclaims; for they say that it refers to John the Baptist, 'the voice of one crying'. Shall we let Jerome, in his usual way, impose blind Jewish fancies upon the passage as its historical sense, and idiocies of his own as its allegorical sense? turning grammar upside down, and understanding of vengeance words that speak of remission of sins? What vengeance, pray, is fulfilled by the preaching of Christ?

Let us look at the words in the Hebrew. 'Comfort ye, comfort ye, My people' (vocative), or 'My people' (accusative),[1] 'saith your God' (v. 1). I presume He is not executing vengeance when he commands comfort! He goes on: 'Speak ye to the heart of Jerusalem, and preach unto her.' 'Speak to the heart' is a Hebraism, meaning, to speak good, sweet, kind words. So in Gen. 34 (v. 3) Shechem speaks to the heart of Dinah, whom he had defiled: that is, he soothed her in her sadness with tender words, as our translator has rendered it. What the good sweet words are that God commands to be preached for their comfort, He now explains, saying: 'that her warfare is accomplished, her iniquity is pardoned; for she hath received of the Lord's hand double for all her sins.' 'Her warfare', which is corrupted in our versions to 'her wickedness',[2] is thought by the bold Jewish grammarians to signify an appointed time. Thus they understand the words in Job 7: 'the life of man on earth is a warfare' (v. 1)—that is, his time is appointed. But I prefer to think that it is called 'warfare' in the simple grammatical sense of the word. So you may understand Isaiah as speaking of the burdensome course of the people under the law, fighting as it were in the arena. In the same way, Paul readily compares preachers and hearers of the word to soldiers, as when he tells Timothy to be a good soldier and war a good warfare (cf. 2 Tim, 2.3; 1 Tim. 1.18); and when he represents the Corinthians as running in a race (cf. 1 Cor. 9.24); and when he says 'no one is crowned, except he strive lawfully' (2 Tim. 2.5). He equips the Ephesians and Thessalonians with arms (Eph. 6.13; 1 Thess. 5.8); and he glories in having 'fought a good fight' (2 Tim. 4.7). And there are similar references elsewhere. So also in 1 Kings 2 it is written in the Hebrew: 'And the sons of Eli slept with the women who fought[3] at the door of the tabernacle of the congregation' (1 Sam. 2.22), whose fighting Moses mentions in Exodus (cf. Exod. 38.8). Hence it is that the God of that people is called the Lord of Sabaoth, that is, the Lord of warfare and of armies.

Isaiah is therefore proclaiming that, because the people were

---

[1] *popule meus, vel populum meum.*   [2] *militia . . . malitia.*   [3] *militantibus* (sic).

crushed under the law as by an unbearable burden, (as Peter informs us in Acts 15 (vv. 7-10), their warfare under the law is to come to an end, and they are to be freed from the law and translated into the new warfare of the Spirit. Moreover, this termination of their harsh warfare, and the replacement of it by a new, free warfare, will not be given them by reason of their merit (for they could not bear the first warfare at all); indeed, it will be given them rather by reason of their demerit, for their warfare is ended by their iniquity being freely forgiven them. There are no obscure or ambiguous words here. He says that their warfare is to be ended precisely by their iniquity being forgiven them; thus plainly implying that those who were militant under the law did not fulfil the law, nor could fulfil it, and only carried on the warfare of sin, and were sinners-militant. It is as if God were saying: 'I am compelled to forgive them, if I would have the law fulfilled by them; indeed, I must also take away the law, for I see that they cannot but sin, and that most of all when they fight—that is, when they labour to fulfil the law in their own strength.' The Hebrew phrase, 'her iniquity is pardoned', indicates free good-pleasure, and that is how iniquity is pardoned: without merit, and indeed, in the presence of demerit. This is the meaning of the words sub-joined: 'For she hath received at the Lord's hand double for all her sins'; that is, not only the remission of sins, but the end of the warfare, as I said. Which means just this: that the law, which is the strength of sin, is taken away; that their sin which is the sting of death, is pardoned; and that they reign in twofold freedom through the victory of Jesus Christ (cf. 1 Cor. 15.55-57). That is the meaning when Isaiah says: 'from the Lord's hand'; they do not obtain it by their own strength or merit, but they receive it as a gift from the Conqueror, Jesus Christ.

'*In* all her sins', says the Hebrew; that is, in Latin, '*for* all her sins', or, '*on account of* all her sins'; as you have it in Hos. 12, 'Israel served *in* a wife' (v. 12), that is, *for* a wife; and in Ps. 16, 'they compassed me about *in* my soul', that is, *for* my soul (cf. Ps. 17.9). Isaiah is depicting our merits, by which we gain this twofold freedom (the end of the warfare of the law, and the pardon of sin); and he shows us that they were all sins, and nothing but sins.

Should I, then, suffer this beautiful passage, which stands unvanquished against 'free-will', to be thus befouled with Jewish dirt by the offices of Jerome and the Diatribe? God forbid! My good friend Isaiah stands victorious over 'free-will', clearly stating that grace is given not to the merits or endeavours of 'free-will', but to its sins and demerits; and that 'free-will' with all its strength can do nothing but carry on the warfare of sin, so that the very law which was thought to be given to help it has proved intolerable to it, and made it more of a sinner as it warred under that law.

The Diatribe argues: '*Though sin abounds by the law*, and *it is where sin abounds that grace also abounds, it does not hence follow that man cannot with God's help make himself acceptable*[1] *before grace, and prepare himself by morally good works for God's favour.*' It will be a surprise to me if the Diatribe says this out of its own head, and did not extract it from some screed that had another destination or source for insertion into its own pages; for it neither sees nor hears what its own words mean. If sin abounds by the law, how is it possible for man to prepare himself by moral works for the favour of God? How can works help him, when the law does not help him? What does it mean for sin to abound by the law, but that works done according to the law are sins? (Of this, elsewhere). What does it mean when it says that man with God's help can prepare himself by moral works? Are we discussing God's help, or 'free-will'? What is not possible by God's help? But it is as I said: the Diatribe sets light by the cause it is pleading; hence the sleepy, snoring style of its discourse. It cites Cornelius the centurion as an example of one whose prayers and alms pleased God before he was baptised or breathed on by the Holy Ghost (cf. Acts 10.4). I, too, have read Luke on the Acts; but I have never found a single syllable to suggest that Cornelius' words were morally good without the Holy Spirit, which is the Diatribe's dream. On the contrary, I find that he was 'a just man, and one that feared God'—so Luke describes him (v. 2). But to call a man without the Holy Spirit 'a just man, and one that feared God', is the same as to call Belial Christ! Moreover, the whole argument of the passage is concerned to show that Cornelius was 'clean' before

[1] *gratum.*

God; the vision sent down to Peter from heaven to reprove him bore witness to that. By such notable deeds and words does Luke call attention to the righteousness and faith of Cornelius. But, for all that, the Diatribe and its beloved Sophists, standing open-eyed under the bright light of Luke's words and of clear fact, continue in blindness; such is their lack of care in reading and marking the Scriptures. And then they have to brand them 'obscure and ambiguous'! Granted, Cornelius was not yet baptised, and had not yet heard the word of Christ's resurrection; but does it hence follow that he was without the Holy Spirit? On these principles you will be saying that John the Baptist and his parents, and the mother of Christ, and Simeon, were without the Holy Spirit! Let us bid such thick darkness farewell!

(iv) *Isa. 40.6-7: man is altogether 'flesh'* (739-745)

The fourth passage is from the same chapter of Isaiah: 'All flesh is as grass, and all the glory of it as the flower of grass: the grass is withered, the flower of grass is fallen: because the Spirit of the Lord hath blown upon it' (vv. 6-7). My friend the Diatribe thinks that this Scripture is somewhat violently dragged into a discussion of grace and 'free-will'. Why, pray? *'Because,'* it says, *'Jerome takes "spirit" as meaning indignation, and "flesh" as meaning man's state of weakness, which has no power against God.'* Again Jerome's tomfooleries are brought before me, instead of Isaiah! And I have to fight more strongly against the disgust which overwhelms me at the Diatribe's carelessness (to use no harsher term) than against the Diatribe itself!

I have said a little earlier what I think of Jerome's idea. Now I ask leave to compare the Diatribe with itself. *'"Flesh",'* it says, *'is man's state of weakness, and "spirit" the Divine indignation.'* Has the Divine indignation nothing else to wither, then, than man's unhappy state of weakness, which it should rather raise up? But here is something prettier still: *'The "flower of grass" is the glory which is born of prosperity in material things.'* The Jews gloried in their temple, circumcision and sacrifices; the Greeks in their wisdom. Therefore, the 'flower of grass', the glory of the flesh, is the righteousness of works and the wisdom of the world. How then is it that the Diatribe calls righteousness and wisdom 'material things'? And what have they to do with Isaiah, who explains his meaning in his own words, saying: 'Surely the people is grass'? He does not say: 'Surely the people's state of weakness is grass', but '*the people*'; and affirms it with an oath. What is 'the people'? Is it only man's state of weakness? I do not know whether Jerome refers 'the weak state of man' to his actual creation, or to his present unhappy lot. But whichever it is, it is certainly a glorious renown and noble spoils that God's indignation gains by withering His own poor creature, unhappy man, instead of scattering the proud, putting down the mighty from their seat, and sending the rich empty away, as Mary puts it in her song (Luke 1.51-53)!

Let us dismiss these disordered fancies, and follow Isaiah. 'The people is grass,' he says. 'The people' is not just flesh, or the weak state of human nature, but comprehends all that is found among the people—rich men, wise men, righteous, saints. (Unless Pharisees, elders, princes, nobles and rich men were no part of the Jewish people?) Their glory is rightly described as 'the flower of grass,' for it was in their kingdom and commonwealth, and most of all in the law, and in God, and in their own righteousness and wisdom, that they gloried; as Paul maintains in Rom. 2, 3 and 9.

So when Isaiah says: 'all flesh', he must mean: 'all the grass', or: 'all the people'; for he does not simply say: 'flesh', but: '*all* flesh'. And to 'the people' belong soul, body, mind, reason, judgment, all that one can search out and specify as being most excellent in man. When he says: 'All flesh is as grass', he exempts nothing but the Spirit that withers it. So too when he says: 'the people is grass', he excludes nothing. Mention 'free-will'—mention anything that can be regarded as highest or lowest among the people—Isaiah calls it all 'flesh' and 'grass'! As is explained by the book's own author, the three terms, 'flesh', 'grass', and 'people', in this passage mean the same thing.

Furthermore, you yourself affirm that the wisdom of the Greeks and the righteousness of the Jews, which were withered by the gospel, were 'grass' and 'the flower of grass'. Do you doubt that the wisdom that there was among the Greeks was the most excellent thing they had? and that the righteousness that there was among the Jews was the most excellent thing they could produce? Tell us, then, of something more excellent! So, whence, then, comes the self-assurance with which you jeer at Philip[1] (I think), saying, '*If any contend that the most excellent thing in man's nature is only "flesh" (that is, ungodly), I shall be happy to agree with him if he will prove his claim by testimonies from Holy Scripture*'? Here you have Isaiah, crying with a loud voice that the people without God's Spirit is 'flesh' (though you will not have it that he does). You have your own admission (thoughtlessly made, perhaps) that the wisdom of the Greeks was 'grass,' or the glory of grass, which is the same as calling it 'flesh.' Or do you maintain that the wisdom of the Greeks had nothing to do with their reason, the *igemonikon*,[2] as you call it, the 'principal part' of man? If you do not deign to listen to me, please listen to yourself, as the force of truth traps you into speaking aright! Then you have John's words: 'That which is born of the flesh is flesh, and that which is born of the Spirit is Spirit' (John 3.6). This passage plainly proves that what is not born of the Spirit is flesh; else the distinction by which Christ divides all men into two classes, 'flesh' and 'spirit', would not stand. But you proudly pass this passage by, as if it did not tell you what you want to know, and hurry off, as usual, elsewhere, pausing only to comment that here John says that believers are born of God and become the sons of God—become, indeed, gods, and new creatures. You disregard the conclusion to which this distinction leads; you casually inform us who are found in the one category, and trust your rhetoric to see you through— as though nobody would notice you thus cunningly and evasively passing by the point!

It is hard at this point to acquit you of deceit and double-dealing. One who handles the Scriptures with such hypocritical artfulness as you do may safely say of himself that he is not yet instructed in the Scriptures, and wants to be instructed, when in fact he wants nothing less, and is merely rattling on like this in order to cast a slur on the clear light that there is in the Scriptures, and to whitewash his own stubbornness! Thus the Jews, even to this day, say that what Christ and the Apostles

---

[1] Melanchthon. [2] τὸ ἡγεμονικόν.

and the whole church have taught is not proved by the Scriptures. Heretics can be taught nothing by the Scriptures. The Papists are still not instructed by the Scriptures, though the very stones cry out the truth. Perhaps you are waiting for a passage to be produced from Scripture that consists of these letters and syllables: 'The principal part of man is flesh', or: 'The most excellent thing in man is flesh', and supposing that you will be undefeated and victorious if such is not forthcoming! —as though the Jews should demand that a statement be produced from the Prophets consisting of these letters: 'Jesus, the carpenter's son, born of the Virgin Mary in Bethlehem, is Messiah and Son of God'! Here, where you are under pressure from a plain statement, you require of us letters and syllables. Elsewhere, when you are worsted by the letters of a statement, you resort to 'figures', 'knots', and 'sound explanations'. Nowhere do you fail to invent something with which to contradict the Scriptures. No wonder; for your whole concern is to find a way of contradicting them! Now you fly to the explanations of the ancients, now to the absurdities of Reason; when neither of these gives relief, you dwell on kindred or alien topics; your only aim is to avoid being held fast by the passage of Scripture that is in hand. What can I say? Proteus is no Proteus compared with you! And yet for all this you cannot escape. What victories did the Arians claim because the syllables and letters of the word *homoousios* were not contained in the Scriptures! It did not worry them that this very thing could be proved most conclusively from other words! Whether this argues a good (not to say, pious) heart, one that desires to be instructed, ungodliness and iniquity themselves may judge!

Take your victory, then; we are beaten; we confess that these letters and syllables ('The most excellent thing in man is flesh') are not found in the Scriptures. But see what a victory yours is! For now we prove that what is most abundantly found in the Scriptures is this: that it is not one part of man, even the most excellent or principal part, that is flesh, but that the whole of man is flesh; and not only so, but the whole people is flesh; and even this is not all, but the whole human race is flesh! Christ says: 'That which is born of the flesh is flesh.' Now cut your knots, fashion your figures, hunt up the explanation of the ancients, or turn elsewhere and for the time being talk about the Trojan war, lest you see or hear the passage in hand!

We, for our part, do not merely believe, but our eyes and experience assure us, that the whole human race is born of the flesh; and so we are bound to believe, on the assurance of Christ, that which we do not see—to wit, that the whole human race is flesh. The Sophists are welcome to doubt and debate whether the ruling[1] part of man is comprehended in the whole man, or the whole people, or the whole human race; we know that the human race is comprehensive of both body and soul, with all their strength and works, all their vices and virtues, all their wisdom and folly, all their righteousness and unrighteousness. All things are flesh, for all things savour of the flesh—that is, of their own—and are, as Paul says in Rom. 3, void of the glory of God and the Spirit of God (Rom. 3.23).

You say: '*Not every energy[2] in man is flesh. There is an energy called the soul, and one called the spirit, by which we aspire to what is upright, as did the philosophers; who taught that we should welcome a thousand deaths sooner than commit a vile action, even if we knew that men would never learn of it and God would pardon it.*'

I reply: One who has sure faith in nothing can easily believe and say anything. I will not ask you, but let your friend Lucian ask you, whether you can point it to anyone out of the entire human race, though he be a Socrates twice or seven times over, who has succeeded in carrying out their teaching as you here state and report it? Why then do you chatter on with empty words? Could they aspire to upright action, when they did not even know what an upright action was? If I should ask you for the most outstanding example of such uprightness, you would say, perhaps, that it was nobly done when men died for their country, for their wives and children, or for their parents; or when they refrained from lying or treachery; or when they endured exquisite torments rather than lie or betray others, as did Q. Scaevola,[3] M. Regulus, and others. But what can you show us in all these men but the external appearance of their works? Have you seen their hearts? Why, it is at once apparent from the look of their works that they did it all for their own glory, so that they were not ashamed to acknowledge and to

---

[1] *egemonica.*   [2] *affectus.*   [3] Actually C. M. Scaevola.

boast that it was their own glory that they sought. The Romans, on their own confession, performed their valiant acts out of a thirst for glory. So did the Greeks. So did the Jews. So does the whole human race. But, upright though this may be in men's eyes, nothing is less upright in the sight of God. It is, indeed, the supreme impiety and the height of sacrilege, inasmuch as they did not do it for the glory of God, nor did they glorify Him as God. By the most ungodly robbery, they robbed God of His glory and took it to themselves, and were never less upright and more vile than when they shone in their highest virtues. How could they work for the glory of God, when they knew neither God nor His glory?—not because it was not visible, but because the flesh did not allow them to behold God's glory, by reason of the mad fury with which they sought their own glory. Here you have your *'spirit that rules'*, your *'principal part of man, which aspires to what is upright'*—a plunderer of God's glory, and a usurper of His majesty! And that applies most of all when men are at their noblest, and are most distinguished for their own highest virtues! Now deny that these men were flesh, and were ruined by ungodly affection!

I do not think that the Diatribe is much offended by the statement that man is 'flesh' or 'spirit'. Latin would here say 'man is *carnal* or *spiritual*.' This peculiarity, like many more, must be conceded to the Hebrew language, that when it says: 'Man is flesh or spirit', it means the same as we mean when we say: 'Man is carnal or spiritual'; just as Latin says: 'The wolf is a disastrous thing[1] for the folds', or: 'Rain is *a welcome thing*[1] for the crops', or: 'this fellow is iniquity and evil itself'.[1] So too Holy Scripture, for the sake of greater intensity,[2] calls man 'flesh'— carnality itself, as it were—because he savours too much— indeed, exclusively—the things of the flesh; and it calls man 'spirit' where he savours, seeks, does and bears nothing but the things of the Spirit.

The Diatribe may raise this still outstanding question: 'Even if the whole of man, and the most excellent thing in man, is called flesh, must all that is called flesh be at once and for that reason called ungodly?' I reply: I call a man ungodly if he is without the Spirit of God; for Scripture says that the Spirit is

---

[1] *triste . . . dulce . . . scelus et ipsa malitia.*   [2] *per Epitasin.*

given to justify the ungodly. As Christ distinguished the Spirit from the flesh, saying: 'That which is born of the flesh is flesh', and adds that what is born of the flesh 'cannot see the kingdom of God', it obviously follows that whatever is flesh is ungodly, under God's wrath, and a stranger to his kingdom. And if it is a stranger to God's kingdom and Spirit, it follows of necessity that it is under the kingdom and spirit of Satan. For there is no middle kingdom between the kingdom of God and the kingdom of Satan, which are ever at war with each other.

These are the arguments which prove that the brightest virtues among the heathen, the best works among the philosophers, the most excellent deeds among men, which appear in the sight of the world to be upright and good, and are so called, are really flesh in the sight of God, and minister to the kingdom of Satan; that is, they are ungodly, sacrilegious, and evil in every respect.

Let us suppose that the Diatribe's views stands good, that not every energy is 'flesh' (that is, ungodly), but there is an energy, called the spirit, which is upright and sound. See what absurdity follows from this—absurdity, not only at the bar of human reason, but in relation to the entire Christian religion and the fundamental articles of faith. If the most excellent thing in man is not ungodly, nor ruined and damned, but only 'the flesh' (that is, the grosser, lower affections), what sort of Redeemer, I ask, shall we make Christ to be? Shall we make the ransom-price of His blood to be of so little worth that it redeemed only the least valuable part of man, man's most excellent part being self-sufficient, and not needing Christ? So from now on I must preach that Christ is the Redeemer, not of the whole man, but only of his least valuable part (that is, his flesh); and that man is his own redeemer in respect of his better part! Choose which you will have. If man's better part is sound, it does not need Christ as its Redeemer. If it does not need Christ, man triumphs above Christ in a glory greater than His; for man takes care of himself in respect of his better part, whereas Christ only cares for his less valuable part. And then the sovereignty of Satan will prove to be nothing, for Satan will rule man's less valuable part only, and man will rule Satan instead in respect of his better part! So that the issue of your doctrine about the principal part of man will be, that man is exalted above both Christ and the devil: that is, man will become God of gods and Lord of lords! What has happened to that 'probable view' which said that 'free-will' can will no good? The Diatribe here maintains that 'free-will' is man's principal part, sound and upright; it does not even need Christ, but can do more than God and the devil can do!

I say this so that you may once more see what a risky business it is to approach the holy things of God in the rash audacity of human reason, without God's spirit. If Christ is 'the Lamb of God that taketh away the sins of the world' (cf. John 1.29), it follows that the whole world is under sin, and condemnation, and the devil. So your distinction between parts that are principal and parts that are not is profitless. 'The world' means men, who savour of the things of the world in every part of them.

'*If the whole man, even when born again by faith, is nothing but "flesh", where is the "spirit" that is born of the Spirit? Where is the child of God? Where is the new creature? I would be glad of information about this.*' Thus speaks the Diatribe.

Whither away? whither away? my best beloved Diatribe! What are you dreaming of? You ask for information as to how the 'spirit' that is born of the Spirit can be 'flesh.' Oh, how gleeful, how sure of victory are you here, scoffing at me as a defeated foe, as though it were impossible for me to stand my ground! At the same time, you seek to exploit[1] the authority of the ancients, who say that some 'seeds of uprightness' are sown in the minds of men.

Now, in the first place, as far as I am concerned you may use or abuse the authority of the ancients to your heart's content; but you must look to what you are believing when you believe men who harp on their own ideas, without the word of God! Maybe your concern about religion does not cause you much anxiety as to what anyone believes, seeing that you so easily believe men, and never stop to see whether what they say is sure or unsure in the sight of God! Moreover, I myself would be glad of information as to when I ever taught what you thus

---

[1] *abuti.* The word means both 'use to the full' and 'abuse'. Erasmus had used it in the first sense: Luther echoes him, insinuating the second.

freely and publicly lay to my charge. Who would be so crazy as to say that he that is born of the Spirit is nothing but flesh? I draw a clear-cut distinction between 'flesh' and 'spirit' as being contrary principles, and I say, according to the Divine oracles, that the man that is not born again through faith is flesh. But one that is born again I no longer call flesh, except in respect of the remnants of the flesh which war against the first-fruits of the Spirit that he has received. I do not think that you meant to fabricate this charge with a view to raising prejudice against me; but you could accuse me of nothing more heinous. Either you understand nothing of my position, or else you find yourself unequal to matters of such magnitude; it may be because you are so overwhelmed and confused by them that you do not sufficiently remember what you say, either against me or for yourself. You speak with a certain degree of forgetfulness once more when you profess to believe, on the authority of the ancients, that there are some 'seeds of uprightness' sown in men's minds; for you asserted earlier that 'free-will' can will no good! How inability to will any good can allow of some 'seeds of uprightness' I do not know. Thus am I constantly obliged to remind you of the state of the question which you took up—because you are constantly forgetting and leaving it, and addressing yourself to matters foreign to your purpose.

(v) *Jer. 10.23: the impotence of man* (745-746)

A further passage is in Jer. 10: 'I know, O Lord, that the way of man is not in himself; it is not in any man to walk and direct his steps' (v. 23). This passage, says the Diatribe, *'relates to the happy outcome of events, rather than to the power of "free-will".'* Here again the Diatribe confidently introduces a gloss, just as it sees fit, as though Scripture were under its own complete jurisdiction! But what need was there for a person of such great authority as yourself to consider the prophet's meaning and intention at all? It is enough that Erasmus says a thing! therefore it is so! If our opponents are allowed to indulge this passion for glossing, what point will they not gain? Let Erasmus teach us how this gloss springs from the sequence of the actual words, and then we will believe him! From the actual sequence of thought, I teach that the words mean this: The prophet, seeing that his earnest instruction of the ungodly is in vain, at once realises that his own word avails nothing unless God teaches within, and therefore, that it is not in the power of man to hear and to will good. Having observed this, he is in terror at the judgment of God, and asks God to correct him if he needs any correction, and not to give him up to be under God's wrath along with the ungodly, whom God suffers to be hardened and to remain in unbelief.

Supposing that the passage is to be understood of the happy or unhappy outcome of events, what if this very gloss should most strongly overthrow 'free-will'? Certainly, this new evasion is fabricated in order to deceive lazy and unwary persons and make them think that an adequate answer has been given, as is the case with that evasion about necessity of consequence. And their attention is so diverted by the new-fangled terms that they do not see how much more thoroughly these evasions entangle and entrap them. If the outcome of these temporal things, over which man was made lord, is not in our own power, how pray, can that heavenly thing, the grace of God, which depends on the will of God alone, be in our power? Can the endeavours of 'free-will' lay hold of eternal salvation, when it cannot keep hold of a farthing, or a hair of the head? When we have no power to hold down the creature, can we have power to hold down the Creator? Why are we so crazy? And this applies much more to the outcome of man's striving after good or evil, seeing that in either case he is much more open to deception, and has much less freedom, than when he strives after money or glory or pleasure. What a fine evasion this gloss is, then; it denies man freedom in trifling issues concerning created things, and proclaims his freedom in supreme issues concerning God! It is like saying, Codrus cannot pay a penny, but he can pay countless thousands of pounds! And I am surprised that the Diatribe, which has hitherto so vigorously flayed Wycliffe's doctrine that all things come to pass by necessity, should now itself grant that the outcome of things is *necessary* as far as we are concerned!

'*Moreover, however much you twist this text to apply it to "free-will"*,' says the Diatribe, '*all acknowledge that no one can hold to a right course of life without the grace of God; nevertheless, we ourselves still strive the while with all our strength, for we pray daily: "O Lord my God, direct my way in Thy sight." He who asks aid does not lay aside endeavour.*'

The Diatribe thinks that it does not matter what it answers, as long as it does not remain silent, but says something; and then it would have what it says appear as a complete answer, such confidence has it in its own authority! It ought to have settled whether we strive by our own strength, and it settles instead that he who prays makes some endeavour. Pray, is it making fun of us? or is it mocking the Papists? He who prays, prays by the Spirit; or, rather, the Spirit himself prays in us, as we are told in Rom. 8 (vv. 26-27). How is the power of 'free-will' proved by the endeavouring of the Spirit? Does the Diatribe regard 'free-will' and the Holy Spirit as identical? Are we now discussing the power of the Holy Spirit? So the Diatribe leaves me this passage of Jeremiah untouched and unconquered, and merely produces out of its own head the gloss: '*we still strive with our own strength.*' And Luther will be obliged to believe it—if he will!

(vi) *Prov. 16.1, 21.1: the sovereignty of God over man* (746-748)

The statement in Prov. 16: 'It is of man to prepare the heart, but of the Lord to govern the tongue' (v. 1), is also referred by the Diatribe to the outcome of events—as if the Diatribe's own statement ought to satisfy me, without any other authority! I am, indeed, abundantly satisfied that, if I allow that the meaning relates to the outcome of events, I clearly come off victorious, according to what I have just said—namely, that, seeing we have no freedom of will in our own sphere of action, much more is true that we have none in the sphere of God's action.

See how acute the Diatribe is: '*How is it of man to prepare the heart, when Luther affirms that all things are controlled by necessity?*' I reply: If the issues of things are not in our power, as you yourself say, how is it of man to control those things? Take to yourself the reply that you gave me! Rather, we must work all we can, just because all things future are to us uncertain; as Ecclesiastes says, 'In the morning sow thy seed, and in the evening hold not thine hand: for thou knoweth not which shall prosper, this or that' (11.6). These things, I repeat, are uncertain as far as our knowing them is concerned, though they are necessary as far as concerns their own outcome. The necessity strikes the fear of God into us, so that we fall not into a presumptuous sense of security, while the uncertainty begets trust, lest we should despair.

The Diatribe, however, goes back to its old theme-song, that much is said in the book of Proverbs in favour of 'free-will,' such as: 'Unfold thy works to the Lord' (cf. 16.3). *'Do you hear it say "thy works"?'* says the Diatribe.

I suppose it makes this claim because there are in that book many imperative and hypothetical verbs, and pronouns in the second person; for it is upon these foundations that it builds its proof of the freedom of the will, like this: 'Unfold'—therefore, you can unfold; 'thy works'—therefore, you perform them. On this principle, you will understand: 'I am thy God' (Isa. 41.10) as meaning: 'you make me your God'! 'Thy faith hath saved thee' (Luke 7.50); *'thy'*, do you hear?—so expound it thus: 'You make your own faith'!—and then you have proved 'free-will'! I am not joking here; I am showing the Diatribe that it is not serious in this business.

The statement in the same chapter, 'The Lord hath made all things for himself; yea, even the wicked for the day of evil' (v. 4), the Diatribe modifies by its own very words as it acquits God of *having made any creature evil*. As though I had spoken of the creation, and not rather of the constant operation of God in created things, the operation by which God moves to action even the ungodly! I dealt with this earlier when discussing Pharaoh.

Nor does the Diatribe find any embarrassment in this text, from the twentieth chapter: 'The king's heart is in the hand of the Lord; he inclineth it whithersoever he will' (21.1). *'He who inclines,'* it says, *'does not forthwith compel.'* As though I were speaking of compulsion, and not rather of necessity of immutability! It is this necessity that is meant by the 'inclining' of God, which is not such a snoring, lazy thing as the Diatribe imagines; it is the most active operation of God, which man cannot avoid or alter, but under which he has, of necessity, the will which God gave him, and which God now makes to act by His own movement. I dealt with this above.

Furthermore, the Diatribe thinks that, since Solomon speaks of 'the king's heart', the passage cannot rightly be turned into a general statement, but means what Job says elsewhere: 'He maketh the hypocrite to reign, because of the sins of the people' (cf. Job 34.30). It finally concedes that the king is inclined to evil by God, but *merely by His permitting the king to give rein to his passions, in order to chasten the people*'! I reply: Whether God 'permits,' or whether he 'inclines,' that permitting or inclining does not come to pass apart from the will and operation of God, for the king's will cannot escape the action of the omnipotent God by which all men's wills, good and bad, are moved to will and to act.

As for my having generalised from the particular will of the king, I do not think it was a foolish or unlearned thing for me to do. For if the king's heart, which appears to be supremely free, and to lord it over others, cannot in fact will except as God inclines it, how much less can any other man? And that conclusion could be validly drawn, not from the king's will only, but from any man's; for if any single man, however undistinguished, cannot will in the presence of God except as God inclines him, the same must be said of all men. Thus, Balaam's inability to say what he wished is a clear proof from the Scriptures that man is not in his own power, nor free in choosing and doing what he does. Were it not so, no such cases would stand in the Scriptures.

(vii) *John 15.5: the meaning of 'nothing'* (748-753)

After this, having said that abundance of such testimonies as Luther gathers might be gathered from the book of Proverbs, but that a 'convenient explanation' could make them stand as well in favour of 'free-will' as against it, the Diatribe cites at last Luther's inescapable, Achillean weapon, the statement in John 15: 'Without me you can do nothing' (v. 5).

I applaud this excellent advocate[1] for 'free-will'! He teaches

[1] *rhetorem.*

us to modify Scripture testimonies by 'convenient explanations'
as we see fit, so that they may really stand in favour of 'free-
will' (that is, may avail, not as they should, but as we would);
and now he pretends to fear this one Achillean text, so that, by
overthrowing it, he may cause the dull reader to hold the rest
of our texts in excessive contempt! But I will look and see by
what power the Diatribe, for all its grandiose heroic talk, is
going to conquer my Achilles; for so far it has not hit a common
infantryman, not even a Thersites, but has most unhappily
used its own weapons to despatch itself!

It catches hold of this little word 'nothing', cuts its throat
with many words and examples, and by means of a 'convenient
explanation' brings it to this: that *'nothing' may mean the same as
'a little imperfect something'*.[1] That is, it says in different words
what in the past the Sophists taught from this passage: 'Without me ye can do nothing'—that is to say, nothing *perfectly*.
This long outworn and rusty gloss the Diatribe renovates by
the power of its rhetoric, and makes play with it as though it
had been the first to produce it and it never was heard of
before. It would set it on show before us as one would a miracle!
Yet all the time it cheerfully omits to give a thought to the
actual text, and to that which precedes and follows the word,
from which our understanding of it must be sought. I make no
comment on its attempt to prove by many words and examples
that the word 'nothing' can be taken in this passage for a 'little
imperfect something'. As though we were arguing about what
can be! What had to be proved was whether it *should* be so taken.
So the whole of this grandiose explanation, if it achieves anything, achieves only this: it makes this passage of John uncertain and ambiguous! And no wonder; for the sole aim of the
Diatribe is to make the Scriptures of God obscure everywhere,
so that it may not be compelled to use them, and to make the
authority of the ancients decisive, so that it may abuse it!
This is a truly amazing religion, which makes the words of man
profitable and the words of God profitless.

The finest thing of all is to see how beautifully consistent this
is: ' *"Nothing" can be taken for "a little something"; and in that sense*'
(says the Diatribe) *'it is most true that without Christ we can do*

---

[1] *modicum et imperfectum.*

nothing; for He is speaking of gospel fruit, which does not appear save in those who abide in the vine, which is Christ,' etc. Here the Diatribe itself admits that fruit does not appear save in those who abide in the vine; and it does so by means of that self-same 'convenient explanation' with which it proves that 'nothing' is 'a little imperfect something'. Perhaps the adverb 'not' should also be 'conveniently explained' to mean that gospel fruit in some measure 'a little imperfect something'—can appear outside Christ; so that we may preach that the ungodly, without Christ, can produce some of the fruits of life even though Satan reigns in them and wars against Christ! that is, that the enemies of Christ may act for Christ! But away with all this. I should like information here as to how the Diatribe can resist heretics, who will employ this rule throughout the Scriptures, and insist on taking 'nothing' and 'not' as meaning 'imperfect', as follows: 'Without Him *nothing* was made' (John 1.3)—that is, a little something! 'The fool hath said in his heart, God is *not*' (Ps. 14.1)—that is, God is imperfect! He hath made us and *not* we ourselves' (Ps. 100.3)—that is, we made a little something! And who can count all the places in Scripture where 'nothing' and 'not' are put? Shall we say at this point: 'we must look for a convenient explanation'? Every heretic finds his own explanation convenient!

This, I suppose, is 'cutting knots'—this opening of the door to such license for corrupt minds and deceiving spirits! To you, who care not a jot for the certainty of holy Scripture, such licence in interpretation would, I suppose, be convenient; but for me, whose task it is to establish consciences, nothing could be more inconvenient, or injurious, or disastrous, than this 'convenience' of yours! Hear, therefore, great conqueror of Luther's Achilles: Unless you prove that 'nothing' in this passage not only *may*, but *must* be taken to mean 'a little something', you have done nothing with your vast profusion of words and examples but fight fire with dry straw! What concern of mine is your '*may* be', when you are required to prove '*must* be'? And unless you do, I stand by the natural grammatical meaning of the word, and deride your armies and your triumphs!

Where now is that 'probable view' which laid it down that

'free-will' can will no good? Perhaps the 'convenient explanation' comes in here, to tell us that 'no good' means 'some good'! It is utterly unheard-of grammar and logic to say that *nothing* is the same as *something*; to logicians, the thing is an impossibility, for the two are contradictory! And where then is our belief that Satan is the prince of this world, and reigns, as Christ and Paul tell us, in the wills and minds of men, who are his prisoners, and serve him? Will this roaring lion, this restless, implacable enemy of the grace of God and the salvation of men, suffer man, who is his slave and part of his kingdom, to make endeavours towards good at any time, or by any movement, whereby he might escape Satan's tyranny? Will he not rather spur and urge man on to will and to do with all his power that which is contrary to grace? Why, the righteous, whose acts are wrought by the Spirit of God, find it hard to resist him and to will and do good, so furiously does he rage against them! You, who imagine that the human will is something placed in an intermediate position of 'freedom' and left to itself, find it easy to imagine that there is at the same time an endeavouring of the will in either direction; for you imagine that both God and the devil are far away, mere spectators, as it were, of this mutable free-will; you do not believe that they are the prompters and drivers of an *enslaved* will, and each waging relentless war against the other! If this alone is believed, then my case stands strong enough, and 'free-will' lies prostrate; as I showed above. Either the kingdom of Satan in man is unreal, in which case Christ will be a liar; or else, if his kingdom is as Christ describes it, 'free-will' will be merely a beast of burden, Satan's prisoner, which cannot be freed unless the devil is first cast out by the finger of God.

By this I think you sufficiently understand, my good Diatribe, what it means, and how much it avails, that your author, disliking Luther's obstinacy in assertion, should regularly observe: '*Luther presses his case very strongly with Scripture texts, but they can be annulled by a single little word.*' Who is unaware that all the Scriptures can be annulled by a single little word? I knew it well enough before ever I heard the name of Erasmus! But the question is, whether it is satisfactory for a Scripture to be annulled by a single little word. Is it rightly annulled? Should it be thus annulled? These are the issues. Let the Diatribe look this way, and it will see how easy it is to annul the Scriptures, and how objectionable is Luther's obstinacy! It will see that both little words, and all the gates of hell, are of no avail at all!

Though I am not bound to prove a negative, yet I will now do what the Diatribe was unable to do for its own affirmative, and evince by force of arguments that 'nothing' in this passage not only *may*, but *must* be taken to mean, not 'a little something', but that which the term naturally conveys. This I will do, over and above the insuperable argument with which I have already won the day—namely, that the usual and natural sense of terms must be retained, unless proof is given to the contrary; which the Diatribe neither has done, nor can do. We evince it first from the nature of the case, as follows: It is plainly proved by Scriptures that are neither ambiguous nor obscure that Satan is by far the most powerful and crafty prince in this world; as I have said. Under his rule the human will is no longer free nor in its own power, but is the slave of sin and of Satan, and can only will what its prince has willed. And he will not let it will any good—though, even if Satan did not rule it, sin itself, whose slave man is, would weigh it down enough to make it unable to will good.

Moreover, the following words of the discourse evince the same point. (The Diatribe proudly disregards them, though I commented pretty copiously upon them in my Assertions.) Christ proceeds thus in John 15: 'If a man abide not in me, he is cast forth as a branch and withers; and men gather them and cast them into the fire, and they are burned' (v. 6). This, I repeat, the Diatribe in its rhetorical virtuosity passed by, hoping that its transition would be beyond the understanding of such unlearned fellows as the Lutherans! But here you see Christ explaining His own simile of the vine and the branch, and declaring plainly enough what he would have understood by the term 'nothing': namely, that man outside Christ is cast forth, and withers. What can being cast forth, and withering, mean, but being delivered up into the devil's power, and growing continually worse? But deterioration is no kind of ability or endeavour! The more the withering branch withers, more and more is it made ready for the fire. Had not Christ himself thus amplified and applied this simile, none would have dared so to amplify and apply it. It holds good, therefore, that 'nothing' in this place must be taken in its proper sense, as the nature of the term conveys it.

Now let us look at the examples by which the Diatribe proves that 'nothing' is in some places taken for 'a little something', so that we may show that in this part also the Diatribe is and achieves—nothing! Even if it were doing anything here, it would still achieve nothing, such a nonentity is the Diatribe in every way and at every point!

'*A man is commonly said to do "nothing",*' it tells us, '*when he does not achieve what he aims at; yet he who endeavours often makes some progress.*' I reply: I never heard it thus 'commonly said'; you have taken the liberty of inventing this usage! Words must be regarded (as the formula runs) in the light of the subject-matter and of the speaker's intention. Nobody calls what he is attempting to do 'nothing'; and he who speaks of 'nothing' is speaking not of the endeavour, but of the effect; it is this that one has in view when one says: 'he does nothing', or 'achieves nothing', that is, he has not attained or accomplished his end. Moreover, supposing that your example holds good (which it does not), it makes more for me than for you. For this is just what I maintain and want to establish—that 'free-will' does many things, which yet are 'nothing' before God! What has it gained by its endeavour, if it does not achieve its aim? And so, wherever the Diatribe turns, it only crashes into and refutes itself—which is the usual fate of those who plead a bad case!

With the same infelicity it quotes this example out of Paul: 'Neither is he that planteth any thing, neither he that watereth; but God that giveth the increase' (1 Cor. 3.7). '*That which is of very little importance, and useless in itself, he calls "nothing",*' says the Diatribe.

Who says that? Are you, Diatribe, telling us that the ministry of the word is *in itself and of very little importance*, when Paul everywhere, and especially in 2 Cor. 3 (vv. 6-9), highly exalts it, and calls it the ministration of life and of glory? Here again you omit to consider the subject-matter and the speaker's intention. As to the giving of increase, the planter and waterer are 'nothing', but as to the planting and watering they are not 'nothing'; for teaching and exhortation is the Spirit's chief work in the church of God. This is Paul's meaning, and this his words clearly enough convey. In any case, supposing that this inept example does hold good, it also will stand on my side. For I maintain that 'free-will' is 'nothing'—that is, useless in itself (as you expound it)—before God! It is of this kind of 'being' that I am speaking; for I am aware that an ungodly will is a *something*, and not a mere non-entity!

There are also the words from 1 Cor. 13: 'If I have not charity, I am nothing' (v. 2). Why the Diatribe quotes this as an example I cannot see, unless it hankered after weight of numbers, or supposed that I was short of weapons with which to transfix it! He who is without charity is in a true and proper sense 'nothing' before God. That is what I say of 'free-will'; so that this example stands on my side against the Diatribe. Perhaps the Diatribe is still unaware of the point at issue between us? I am not speaking of 'natural being', but of 'gracious being',[1] as they call it. I know that 'free-will' can do some things by nature; it can eat, drink, beget, rule, etc. The Diatribe need not mock me in its ravings—its talking-fit, so to speak—by saying that, if I press the term 'nothing', then 'free-will' may not even sin without Christ; Luther granted all the time that 'free-will' avails for nothing but sin! Thus has it pleased the wise Diatribe to play the fool even in a serious matter. I say that man without the grace of God nonetheless remains under the general omnipotence of the God who effects, and moves, and impels all things in a neces-sary, infallible course; but the fact of man's thus being carried along is 'nothing'—that is, avails nothing in God's sight, nor is reckoned to be anything but sin. Thus he who is without charity is 'nothing' in grace. Now, the Diatribe itself acknow-ledges that here we are dealing with gospel 'fruit,' which does not appear without Christ. Why then does it at once turn aside from the point at issue, start up an irrelevant theme, and raise quibbles about natural working and human 'fruit'? Surely because one who is devoid of truth is never consistent with himself!

So it is with the words of John 3: 'A man can receive *nothing*

---

[1] *de esse naturae . . . de esse gratiae.*

except it be given him from above' (v. 27). John here speaks of man (who is certainly *something* already), and denies that he receives *anything* (that is, the Spirit with His gifts; for it is of that, not of nature, that he is speaking). He did not need the Diatribe to teach him that man already has eyes, nose, ears, mouth, hands, mind, will, reason, and all that is in man! Or does the Diatribe suppose the Baptist to have been so raving mad that when he mentioned 'man', he was thinking of the 'chaos' of Plato, or the 'vacuum' of Leucippus, or the 'infinite' of Aristotle, or some other *nothing*, which might at last become a *something* by a gift from heaven? And this, I suppose, is 'producing examples from the Scriptures'—this deliberate fooling on so vital a subject!

What, then, is the point of that mass of words which tells us that fire, and escape from evil, and striving after good, and all the rest, are from heaven—as though anyone were unaware of that, or denied it? We are speaking of grace, and, as the Diatribe itself has said, of Christ, and of gospel fruit; yet it spends all its time babbling about nature, thus dragging out the argument, and fogging the unlearned reader! Meanwhile, it not only fails to produce a single case in which 'nothing' is taken for 'a little something' (which it was it undertook to do); it also openly betrays that it has no understanding or concern as to what Christ and grace are, or how grace differs from nature, and even the least learned Sophists knew that; it is a distinction which they have laboured, by incessant repetition in their schools! At the same time, the Diatribe wholly fails to see that all its examples make for me and against itself. For the Baptist's word means that man can receive nothing unless it is given him from above; so that 'free-will' is nothing!

This is how my Achilles is conquered—weapons are handed to it by the Diatribe, whereby it despatches the Diatribe, unarmed and defenceless! This is how the Scriptures with which Luther, the obstinate assertor, presses his case are 'annulled by a little word'!

(viii) *That 'free-will' does not follow from man's co-operation with God* (753-755)

After this, the Diatribe lists many similes, by which it accomplishes nothing beyond whirling the witless reader away to irrelevant matters, after its fashion; for it continues utterly oblivious of the matter in hand. Thus: '*God indeed preserves the ship, but the sailor steers it to harbour; so the sailor does something.*' This simile distinguishes the work of preserving, which is God's, from the work of steering, which is the sailor's. If it proves anything, it proves this: that *all* the work of preserving is God's, and *all* the work of steering is man's. And yet it is 'a beautiful and apt simile'! Again: '*The husbandman gathers the increase, but God gave it.*' Here once more it attributes different operations to God and to man—unless it means to identify the husbandman with the Creator Who gave the increase! Even allowing, however, that the same works are here attributed to both God and man, what do these similes prove? Merely that the creature co-operates with the operation of God! And are we now debating co-operation? Are we not rather debating the power and operation that properly belongs to 'free-will'? Whither has our rhetorician fled, he that was going to talk about palm trees, and in fact talks about nothing but marrows? 'He started a vase; then why does a pitcher result?'[1] I also am aware that Paul co-operates with God in teaching the Corinthians; he preaches without, and God teaches within. The work of each is in that case distinct. In like manner, Paul co-operates with God when he speaks in the Spirit of God; and here the work is the same. What I assert and maintain is this: that where God works apart from the grace of His Spirit, He works all things in all men, even in the ungodly; for He alone moves, makes to act, and impels by the motion of His omnipotence, all those things which He alone created; they can neither avoid nor alter this movement, but necessarily follow and obey it, each thing according to the measure of its God-given power. Thus all things, even the ungodly, co-operate with God. And when God acts by the Spirit of His grace in those whom He has justified, that is, in His own kingdom, He moves and carries

[1] Hor., *Ars Poet.*, 217.

them along in like manner; and they, being a new creation, follow and co-operate with Him, or rather, as Paul says, are made to act by Him (Rom. 8.14).

But this is not the place for these matters. We are not now discussing what we can do by God's working in us, but what we can do by ourselves; that is, whether, created as we are from nothing, we can through this general movement of omnipotence do or attempt anything of ourselves to prepare ourselves for new creation by the Spirit. The Diatribe should have spoken to this point, and not turned aside elsewhere!

What I say on this point is as follows: Man, before he is created to be man, does and endeavours nothing towards his being made a creature, and when he is made and created he does and endeavours nothing towards his continuance as a creature; both his creation and his continuance come to pass by the sole will of the omnipotent power and goodness of God, Who creates and preserves us without ourselves. Yet God does not work in us without us; for He created and preserves us for this very purpose, that He might work in us and we might co-operate with Him, whether that occurs outside His kingdom, by His general omnipotence, or within His kingdom, by the special power of His Spirit. So, too, I say that man, before he is renewed into the new creation of the Spirit's kingdom, does and endeavours nothing to prepare himself for that new creation and kingdom, and when he is re-created he does and endeavours nothing towards his perseverance in that kingdom; but the Spirit alone works both blessings in us, regenerating us, and preserving us when regenerate, without ourselves; as James says: 'Of His own will begat He us with the word of His power, that we should be the firstfruits of His creation' (Jas. 1.18). (James is speaking of the renewed creation.) But He does not work in us without us, for He re-created and preserves us for this very purpose, that He might work in us and we might co-operate with Him. Thus he preaches, shows mercy to the poor, and comforts the afflicted by means of us. But what is hereby attributed to 'free-will'? What, indeed, is left it but— nothing! In truth, nothing!

Peruse, now, the five or six pages in which, by means of

similes of this kind, and beautiful passages and parables quoted from the Gospel and Paul, the Diatribe does nothing but inform us that *'countless passages'* (its very words) *are found in the Scriptures that speak of the co-operation and help of God.* If I then conclude from these that man can do nothing without the help of God's grace; therefore, no works of man are good; the Diatribe contrariwise concludes, by a rhetorical inversion *'Nay there is nothing that man cannot do with the help of God's grace; therefore, all the works of man can be good. Thus, all the passages in the Divine Scriptures that mention such help are they that establish "free-will"; and these are countless. Therefore, if the matter is assessed by the number of testimonies, victory is mine.'* So speaks the Diatribe.

Do you think the Diatribe was quite sober, or in its right mind, when it wrote this? For I will not put it down to wickedness and villainy—unless perhaps its intention is to bore me to death by its characteristic habit of always dealing with something other than its stated theme! But if the Diatribe has enjoyed itself by trifling on such a vital matter, then let me too enjoy myself by publicly exposing its wilful stupidities.

In the first place I do not dispute, nor am I unaware, that all man's works *can* be good, if they are done with the help of God's grace, and that there is nothing that man cannot do with the help of God's grace. But I cannot be sufficiently astonished at the careless oversight which leads you, who set out to write about the power of 'free-will', to write instead about the power of God's grace. And then—as if all men were stocks and stones —you have the audacity to assert publicly that 'free-will' is established by those passages of Scripture that commend the assistance of God's grace! Not only do you dare to do that, but you go on to hymn your own praises—a swaggering conquering hero! Now in truth I know from your own word and deed what 'free-will' is, and what it can do—it can *rave*! Pray, what can it be in you that talks at this rate, if not just 'free-will'? But listen to your conclusions! *'The Scripture commends God's grace; therefore, it proves "free-will".' 'It commends the help of God's grace; therefore, it establishes "free-will".'* By what logic did you learn these inferences? Why not the opposite—'grace is preached; therefore, "free-will" is done away'? 'The assistance of grace is commended; therefore "free-will" is abolished'? To what end is grace given? Is it that grace may be, as it were, the fancy dress in which 'free-will', proud and self-sufficient in its strength, blithely disports itself on May-days?[1] Wherefore, though I am no rhetorician, I am going to invert your reasoning, by a sounder rhetoric than yours, as follows: 'All the passages in the Holy Scriptures that mention assistance are they that do away with "free-will", and these are countless. Therefore, if the matter is assessed by the number of testimonies, victory is mine. For grace is needed, and the help of grace is given, because "free-will" of itself can do nothing; as the Diatribe itself states in that "probable view", it cannot will any good. Therefore, when grace is commended and the assistance of grace is proclaimed, the impotence of "free-will" is thereby declared.' This is a sound inference, and a settled conclusion, which the very gates of hell shall not overthrow.

Here I shall terminate the defence of those arguments of mine which the Diatribe sought to refute, lest my book should swell to undue size. Anything else that merits notice will be dealt with in the course of what we have to assert. Erasmus repeats in his peroration that, *if my view stands, all the precepts, threats and promises are in vain, and no place is left for merit or demerit, reward or punishment; and it is difficult to defend the mercy, let alone the justice of God, if God damns sinners of necessity; and other inconveniences follow which have so impressed great men as to overwhelm them.* On all these matters I have spoken my mind already. And I do not accept or tolerate that middle way[2] which Erasmus (I think, with good intentions) recommends to me, namely, to *allow a very little[3] to 'free-will', so that the contradictions of Scripture and the aforementioned inconveniences may be more easily removed.* The case is not bettered by this middle way, nor is anything gained. For, unless you attribute all and everything to 'free-will', in the way that the Pelagians do, the contradictions in the Scripture still remain, merit and reward are done away, the mercy and justice of God are done away also, and all the inconveniences which we intend to avoid by allowing to 'free-will' this tiny, ineffective power continue with us; as I explained above. So

---

[1] *diebus bachanalibus.*   [2] *mediocritatem.*   [3] *perpusillum.*

we have to go to extremes, deny 'free-will' altogether, and ascribe everything to God! Thus will the Scriptures be free from contradictions; and the inconveniences, if not removed, may be borne with.

(ix) *Conclusion of this section* (756)

This I beg of you, my good Erasmus—do not think that I maintain this cause at the prompting of passion rather than of judgment. I do not tolerate the insinuation that I am hypocrite enough to write one thing and believe another, nor have I been carried by the heat of battle (as you write of me) to the point where I now deny 'free-will' for the first time, having previously ascribed something to it. I know that you will not be able to point to such an ascription anywhere in my books. There are in existence expositions and discussions[1] of mine in which I have constantly asserted, up to this very hour, that 'free-will' is a nonentity, a *thing* (I have used that word) *consisting of a name alone.* Conquered by truth and forced into the lists of the challenge of debate, this was my conviction; and thus have I written. As to my having argued somewhat vigorously, I acknowledge my fault, if it is a fault—but no; I have wondrous joy that this witness is borne in the world of my conduct in the cause of God. May God Himself confirm this witness in the last day! Who would then be happier than Luther —commended by the testimony of all his age as having maintained the cause of truth, not lazily, nor deceitfully, but with vigour enough and to spare! Then shall I happily escape Jeremiah's threat, 'Cursed he be that doeth the work of the Lord carelessly' (Jer. 48.10)!

If I seem too bitter against your Diatribe, you must pardon me. I do not act so out of ill-will; but I was concerned that by the weight of your name you were greatly jeopardising the cause of Christ (though you can really effect nothing against it by your learning). And who can always so govern his pen as not on occasion to show warmth? Even you, who in your passion for restraint almost freeze in this book, not infrequently

---

[1] *themata et problemata.*

hurl fiery, gall-dipped darts against me, so that were your reader not very fair-minded and sympathetic, he would think you venomous. But these things have no bearing on our debate, and we must freely pardon each other in them; for we are but men, and there is nothing in us that is not characteristic of mankind.

VII

THE BIBLE DOCTRINE OF THE BONDAGE OF THE WILL (*W.A.* 756-786)

(i) *Rom. 1.18ff.: the universal guilt of mankind disproves 'free-will'* (756-760)

WE come now to the last part of this book, in which, as I promised, I am to bring into the field my own resources against 'free-will'. Not that I shall bring them all; who could do that in this small book, when the entire Scripture, every jot and tittle of it, stands on my side? And there is no need; for 'free-will' lies vanquished and prostrate already. Twice have I overthrown it: first, by proving that all that it thought made for it actually stands against it; then, by showing that the arguments which it sought to refute still continue impregnable. And, even were it as yet unconquered, no more need be done than to lay it low with a single stroke or two; for when with one weapon you have despatched your enemy, there is no need to go on hacking him with many more. We shall now, therefore, be briefer, if our subject will allow of it. Out of a host of armies, I shall bring into the fray two generals, with a few of their legions only—I mean, Paul and the evangelist John.

Paul, writing to the Romans, enters upon his argument for the grace of God against 'free-will' as follows: 'The wrath of God' (he says) 'is revealed from heaven against all ungodliness and unrighteousness of men, who hold down the truth in unrighteousness' (Rom. 1.18). Do you hear this general judgment against all men, that they are under the wrath of God? What does this mean, but that they merit wrath and punishment? He assigns the reason for the wrath by saying that they do only that which merits wrath and punishment—that they are all ungodly and unrighteous, and hold down the truth in unrighteousness. Where now is the power of 'free-will' to endeavour after some good? Paul makes it merit the wrath of God, and pronounces it ungodly and unrighteous! And that which deserves wrath and is ungodly is endeavouring and availing, not for grace, but against it.

Here someone will smile at Luther's sleepy-headedness in not studying Paul closely enough. He will say that Paul is here speaking, not of all men, nor of all their activities, but only of those that are ungodly and unrighteous and who, as his own words put it, 'hold down the truth in unrighteousness'; and that it does not hence follow that all men are such.

On this I would comment that, in Paul, the words 'against all ungodliness of men' means the same as 'against the ungodliness of all men', because Paul almost everywhere uses Hebrew idiom. Thus the sense is: 'all men are ungodly and unrighteous, and hold down the truth in unrighteousness; all, therefore, merit wrath.' Furthermore, there is in the Greek no relative pronoun ('*of those* who'), but an article, like this: 'the wrath of God is revealed from heaven against all ungodliness and unrighteousness of men-holding-down-the-truth-in-unrighteousness.' So that this phrase stands as a description[1] of all men, that they 'hold down the truth in unrighteousness'; just as it is a description when it says, 'Our Father, which art in heaven', which might be otherwise expressed thus: 'Our heavenly Father', or: 'Our Father in heaven'. The design of the words is to mark off those who believe and are godly.

This explanation of mine might seem frivolous and empty, did not Paul's own argument require and evince it. A little before, he had said: 'The gospel is the power of God unto salvation to every one that believeth, to the Jew first and also to the Greek' (v. 16). There are no obscure or ambiguous words here: the gospel of the power of God is necessary 'to Jews and Greeks', that is, to all men, that they may by believing be saved from the wrath revealed. Paul proclaims that the Jews, for all their mighty righteousness, knowledge of God's law and power of 'free-will', differ not a whit from other men in their destitution and need of the power of God for salvation from the wrath revealed; he represents that power as necessary to them; does he not hereby adjudge them to be under wrath? What men will you instance, now, as not being subject to the wrath of God,

[1] *epitheton.*

when you are compelled to believe that the noblest men in the world, that is, the Jews and the Greeks, were subject to it? Whom among the Jews and the Greeks themselves will you exempt, when Paul embraces them all without distinction in a single phrase, and passes on them all the same verdict? Must we suppose that out of those two outstanding nations there were none that aspired to uprightness? none that endeavoured with all the strength of 'free-will'? Yet Paul does not hesitate to consign them all under wrath and proclaim them all ungodly and unrighteous. And must we not suppose that the other apostles, each in his own sphere, consigned all other nations under this wrath in similar terms?

This passage in Paul, therefore, stands strong in its insistence that even in the most excellent men, however endowed with law, righteousness, wisdom and all virtues, 'free-will', their most excellent part, is nonetheless ungodly, and unrighteous, and merits God's wrath. Otherwise Paul's argument is without force. But if it is a valid argument, then his division leaves no middle state; for by it he assigns salvation to those who believe the gospel and wrath to all the rest. He makes believers righteous, and unbelievers ungodly, unrighteous, and under wrath. He means just this: the righteousness of God is revealed in the gospel to be 'from faith'; therefore, all men are ungodly and unrighteous. God would be foolish to reveal righteousness to men who knew it, or had the seeds of it, already; since He is not foolish, and yet does reveal to them the righteousness of salvation, it is apparent that 'free-will', even in the noblest men, not only does not possess and cannot effect anything, but does not even know what is righteous in God's sight. Or may it be that the righteousness of God is not revealed to these noblest men, but to the most ignoble only? But that is contradicted by Paul's boast that he is debtor to Jews and to Greeks, to the wise and to the unwise, to the Greeks and to the barbarians. So in this passage Paul simply lumps all men together, and concludes them, one and all, to be ungodly, unrighteous, ignorant of righteousness and of faith; so impossible is it that they can will or do any good. And this conclusion is confirmed by the fact that God reveals the righteousness of salvation as to men who sit ignorantly in darkness; of themselves, therefore, they know nothing of it; and if they are ignorant of the righteousness of salvation, they are certainly under wrath and condemnation, and by reason of their ignorance they cannot thence extricate themselves, nor endeavour so to do. How can you endeavour, if you do not know what, or how, or why, or to what extent, you must endeavour?

The facts of experience support this conclusion. Show me out of the whole race of mortal men one, albeit the most holy and righteous of them all, to whose mind it ever occurred that the way to righteousness and salvation was simply to believe on Him who is both God and man, who died for men's sins, and was raised, and is set at the right hand of the Father! Show me one who dreamed of this wrath of God which Paul here says is revealed from heaven! Look at the greatest philosophers! What thoughts had they of God? What have they left in writing about the wrath to come? Look at the Jews, incessantly instructed by a host of signs and prophets; what did they think of this Way? Not only did they not receive it, but they so hated it that no nation under heaven has persecuted Christ more bitterly to this day. Yet who would dare to say that amid so great a people there was not one who exercised 'free-will' and made endeavour with all its power? How is it, then, that they all endeavour the opposite way, and that that which was the most excellent part of the most excellent men not only did not follow this method of righteousness, not only was ignorant of it, but when it was revealed and proclaimed to them, thrust it away with the greatest hate and wished for its ruin? So much so that in 1 Cor. 1 (v. 23) Paul speaks of that Way as being 'to the Jews a stumbling-block, and to the Gentiles[1] foolishness.' Since he speaks of Jews and Gentiles[1] as on the same footing, and since it is certain that Jews and Gentiles[1] constitute the chief peoples under heaven, it is also certain that 'free-will' is nothing but the greatest enemy of righteousness and man's salvation. There must have been some among the Jews and the Gentiles who wrought and endeavoured with all the power of 'free-will'; and yet by that very endeavouring they merely waged war against grace.

Now come and tell us that 'free-will' endeavours towards

1 = 'Greeks.'

good, when goodness and righteousness themselves are a stumbling-block and foolishness to it! Neither can you say that this applies to some, but not all. Paul speaks of all as on the same footing when he says: 'to the Jews a stumbling-block and to the Gentiles foolishness,' and he excepts none but believers. 'To us,' he says, that is, 'who are called,' and saints, 'it is the power and wisdom of God' (vv. 18, 24). He does not say: to some Gentiles and to some Jews, but simply: to Gentiles and Jews who are not of us. He separates believers from unbelievers by a clear division, leaving no middle state. We are discussing Gentiles who work without grace; and Paul is saying that to them the righteousness of God is foolishness which they abhor. And this is your 'praiseworthy endeavour of "free-will" towards good'!

Furthermore: see whether Paul himself does not specifically instance the noblest among the Greeks when he says that the wiser ones among them 'became fools, and their heart was darkened', and that 'they became vain in their own reasonings'[1]—that is, by their own subtle disputations (Rom. 1.21). Does he not here, pray, touch on the noblest and most excellent thing in the Greeks, when he touches on their reasonings? These were their finest and best thoughts and opinions, which they took for solid wisdom. But, as elsewhere he calls this wisdom that was in them 'foolish', so here he says it was 'vain', and by its many endeavours grew worse, till at last with darkened hearts they worshipped idols and committed consequent enormities, which he goes on to mention. If, now, the best effort and performance of the best of the Gentiles is evil and ungodly, what do you think of the rest of men, the inferior Gentiles, as it were? And here Paul makes no distinction among the best of them, but condemns their pursuit of wisdom without respect of persons. But if the actual performance and effort is condemned, then all who made that effort, though they did so with all the power of 'free-will' are condemned too. Their very best endeavour, I repeat, is declared defective; how much more, then, they that were exercised in it?

In the same way, making no difference, he goes straight on to reject those Jews who are Jews in the letter but not in the Spirit. 'Thou by the letter and circumcision dishonourest God,'

[1] dialogismis.

he says (Rom. 2.23, 27). Again: 'He is not a Jew, which is one outwardly, but he who is a Jew inwardly' (vv. 28-29). What can be clearer than this division? The Jew outwardly is a transgressor of the law. How many Jews do you think there were without faith who were yet most wise, most religious and most upright persons, and aspired after righteousness and truth with the highest endeavour? The apostle often bears record of them that 'they have a zeal of God', 'they follow after the righteousness of the law', 'day and night they strive to come to salvation', they live 'blameless' (Rom. 10.2, 9.31; Acts 26.7; Phil. 3.6). Nonetheless, they are transgressors of the law, because they are not Jews in spirit, and, indeed, obstinately resist the righteousness of faith. What conclusion remains, then, but that 'free-will', when at its best, is then at its worst, and the more it endeavours the worse it grows and is? The words are plain; the division is clear-cut; nothing can be said against it.

(ii) *Rom. 3.9ff., 19ff.: the universal dominion of sin disproves 'free-will'* (760-764)

But let us hear Paul interpret himself. In the third chapter, by way of peroration, he says: 'What then? are we better than they? In no wise; for we have proved both Jews and Gentiles to be all under sin' (v. 9). Where is 'free-will' now? All Jews and Greeks, he says, are under sin! Are there any 'figures' or 'knots' here? What can the whole world's 'explanation' avail against this perfectly clear statement? By saying 'all' he excepts none. By describing them all as 'under sin', that is, slaves of sin, he leaves them no goodness. Where did he give this proof that all Jews and Gentiles are under sin? Precisely where I called attention to it, that is, where he says: 'The wrath of God is revealed from heaven against all ungodliness and unrighteousness of men.' He there proceeds to prove from experience that men were unthankful to God and enslaved to a host of vices and are, as it were, forced by the fruits of their own ungodliness to admit that they will and do nothing but evil. Then he judges the Jews separately, saying that the Jew in the letter is a transgressor of the law, and proving it in a similar way from the fruits of experience, thus: 'Thou that preachest a man should not steal stealest thyself; thou that abhorrest idols dost commit sacrilege' (Rom. 2.21-22); and he exempts none at all but those who are Jews in spirit. You cannot find a way out by saying: though they are under sin, yet the best part in them, that is, reason and will, makes endeavours towards good. For if the endeavour that remains to them is good, Paul's statement that they are under sin is false. When he names 'Jews and Gentiles', he includes all that is in Jews and Gentiles—unless you are going to turn Paul upside down and make out that what he wrote means this: 'the flesh of all Jews and Gentiles, that is, their grosser affections, are under sin.' But wrath is revealed from heaven against them, and unless they are justified by the Spirit it will damn them, whole and entire; which would not be, were they not under sin, whole and entire!

Let us see how Paul proves his view from the Holy Scriptures, and whether 'words have more force in Paul than in their own place'! 'Thus it is written,' he says: 'there is none righteous, there is none that understandeth, none that seeketh after God. They are all gone out of the way, they are all together become unprofitable, there is none that doeth good, no, not one,' etc. (Rom. 3.10-12). Here let him that can give me a 'convenient explanation', or invent 'figures', or contend that the words are ambiguous and obscure! Let him that dares defend 'free-will' against these indictments, and I will gladly give way and recant, and be a confessor and assertor of 'free-will' myself! It is certain that these words apply to all men, for the prophet introduces God as looking down from heaven upon all men and pronouncing this sentence upon them. That is how he puts it in Psalm 13: 'God looked down from heaven upon the children of men to see if there were any that did understand or seek after God. But they are all gone out of the way,' etc. (Ps. 14.2-3). Lest the Jews should think that this did not apply to them, Paul anticipates them by asserting that it applies to them most of all: 'We know,' he says, 'that what things soever the law saith, it says to them that are under the law' (v. 19). That was what he meant when he said: 'To the Jew first, and also to the Greek'. You hear, then, that all the children of men, all that are under the law, that is, Gentiles as well as Jews, are accounted before God to be unrighteous, not understanding, not seeking after

God, no, not one of them; they all go out of the way and are unprofitable. And I think that among the children of men, and those that are under the law, are numbered the 'best and most upright', who endeavour after what is upright and good with all the power of 'free-will', and of whom the Diatribe boasts as having the knowledge and seeds of uprightness implanted in them! (Or perhaps it would claim that such are the children of angels?)

How then are endeavours after good made by those who one and all are ignorant of God, and neither regard nor seek God? How have they a power that is profitable for good, when they all go out of the way from good, and are utterly unprofitable? Do we not know what it means to be ignorant of God, not to understand, not to seek God, not to fear God, to go out of the way and to be unprofitable? Are not the words perfectly clear? and do they not teach that all men are ignorant of God and despise God, and moreover go out of the way after evil, and are unprofitable for good? Paul is not here speaking of ignorance in seeking food, or of contempt for money, but of ignorance and contempt of religion and godliness. And doubtless that ignorance and contempt are not seated in the flesh, in the sense of the lower and grosser affections, but in the highest and most excellent powers of man, in which righteousness, godliness, and knowledge and reverence of God, should reign—that is, in reason and will, and so in the very power of 'free-will', in the very seed of uprightness, the most excellent thing in man!

Where are you now, my good Diatribe? You promised earlier that you would freely acknowledge that the most excellent thing in man is 'flesh' (that is, ungodly), if this were proved by the Scriptures! Acknowledge it now, then, as you hear that the most excellent thing in all men is not only ungodly, but ignorant of God, scornful of God, turned to evil, and unprofitable for good! What is it to be unrighteous, if not for the will (which is one of man's most excellent parts) to be unrighteous? What is it not to understand God and good, if not for the reason (which is another of man's most excellent parts) to be ignorant of God and good, that is, blind to the knowledge of godliness? What is it to go out of the way and be unprofitable, if not for men to have no power for good in any part of themselves, least

of all in their most excellent parts, but only power to do evil?
What is it not to fear God, if not for men to despise God with
all their faculties, and with their noblest most of all? And to
despise God is to despise all the things of God, His words,
works, laws, precepts and will! What, now, can reason propose
that is right, when it is thus blind and ignorant? What can the
will choose that is good, when it is thus evil and unprofitable?
or, rather, what can the will pursue, when reason can propose
to it nothing but the darkness of its own blindness and ignorance? Where reason is in error and the will turned away, what
good can man attempt or perform?

Perhaps some bold spirit will here play the Sophist and say:
though the will goes out of the way and reason does not know
how to act, yet the will is able to make some endeavour, and
reason to acquire some knowledge, by its own strength; for we
are able to do much that in fact we do not do; and it is, of
course, the degree of potency, and not its act, that concerns us.[1]

I reply: The words of the prophet cover both the act and
potency. To say: man does not seek God, is the same as saying:
man cannot seek God, as you may hence gather: If there were
potency or power in man to will good, the movement of Divine
omnipotence would not suffer it to remain inactive or keep
holiday, as I explained above, and it could not but be moved
to action in some men, or at least in some individual man, and
be exhibited in some employment. But this does not happen;
for God looks down from heaven, and does not see even one
who attempts to seek after Him. Whence it follows that power
to attempt or purpose to seek after him is nowhere to be found;
but all men instead go out of the way. Moreover, if Paul were
not understood to affirm lack of potency, his argument would
be without force; for Paul's whole aim is to make grace necessary to all men, and if they could initiate something by themselves, they would not need grace. As it is, however, they need
grace, just because they cannot do this. So you see that by the
terms of this passage 'free-will' is utterly laid low, and nothing
good or upright is left to man; for he is declared to be unrighteous, ignorant of God, a despiser of God, turned away from Him
and unprofitable in His sight. And the prophet's words have

[1] *de vi potentiae scilicet, non de actu disputamus.*

force enough in their own place, as well as in Paul's quotation of them! It is no small thing when man is said to be ignorant of God and to despise Him; for this is the fountain-head of all iniquities, the sink of sins, yes, a hell of evil! What evil is not present where there is ignorance and contempt of God? In short, the rule of Satan over men could not be depicted in fewer yet fuller words than by saying that they are ignorant of, and despise, God! Here is unbelief, disobedience, sacrilege, blasphemy towards God, cruelty and mercilessness towards one's neighbour, and love of self in all the things of God and of man! Here you have the glory and potency of 'free-will'!

Paul now proceeds to put on record that he is speaking of every man, and of the best and most excellent men most of all. These are his words: 'that every mouth may be stopped, and all the world become guilty before God; for by the works of the law shall no flesh be justified in His sight' (Rom. 3.19-20).

How, pray, are all mouths stopped, if a power that gives us a degree of ability is left to us? One could then say to God: it is not the case that there is nothing at all here; here is something which You cannot condemn, seeing that You have given it a degree of ability. Its mouth at least will not be silenced, nor will it be subject to Your wrath. For if the power of 'free-will' is unimpaired and capable of effective action, it is false to say the whole world is guilty and answerable before God. This power is no small thing in a small corner of the world, but is the most excellent thing and the most universal; and its mouth must not be stopped! If its mouth ought to be stopped, then it ought to take its place with 'all the world' as guilty, and answerable before God. But by what right can it be called guilty, if it is not unrighteous and ungodly, that is, meriting punishment and vengeance? I should like to see the 'explanation' by which this power in man may be cleared of the guilt that is binding upon all the world before God, or the artifice by which it may be exempted from inclusion in 'all the world'! Paul's words: 'They are all gone out of the way; all the world is guilty; there is none righteous', are awful thunderclaps and piercing thunderbolts; they are in truth what Jeremiah calls 'the hammer that breaketh the rock in pieces' (cf. Jer. 23.29). They break in pieces not only all that is in one man, or in some men, or in some part of them, but all that is in the whole world, in every man without any exception; so that the whole world should tremble, and fear, and flee at these words. For what mightier or more awful utterances could there be than these: 'all the world is guilty, all the children of men are turned away and unprofitable; there is none that fears God; there is none that is not unrighteous; none understandeth; none seeketh after God'? Nevertheless, such was and is the hardness and senseless obstinacy of our hearts that we do not hear nor feel the force of these thunderclaps and thunderbolts, but exalt and set up 'free-will' and its powers in the face of them all. Thus we have in truth fulfilled the words of the first chapter of Malachi: 'They build, but I will throw down!' (v. 4). With the same majesty of utterance it is also said: 'By the deeds of the law shall no flesh be justified in his sight' (Rom. 3.20). 'By the deeds of the law' is a mighty phrase, as is: 'all the world' and: 'all the children of men.' For it should be observed that Paul avoids naming persons and mentions men's pursuits only, intending thus to include all persons and all that is most excellent in them. Had he said, *the Jewish people*, or *the Pharisees*, or *certain ungodly persons*, are not justified, he might have appeared to be leaving out some who by the power of 'free-will,' and by the help of the law, were not altogether unprofitable. But when he condemns the very works of the law, and makes them ungodly in God's sight, it becomes clear that he is condemning all that were mighty in zeal for the works of the law. And none were zealous for the works of the law but the best and most excellent men, and that only with their best and most excellent faculties, that is, their reason and their will. If, then, those who exercised themselves in the works of the law with the highest zeal and endeavour of reason and will, that is, with all the power of 'free-will,' and had the help of the law as a God-given aid, instructing and spurring them on—if *they* are condemned for ungodliness, as not being hereby justified, and are declared to be 'flesh' in God's sight, what then is left in the entire human race which is not 'flesh' and ungodly? For all who are of the works of the law are condemned alike. It makes no difference whether they exercised themselves in the law with the highest zeal, or with lukewarm zeal, or with none at all. They all could perform only works of the law; and works of the law do not justify; and if they do not justify, they prove those who work them to be ungodly, and leave them so; and the ungodly are guilty, and merit the wrath of God! These things are so clear that none can whisper a word against them.

(iii) *That the 'works' which justify are not merely ceremonial works* (764-766)

Paul's meaning is commonly escaped and avoided by saying that what he calls 'works of the law' are ceremonial works, which since the death of Christ are death-dealing. I reply: This is the error of ignorant Jerome, which, for all Augustine's strenuous resistance, spread throughout the world when God withdrew, and Satan prevailed, and has continued to this day; with the result that it has been impossible to understand Paul, and the knowledge of Christ has been inevitably obscured. Had there been no other error in the church, this one was sufficiently potent and destructive to wreck the gospel. Unless extraordinary grace has interposed, Jerome deserved hell rather than heaven for it—so far am I from having the audacity to canonise him and call him a saint! It is not true that Paul is here speaking only of ceremonial works; else, how will his argument to prove that all are unrighteous and need grace, stand good? For one could then say: Granted, we are not justified by ceremonial works; but a man can be justified by the moral works of the Decalogue. So your syllogism has not proved that grace is necessary to all men. And how profitable, in that case, grace would be, delivering us merely from ceremonial works, which are the easiest works of all, and can be screwed out of us by plain fear or self-love!

Moreover, it is erroneous to say that ceremonial works are deadly and unlawful since the death of Christ. Paul never said that. What he says is that they do not justify, or in any way help man to free himself from ungodliness in God's sight. It is fully compatible with this that one can do them without doing anything unlawful. Eating and drinking are works which do not justify or commend us to God, yet he who eats and drinks does not therefore do something unlawful.

And there is a further error here: Ceremonial works were as much commanded and made obligatory in the old law as was the Decalogue; therefore, the latter had neither more nor less force than the former. Paul speaks to the Jews first, as he says in Rom. 1 (v. 16); so none need doubt that by 'the works of the law' all the works of the entire law are meant. Indeed, they could not be called 'the works of the law' if the law was abrogated and death-dealing, for an abrogated law is law no more, as Paul well knew. When he speaks of 'the works of the law', therefore, he is speaking, not of a law that is abrogated, but of a law that is in force and authoritative. Otherwise, how easily he might have said: 'The law itself is now abrogated!'—which would have been a plain, clear statement of the case. But let us appeal to Paul himself, his own best interpreter. In Gal. 3, he says: 'As many as are of the works of the law are under the curse; for it is written, Cursed is everyone that continueth not in all things which are written in the book of the law, to do them' (v. 10). Paul is here urging the same point as in Romans, and in the same words; and you see that when he makes mention of the works of the law he speaks of all the laws that are written in the book of the law. Moreover—what is still more remarkable —Paul cites Moses as cursing those who continue not in the law, whereas he himself pronounces accursed those who are of the works of the law; thus adducing a passage with a different scope from his own expressed view, the former being negative and the latter affirmative. This he does, however, because the real position in the sight of God is that those who are most zealous in the works of the law are furthest from fulfilling the law; for they are without the Spirit, Who alone fulfils the law. Men may try to keep it in their own strength, but they can accomplish nothing. Thus, both statements are true—that of Moses, that they are accursed who 'continue not', and that of Paul, that they are accursed who 'are of the works of the law'. Both speakers require that men should have the Spirit, without Whom works of law, however many are done, do not justify, as Paul says; so that men do not continue in all things that are written, as Moses says.

In a word: Paul fully confirms what I say by his division. He divides workers at the law into two classes, those who work after the Spirit and those who work after the flesh, leaving no middle state. He says: 'By the deeds of the law shall no flesh be justified.' What is this, but to say that when men work at the law without the Spirit, being themselves flesh, that is, ungodly and ignorant of God, their works profit them nothing? In Gal. 3, he makes use of the same division when he says: 'Received ye the Spirit by the works of the law, or by the hearing of faith?' (v. 2). Again, in Rom. 3 he says: 'But now the righteousness of God has been revealed without the law'; and again: 'We conclude that a man is justified by faith without the works of the law' (vv. 21, 28). From all these passages it is clear and plain that in Paul the Spirit is set in opposition to the works of the law, as He is to all other things that are not spiritual, and to all the powers and qualities of the flesh. So it is certain that Paul's view here accords with Christ's teaching in John 3 (v. 6), that everything which is not of the Spirit is flesh, however specious, holy and excellent it may be, even the most glorious works of God's law, by whatever powers wrought. For the Spirit of Christ is needed, and without Him all is nothing but a matter for condemnation.

Let it be settled, then, that Paul by 'the works of the law' means, not ceremonial works, but all the works of all the law. Then it will also be settled that all works of law that are wrought without the Spirit are condemned. But the power of 'free-will' (which is the matter in dispute), though no doubt the most excellent thing in man, is without the Spirit. That he is 'of the works of the law' is the finest thing that can be said of a man. But Paul does not say, 'who are of sins, and of ungodliness, contrary to the law'; he says, 'who are of the works of the law'— that is, the best devotees of the law, who, over and above the power of 'free-will', are also aided—that is, instructed and encouraged—by the law itself. If, now, 'free-will,' when aided by the law, and occupied in the law with all its powers, profits nothing and fails to justify, but is left in ungodliness in the flesh, what must we think it could do on its own, without the law? 'By the law is the knowledge of sin,' says Paul (Rom. 3.20). Here he shows how much and how far the law profits, teaching that 'free-will' is of itself so blind that it does not even know what sin is, but needs the law to teach it! And what can a man essay to do in order to take away sin, when he does not know what sin is? Surely this: mistake what is sin for what is not sin, and what is not sin for what is sin! Experience informs us clearly enough how the world, in the persons of those whom it accounts its best and most zealous devotees of righteousness and godliness, hates and hounds down the righteousness of God preached in the gospel, and brands it heresy, error, and other opprobrious names, while flaunting and hawking its own works and devices (which are really sin and error) as righteousness and wisdom. By these words, therefore, Paul stops the mouth of 'free-will', teaching that by the law it is shown sin, as being ignorant of its sin; so far is he from allowing it any power to make endeavours towards good.

(iv) *That the law is designed to lead to Christ by giving knowledge of sin* (766-767)

And here is the solution of the question which the Diatribe repeats so often all through the book: '*if we can do nothing, what is the purpose of all the laws, precepts, threats and promises?*' Paul here gives the answer: 'by the law is the knowledge of sin.' His answer to the question is far different from the ideas of man, or of 'free-will'. He does not say that 'free-will' is proved by the law, nor that it co-operates unto righteousness; for by the law comes, not righteousness, but knowledge of sin. This is the fruit, the work, the office of the law; it is a light to the ignorant and blind, but one that displays disease, sin, evil, death, hell and the wrath of God. It does not help nor set them free from these things; it is content merely to point them out. When a man discovers the sickness of sin, he is cast down and afflicted; nay, he despairs. The law does not help him; much less can he heal himself. Another light is needed to reveal a remedy. This is the voice of the gospel, which displays Christ as the Deliverer from all these evil things. But neither reason nor 'free-will' points to Him; how could reason point to Him, when it is itself darkness and needs the light of the law to show it its own sickness, which by its own light it fails to see, and thinks is sound health?

So too in Galatians, dealing with the same point. Paul

asks: 'Wherefore then serveth the law?' (3.19). He does not answer, as the Diatribe does, that it proves the existence of 'free-will', but says 'it was added because of transgressions, until the seed should come to whom He had made promise.' 'Because of transgressions,' he says; not, indeed, to restrain them, as Jerome dreams, for Paul is arguing that the removing and restraining of sins by the gift of righteousness was promised to the seed that was to come; but to increase transgressions, as he says in Rom. 5: 'The law entered, that sin might abound' (v. 20). But that sins were not committed in abundance without the law; but then they were not known to be transgressions and sins of such awful import, and the most and greatest of them were held to be righteousness! As long as sins are unknown, there is no room for a cure, and no hope of one; for sins that think they betoken health and need no physician will not endure the healer's hand. The law is therefore necessary to give knowledge of sin, so that proud man, who thought he was whole, may be humbled by the discovery of his own great wickedness, and sigh and pant after the grace that is set forth in Christ.

See, then, how simple the statement is: 'By the law is the knowledge of sin.' Yet this text alone has power enough to confound and overthrow 'free-will'. For if it is true that 'free-will' of itself does not know what sin and evil are, as the apostle says here and in Rom. 7 ('I had not known that covetousness was sin, except the law had said, "Thou shalt not covet"' [vv. 7, 8]), how can it ever know what righteousness and good are? And if it is ignorant of righteousness, how can it endeavour to attain it? We do not know the sin in which we were born, in which we live, and move, and have our being, and which, moreover, lives, moves and reigns in us; how then should we know that righteousness which reigns outside us in heaven? Paul's words make this wretched 'free-will' to be utterly and completely non-existent!

(v) *Rom. 3.21-26: the doctrine of salvation by faith in Christ disproves 'free-will'* (767-769)

This being so, Paul now proclaims with full confidence and

weight of authority: 'But now the righteousness of God without the law, is manifested, being witnessed by the law and the prophets; even the righteousness of God which is by faith of Jesus Christ unto all and upon all them that believe in Him: for there is no difference, for all have sinned and are without the glory of God; being justified freely by His grace through the redemption that is in Christ Jesus, Whom God hath set forth to be a propitiation through faith in His blood,' etc. (Rom. 3.21-5). Here Paul utters very thunderbolts against 'free-will'. First: 'The righteousness of God without the law,' he says, 'is manifested.' He distinguishes the righteousness of God from the righteousness of the law; because the righteousness of faith comes by grace, without the law. His phrase 'without the law' can mean only that Christian righteousness exists without the works of the law, the works of the law availing and effecting nothing towards its attainment. So he says, just below: 'We concluded that a man is justified by faith without the deeds of the law' (v. 28). Earlier, he had said: 'By the deeds of the law shall no flesh be justified in His sight' (v. 20). From all this it is very plain that the endeavour and effort of 'free-will' are simply null; for if the righteousness of God exists without the law, and without the works of the law, how shall it not much more exist without 'free-will'? For the supreme concern of 'free-will' is to exercise itself in moral righteousness, the works of that law by which its blindness and impotence are 'assisted'. But this word 'without' does away with morally good works, and moral righteousness, and preparations for grace. Imagine any power you can think of as belonging to 'free-will', and Paul will still stand firm and say: 'the righteousness of God exists without it!' And though I should grant that 'free-will' by its endeavours can advance in some direction, namely, in the direction of good works, or the righteousness of the civil or moral law, yet it does not advance towards God's righteousness, nor does God deem its efforts in any respect worthy to gain His righteousness; for He says that His righteousness stands without the law. And if 'free-will' does not advance towards God's righteousness, what will it gain even if by its works and endeavours it advances towards angelic holiness?—if that were possible. I do not think there are any obscure and ambiguous words here, nor that room is left here for any figures of speech. Paul clearly distinguishes the two righteousnesses, assigning the one to the law and the other to grace; and he declares that the latter is given without the former and without its works, and that the former without the latter does not justify or avail anything. I should like to see how 'free-will' can stand and be defended against these texts!

Another thunderbolt is Paul's statement that the righteousness of God is manifested and avails 'unto all and upon all them that believe' in Christ, and that 'there is no difference'. Here again in the plainest words he divides the whole human race into two. To believers he gives the righteousness of God; to unbelievers he denies it. Now, nobody is fool enough to doubt that the power and endeavour of 'free-will' is something distinct from faith in Jesus Christ! But Paul denies that anything apart from this faith is righteous before God. And if it is not righteous before God, it must be sin; for with God there remains nothing intermediate[1] between righteousness and sin that is, as it were, neutral, being neither righteousness nor sin. Otherwise, Paul's entire argument would be wholly ineffective, for its starting-point is just this dichotomy—all that is wrought and done among men is either righteousness or sin in God's sight: righteousness, if faith is with it; sin, if faith is lacking. With men, indeed, it is the case that actions in which men who owe nothing to each other confer nothing on each other are called 'intermediate' and 'neutral'. But the ungodly man sins against God, whether he eats, or drinks, or whatever he does, because he abuses God's creation by his ungodliness and persistent ingratitude, and does not from his heart give glory to God for a single moment.

This statement is also a mighty thunderbolt: 'All have sinned and are without the glory of God: for there is no difference.' What, pray, could be more plainly said? Produce a man who works by 'free-will', and tell me whether he sins in his endeavours. If he does not sin, why does Paul not exempt him? Surely, he says 'all' does not exempt any, in any place, at any time, in any work, in any effort? So if you except anyone for any design or work, you make Paul a liar; for in all that Paul says he

---

[1] *medium*

includes this man, who works and endeavours by 'free-will', among the 'all', when he should have respected his person and not numbered him among sinners in such a blithe and sweeping style!

His statement, that all are 'devoid of the glory of God', teaches the same truth. You can take 'the glory of God' here in two ways, actively and passively. This is Paul's manner in the Hebraisms which he often employs. Actively, 'the glory of God' is that by which He glories in us; passively, it is that by which we glory in God. It seems to me that the phrase should here be taken passively; just as 'the faith of Christ', which in Latin idiom would denote 'faith which Christ has', means, according to Hebrew idiom, 'faith which we have in Christ', and 'the righteousness of God', which in Latin idiom would denote a righteousness which God has, means, according to Hebrew idiom, a righteousness which we have from God and in God's sight. Similarly, we take 'the glory of God', not in the Latin, but in the Hebrew way, as meaning the glory which we have in God and before God; which could be called, our glory in God.

Now, he who glories in God is he who knows for sure that God looks on him with favour, and deigns to regard him kindly, so that what he does is pleasing in God's sight, and what does not please God is borne with and pardoned. If, now, the endeavour and effort of 'free-will' is not sin, but is good in God's sight, it can certainly glory, and in its glorying confidently say: this pleases God, God looks with favour on this, this God deigns to accept, or at any rate He bears with it and pardons it. This is the glory of those who have faith in God. To those that are without it belongs confusion of face, rather than glory, in God's presence. But Paul here says that men are wholly devoid of this glory. And experience proves that they are. Inquire of all the 'free-will'-endeavourers throughout the world, and if you can show me one who, seriously and from his heart, can say of any of his efforts and endeavours: 'I know that this pleases God,' I will confess defeat, and yield you the palm. But I know that none will be found. And if this glory is wanting, so that a man's conscience dare not say with sure confidence: 'this pleases God,' it is certain that he does not please God! For as he believes, so is he; he does not believe that he undoubtedly pleases God, but it is necessary that he should; for it is precisely the sin of unbelief to doubt of the favour of God, inasmuch as God would have His favour believed in with the fullest certainty of faith. Thus I prove, on the testimony of their own consciences, that 'free-will', being without the glory of God, is, with all its powers, efforts and endeavours, perpetually guilty of the sin of unbelief.

(vi) *That the Pelagian doctrine of merit is less vicious than that of the Scholastics and Erasmus* (769-771)

And what will the guardians of 'free-will' say to what follows: 'being justified freely by His grace'? What does 'freely' mean? What does 'by His grace' mean? How will endeavour, and merit, accord with freely given righteousness? Perhaps they will here say that they assign to 'free-will' as little as possible, not by any means condign merit.[1] But these are empty words; for what is being sought by means of 'free-will' is that merit may have its place. The Diatribe itself argued and expostulated throughout in this strain: '*If there is no freedom of will, what place is there for merit? If there is no place for merit, what place is there for reward? To what will it be ascribed, if man is justified without merit?*' Paul here gives the answer—there is no such thing as merit at all, but all that are justified are justified freely, and this is ascribed to nothing but the grace of God. And when righteousness is given, then the kingdom and eternal life are given with it. Where is your endeavour now? and your effort? and your good works? and the merits of 'free-will'? What use are they? You cannot plead obscurity and ambiguity; the matter and the words are as plain and simple as can be. Granted that your friends assign to 'free-will' 'as little as possible', nonetheless they teach us that by that little we can attain righteousness and grace: and they solve the problem as to why God justifies one and abandons another simply by presupposing 'free-will', and saying: 'The one endeavoured and the other did not; and God regards the one for his endeavour and despises the other; and He would be unjust were He to do anything else!' Though in

---

[1] See p. 48f., *supra.*

what they say and write they profess that they do not attain
grace to condign merit, nor call the merit in question 'condign',
they are only trying to fool us by a word, for they hold the
thing none the less. What can excuse their not calling it condign merit, when they assign to it all that pertains to condign
merit? saying that he who endeavours finds grace in the sight
of God, whereas he who does not endeavour does not find it?
Is this not clearly a description of condign merit? Do they not
make God a respecter of works, merits, and persons, when they
say that one man is without grace by his own fault, because he
did not endeavour, whereas another, because he endeavours,
obtains grace which he would not have obtained had he not
endeavoured? If this is not condign merit, I should like to be
told what condign merit may be said to be! You could play on
any word like this; you could say: 'It is not indeed, condign
merit, but has the same effect as condign merit'; 'the thorn is
not a bad tree, but has just the same effect as a bad tree'; 'the
fig-tree is not a good tree, but has the same effect as a good tree';
'the Diatribe is not, indeed, ungodly, but says and does just
what the ungodly do'!

The guardians of 'free-will' have exemplified the saying: 'out of
the frying-pan, into the fire.'[1] In their zeal to disagree with the
Pelagians, they start denying condign merit, and by the very
form of their denial they set it up more firmly! By word and
pen they deny it, but really, in their hearts, they establish it,
and are worse than the Pelagians upon two accounts. In the
first place, the Pelagians confess and assert condign merit
straightforwardly, candidly and honestly, calling a spade a
spade[2] and teaching what they really hold. But our friends here,
who hold and teach the same view, try to fool us with lying
words and false appearances, giving out that they disagree with
the Pelagians, when there is nothing that they are further from
doing! 'If you regard our pretences, we appear as the Pelagians'
bitterest foes; but if you regard the facts and our hearts, we are
Pelagians double-dyed.' Then, in the second place, this
hypocrisy of theirs results in their valuing and seeking to
purchase the grace of God at a much cheaper rate than the

---

[1] *Incidit in Scyllam, dum vult vitare Charybdim.*
[2] *appellantes scapham scapham, ficum ficum.*

Pelagians. The latter assert that it is not by a feeble something within us that we obtain grace, but by efforts and works that are complete, entire, perfect, many and mighty; but our friends here tell us that it is by something very small, almost nothing, that we merit grace.

Now, if there must be error, those who say that the grace of God is priced high, and account it dear and costly, err less shamefully and presumptuously than those who teach that its price is a tiny trifle, and account it cheap and contemptible. Paul, however, pounds both errors to a single pulp with one word when he says that all are justified freely, without the law, and without the works of the law. The assertion that justification is free to all that are justified leaves none to work, merit or prepare themselves, and leaves no work that can be said to carry either congruent or condign merit. By the one cast of this thunderbolt, Paul shatters both the Pelagians with their total merit and the Sophists with their tiny merit. Free justification does not permit you to set men working for it, for free donation and preparation by working are manifestly incompatible. Furthermore, justification by grace does not permit you to regard the worthiness of any person, as Paul later says in the eleventh chapter: 'If by grace, then it is no more of works; otherwise, grace is not grace' (v. 6). So, too, he says in the fourth chapter: 'Now to him that worketh the reward is reckoned, not of grace, but of debt' (v. 4). And so my good Paul, the scourge of 'free-will', stands undefeated! He lays low two armies with a single word! For if we are justified without works, all works are condemned, whether small or great; Paul exempts none, but thunders impartially against all.

Now see here how sleepy-headed all our opponents are, and how little it helps a man to rely on the ancient fathers, for all their repute down the course of the ages! Were they not all equally blind to, yes, and heedless of, Paul's clearest and plainest words? What, pray, can be said for grace against 'free-will' clearly and plainly, if Paul's discourse here is not clear and plain? He exalts grace against 'free-will' in categorical terms:[1] using the clearest and simplest words, he says that we are justified freely, and that grace is not grace if procured by works.

[1] *per contentionem.*

With the greatest plainness he excludes all works in the matter of justification, and so sets up grace alone, and justification that is free. Yet in this light we still seek darkness, and because we cannot give ourselves great credit, yes, all the credit, for justification, we try to give ourselves some tiny little credit—solely in order that we may gain the point that justification by the grace of God is not free and without works! As though Paul's denial that any of our greater works contributes to our justification were not much more a denial that our tiny little works do so! Especially when he has laid it down that we are justified only by God's grace, without any works—indeed, without the law, in which all works, great, small, congruently or condignly meritorious, are contained. *Now* go and boast of the authority of the ancients and trust what they say—now that you see that they one and all disregarded the supremely plain and clear teaching of Paul! They fled from this morning star, yes, this sun, as if their lives depended on it; for they were in the grip of their own carnal ideas, and thought it absurd that no room should be left for merit.

(vii) *Rom. 4.2-3: the total irrelevance of works to man's righteousness before God* (771-772)

Let us cite the example that Paul goes on to cite, that of Abraham. He says: 'If Abraham were justified by works he hath whereof to glory; but not before God. For what saith the Scripture? Abraham believed God, and it was reckoned unto him for righteousness' (Rom. 4.2-3). Here, too, please take note of Paul's distinction as he recounts Abraham's twofold righteousness. The one is of works; that is, moral and civil. But Paul says that this did not justify Abraham in the sight of God, even though it made him righteous in the eyes of men. He has glory before men by reason of that righteousness, but is yet without the glory of God. None can say that it is the works of the law, or ceremonial works, that are here condemned, for Abraham lived many years before the law. Paul simply speaks of Abraham's works, and those his best works; for it would be absurd to argue as to whether a man is justified by evil works. If, now, Abraham is righteous by none of his works, so that, unless he puts on another righteousness (that of faith), both he and all his works are left under the power of ungodliness, it is apparent that no man can make any advance towards righteousness by his works; and it is further apparent that no works, efforts or endeavours of 'free-will' are of any avail in God's sight, but that they are all adjudged ungodly, unrighteous, and evil. For if a man himself is not righteous, neither are his works and endeavours righteous; and if they are not righteous, they merit damnation and wrath.

The other righteousness is that of faith, and consists, not in any works, but in the gracious favour and reckoning of God. See how Paul stresses the word 'reckoned'; how he insists on it, and repeats it, and enforces it. 'To him that worketh,' he says, 'the reward is *reckoned*, not of grace, but of debt. But to him that worketh not, but believeth on him that justifieth the ungodly, his faith is *reckoned* for righteousness,' according to the purpose of God's grace. Then he quotes David as saying the same about the reckoning of grace. 'Blessed is the man to whom the Lord has not imputed sin,' etc. (vv. 4ff.). He repeats the word 'reckon' in this chapter about ten times.

In short, Paul sets 'him that worketh' and 'him that worketh not' side by side, and leaves none in the middle between them. He declares that righteousness is not reckoned to him that worketh, but is reckoned to him that worketh not, if only he believes. There is no way by which 'free-will', with its effort and endeavour, can dodge or escape; it must either be numbered with 'him that worketh', or with 'him that worketh not'. If with 'him that worketh', you have heard Paul say that righteousness is not reckoned to it. If with 'him that worketh not, but believeth' on God, righteousness is reckoned to it. But then it will not be the power of 'free-will', but a new creation by faith. And if righteousness is not reckoned to 'him that worketh', it becomes clear that his works are nothing but sins, evil and ungodly in God's sight.

No impudent Sophist can here object that, though man be evil, yet his work need not be evil. For Paul specifies not 'man' simply, but 'him that worketh', his intention being to declare in the plainest words that man's actual works and efforts are condemned, whatever they are and by whatever name or appearance they go. It is of good works that he speaks, for he is arguing about justification and merit. And when he speaks of 'him that worketh', he speaks comprehensively of all who work and of all the works that they do, but especially of their good and upright works. Otherwise, his distinction between 'him that worketh' and 'him that worketh not' would not hold water.

(viii) *Of other arguments against 'free-will', not here developed* (772-773)

I here pass by arguments of great strength drawn from the purpose of grace, from the promise, from the power of the law, from original sin, and from God's election; every one of which by itself could utterly overthrow 'free-will', thus:

If the source of grace is the predestinating purpose of God, then it comes by necessity, and not by any effort or endeavour on our part, as I showed above.

Again: If God promised grace before the law, as Paul argues here and in Galatians, then it does not come by works or by law, else the promise would come to nothing; and faith also (by which Abraham was justified before the law was given) would come to nothing, should works avail.

Again: since the law is the strength of sin, displaying it without removing it, it makes the conscience guilty before God and threatens wrath. This is Paul's meaning when he says: 'the law worketh wrath' (Rom. 4.15). How then could righteousness be procured by the law? And if we get no help from the law, how can we get help from the power of our will alone?

Again: since by the single offence of the one man, Adam, we all lie under sin and condemnation, how can we set our hand to anything that is not sinful and damnable? When he says 'all', he excepts none; not the power of 'free-will', nor any worker, whether he works and endeavours or not; he is of necessity included with the rest among the 'all'. Neither should we sin or be condemned by reason of the single offence of Adam, if that offence were not our own; who could be condemned for another's offence, especially in the sight of God?

But his offence becomes ours; not by imitation, nor by any act on our part (for then it would not be the single offence of Adam, since we should have committed it, not he), but it becomes ours by birth. (We must, however, discuss this elsewhere.) Original sin itself, then, does not allow 'free-will' any power at all except to sin and incur condemnation.

These arguments, I repeat, I pass by; both because they are so very plain and powerful, and also because I have said something of them above. If, indeed, I wanted to review all the passages in Paul alone that overthrow 'free-will', I could do nothing better than give a running commentary on his entire writings, showing that the boasted power of 'free-will' is refuted by almost every word—as I have done already in the case of these third and fourth chapters of Romans. I chose to deal with them particularly, because I wanted to show up the sleepy-headedness of all those friends of ours who read Paul in such a fashion that the last things they see in these perfectly plain passages are the mighty arguments against 'free-will' to which I have referred; and I wished also to expose the folly of their confidence in the authority and writings of the ancient doctors, and to leave them to think over what force the forementioned clear arguments would have, if handled with care and judgement.

(ix) *Of Paul's cogency against 'free-will'* (773-774)

Speaking for myself, I am astounded that, when Paul so often uses these comprehensive terms, 'all', 'none', 'not', 'never', 'without', as in: 'they are *all* gone out of the way, there is *none* righteous, *none* that doeth good, no, not one'; '*all* are sinners condemned by the offence of one'; 'we are justified by faith *without* the law, *without* works' (so that he who would alter Paul's language could not thereby increase the clarity and plainness of his speech)—I am amazed, I repeat, how it has happened that in face of these comprehensive terms and statements, others that are contrary, yes, contradictory to them should have won acceptance, such as: 'Some are not gone out of the way, are not unrighteous, are not evil, are not sinners, are not condemned; there is something in man that is good and

strives after good'; as though he who strives after good, whoever he may be, is not covered by the terms: 'all', 'none', and
'not'! Personally, I could find nothing, even if I wished, to
advance in reply against Paul, but would be forced to include
the power of my own 'free-will', and its endeavour with it,
among the 'all' and 'none' of which Paul speaks—unless we are
to introduce a new grammar, and a new mode of speech! Had
Paul used such an expression once, or in one place only, it
might have been permissible to suspect a figure of speech and
to isolate and strain the words. But as it is, he uses such expressions constantly, in both affirmative and negative sentences, and
everywhere expresses his views by categorical statement and
comprehensive contrast; so that not only the natural force of
words and the actual flow of speech, but also that which comes
before and after, the whole surrounding context, and the scope
and contents of his entire argument, unite to prove what his
meaning is: Paul intends to say that apart from faith in Christ
there is nothing but sin and condemnation.

I promised to refute 'free-will' in such a way that none of my
opponents would be able to resist, and this, I think, I have
done; even if they will not own themselves beaten and come
over to my view, or be silent. That, after all, it is not in my
power to bring about; it is the gift of the Spirit of God.

(x) *Rom. 8.5: the state of man without the Spirit* (774-775)

Before we hear the evangelist John, let me add a crowning
testimony from Paul (and if this does not suffice, I am ready to
marshal the whole of Paul against 'free-will' by means of a
running commentary on all he wrote!). In Rom. 8, dividing
the human race into two, 'flesh' and 'spirit', as Christ does in
John 3 (v. 6), he says: 'They that are after the flesh do mind
the things of the flesh, but they that are after the Spirit do mind
the things of the Spirit' (v. 5). That Paul here calls all 'carnal'
that are not 'spiritual' is plain, both from the opposition of
'spirit' and 'flesh' in the division itself, and from Paul's own
next words: 'But ye are not in the flesh, but in the Spirit, if so
be that the Spirit of God dwell in you. Now if any man have
not the Spirit of Christ, he is none of his' (v. 9). What is the

meaning of: 'Ye are not in the flesh, if the Spirit is in you,' but those who have not the Spirit are of necessity in the flesh? And he that is not Christ's, whose else is he but Satan's? It stands good then, that those who lack the Spirit are in the flesh, and under Satan.

Now let us see what Paul thinks about endeavour and the power of 'free-will' in carnal men. 'They that are in the flesh cannot please God.' Again: 'The carnal mind is death.' Again: 'The carnal mind is enmity against God.' Once more: 'It is not subject to the law of God, neither indeed can be' (vv. 5-8). Let the guardian of 'free-will' answer the following question: How can endeavours towards good be made by that which is death, and displeases God, and is enmity against God, and disobeys God, and cannot obey him? Paul did not mean to say that the carnal mind is *dead*, and *at enmity* with God, but that it is *death itself* and *enmity itself*, which cannot possibly be subject to the law of God or please God; as he had said a little before ('For what the law *could not do*, in that it was weak through the flesh, God did,' etc. (v. 3)).

I, too, know of Origen's fancy about the 'threefold affection', one called 'flesh', another 'soul', and the other 'spirit', the soul being in the middle between the other two, and able to turn either flesh-wards or spirit-wards. But these are just his own dreams; he retails them, but does not prove them. Paul here calls everything without the Spirit 'flesh', as I have shown. Therefore, the highest virtues of the best men are 'in the flesh'; that is, they are dead, and at enmity with God, not subject to God's law nor able to be so, and not pleasing God. Paul does not say merely that they are not subject, but that they cannot be subject. So also Christ says in Matt. 7: 'An evil tree cannot bring forth good fruit' (v. 18). And in Matt. 12: 'How can ye, being evil, speak that which is good?' (v. 34). Here you see that not only do we speak evil, but we cannot speak good. And though He says elsewhere that we, though evil, know how to give good things to our children (cf. Matt. 7.11), yet He denies that we do good, even by our giving of good things, because the good things which we give are God's creatures, and we, being evil, cannot give those good things in good fashion. He addresses this word to all men, even to His own disciples. So that this pair of statements by Paul, that 'the righteous lives by faith' (Rom. 1.17), and that 'whatsoever is not of faith, is sin' (Rom. 14.23), stand confirmed. The latter follows from the former; for if it is only by faith that we are justified, it is evident that they who are without faith are not yet justified; and those who are not justified are sinners; and sinners are evil trees, and can only sin and bear evil fruit. Wherefore, 'free-will' is nothing but the slave of sin, death and Satan, not doing anything, nor able to do or attempt anything, but evil!

(xi) *Rom. 10.20, 9.30-31: salvation by grace has no reference to previous endeavour* (775-776)

Add to this the instance quoted in the tenth chapter of Romans from Isaiah: 'I was found of them that sought me not, I manifested myself to them that asked not after me' (v. 20; Isa. 65.1). Paul says this of the Gentiles—that it was given to them to hear and know Christ when previously they could not even think of Him, much less seek Him or prepare themselves for Him by the power of 'free-will'. From this instance it is clear enough that grace comes so freely, that no thought of it, and certainly no endeavour or desire after it, precedes its coming. And take the case of Paul, when he was Saul—what did he do with all the power of his 'free-will'? Certainly, if his state of mind be regarded, his heart was set on what was best and highest. But look at the endeavour whereby he found grace! Not only did he not seek grace, but he received it through his own mad fury against it!

Of the Jews, on the other hand, Paul says in chapter 9: 'The Gentiles, which followed not after righteousness, have attained unto the righteousness which is by faith. But Israel, which followed after the law of righteousness, hath not attained unto the law of righteousness' (vv. 30-31). What word can any defender of 'free-will' breathe against this? The Gentiles, when filled with ungodliness and every vice, receive righteousness freely by the mercy of God; the Jews, who follow after righteousness with the greatest effort and endeavour, do so in vain. Is not this just to say that the endeavours of 'free-will' after the highest are vain, and that by them it rather grows worse and is carried away backwards? None can say that the Jews' efforts were not made with the highest power of 'free-will'. Paul himself bears record of them in the tenth chapter, that 'they have a zeal of God, but not according to knowledge' (v. 2). So nothing that is assigned to 'free-will' was lacking to the Jews; yet nothing resulted—indeed, the reverse of what they sought resulted! In the Gentiles, nothing that is assigned to 'free-will' was present; yet for them the righteousness of God resulted. What is this but proof positive, by the very clear example of the two nations and the very plain testimony of Paul, that grace is given freely to the undeserving and utterly unworthy, and is not attained by any of the efforts, endeavours, or works, small or great, of even the best and most upright men who seek and follow after righteousness with flaming zeal?

(xii) *John 1.5, 10-13, 16: salvation for a sinful world is by the grace of Christ through faith alone* (776-778)

Now let us come to John, who is also an eloquent and powerful scourge of 'free-will'.

Right at the outset, he assigns to 'free-will' such blindness that it does not even see the light of truth, so far it is from being able to strive after it. He says: 'The light shineth in darkness, but the darkness comprehendeth it not' (John 1.5). And straight after: 'He was in the world, and the world knew him not; He came unto his own, and his own knew him not' (vv. 10-11). What do you think he means by 'world'? Will you exempt any man from being so called, save him that is new created by the Holy Ghost? The use of this term, 'world', is characteristic of this Apostle; and by it he simply means, the whole human race. So whatever he says of the 'world' must be understood of 'free-will', as being the most excellent thing in man. According to this apostle, then, the 'world' does not know the light of truth; the 'world' hates Christ and His; the 'world' neither knows nor sees the Holy Spirit; the whole 'world' is set in wickedness; all that is in the 'world' is the lust of the flesh and of the eyes, and the pride of life. 'Love not the world.' 'Ye are of the world' says Christ; 'the world cannot hate you, but me it hateth, because I testify that its works are evil' (cf. John 15.19, 14.17; 1 John

5.19, 2.16, 2.15; John 8.23, 7.7). All these and many similar passages are proclamations of what 'free-will' is—the principal part of the 'world', ruling under Satan's command! John himself speaks of the 'world' antithetically, so that the 'world' means whatever is not taken out of the world to be under the Spirit. Thus Christ says to his apostles: 'I have taken you out of the world, and set you,' etc. (John 15.19). If, now, there were any in the world who endeavoured after good by the power of 'free-will' (as there should be, if 'free-will' had any power), then, out of respect for them, John should have modified his statement, so as not, by generalising, to implicate them in all the evil deeds with which he charges the world. But this he does not do; from which it is clear that he is making 'free-will' guilty of all that is charged against the world. And his reason is, that the world does all that it does by the power of 'free-will', that is, by will and reason, its own most excellent parts.

He goes on: 'But as many as received him, to them gave he power to become the sons of God, even to them that believe on his name: which were born, not of blood nor of the will of the flesh, nor of the will of man, but of God' (1.12-13). By this exhaustive division he rejects from the kingdom of Christ 'blood', 'the will of the flesh', and 'the will of man'. 'Blood' means, I think, the Jews; that is, those who expected to be the children of the kingdom because they were the children of Abraham and the fathers, and so gloried in their 'blood'. 'The will of the flesh' I understand as the efforts which the people exerted in the works of the law; for 'flesh' here means carnal men without the Spirit, who were certainly possessed of will and endeavour, but who, because the Spirit was not in them, possessed them in a carnal manner only. 'The will of man' I understand in a general sense, of the efforts of all men, that is, the nations, or any man whatsoever, whether in the law or without the law. So the sense is: the sons of God became such, not by carnal birth, nor by zeal for the law, nor by any other human effort, but only by being born of God. Now, if they are not born of the flesh, nor trained by the law, nor prepared by any human discipline, but are born again of God, it is apparent that 'free-will' avails nothing here. 'Man', I think, is used in the Hebrew way, to mean 'any man', or 'all men', just as 'flesh' is used antithetically to mean 'people without the Spirit'. 'Will', I think, is used to denote the highest power in man— that is, the principal part, 'free-will'. But even supposing that I do not hit the precise meaning of the individual words, the substance of the matter is still perfectly plain—that John by this division is rejecting everything that is not 'born of God'; which, as he himself explains, is something that results from 'believing on his name.' 'The will of man', or 'free-will', which is neither new birth from God nor yet faith, is therefore necessarily included in this rejection. If 'free-will' could avail anything, John ought not to reject 'the will of man', nor should he draw men away from it and direct them to faith and new birth alone, lest the words of Isa. 5 should be pronounced against him: 'Woe unto you that call good evil!' (v. 20). But as it is, seeing that he rejects alike 'blood', 'the will of the flesh', and 'the will of man', it is certain that the will of man is of no more avail to make men the sons of God than 'blood' or carnal birth. And none doubts that carnal birth does not make sons of God; for Paul says: 'They which are the children of the flesh, these are not the children of God' (Rom. 9.8), and proves it by the cases of Ishmael and Esau.

The same John introduces the Baptist speaking of Christ thus: 'And of his fulness have we all received, and grace for grace' (1.16). He says that we receive grace out of the fulness of Christ—but for what merit or effort? 'For grace,' he says; that is, the grace of Christ; as Paul says: 'The grace of God, and the gift of grace, which is by one man, Jesus Christ, hath abounded unto many' (Rom. 5.15). Where now is the endeavour of 'free-will' that secures grace? John is here saying, not only that grace is not received by any effort of our own, but that it comes by the grace of another, that is, 'one man, Jesus Christ'. So, either it is false that we receive our grace for the grace of another, or else it is apparent that 'free-will' is nothing; for these two positions cannot stand together, that the grace of God is *both* so cheap that it may be gained anywhere and everywhere by a little endeavour on the part of any man, *and* so dear that it is given to us only in and through the grace of this one great man!

And I could wish that the guardians of 'free-will' would be

taught by this passage to recognise that when they assert 'free-will' they are denying Christ. For if I obtain the grace of God by my own endeavour, what need have I of the grace of Christ for the receiving of my grace? When I have the grace of God, what do I need besides? The Diatribe said, and all the Sophists say, that we obtain the grace of God by our own endeavour, and are thereby made ready to receive it, not, indeed, as of *condignity*, but as of *congruity*.[1] This is plainly to deny Christ. It is for His grace, the Baptist says here, that we receive grace. Earlier on, I confuted their fabrication about 'condignity' and 'congruity', showing that these are empty words, but that what they really believe in is condign merit, and that their view involves greater impiety than that of the Pelagians; as I said. Thus it is that the ungodly Sophists, together with the Diatribe, deny the Lord Christ, who bought us, more than ever the Pelagians or any heretics did! So utterly does grace refuse to allow any particle or power of 'free-will' to stand beside it!

That the protectors of 'free-will' deny Christ is proved, not by this Scripture only, but by their own lives. By this doctrine they have made Christ to be, no longer a sweet Mediator, but a dreadful Judge, whom they strive to placate by the intercessions of the Mother and of the Saints, and by devising many works, rites, observances and vows, by which they aim to appease Christ so that He may give them grace. They do not believe that He intercedes before God and obtains grace for them by His blood, and 'grace' (as is here said) 'for grace'. And as they believe, so it is unto them. Christ is in truth an inexorable judge to them, and deservedly so; for they abandon Him in His office as a Mediator and kindest Saviour, and account His blood and grace as of less worth than the efforts and endeavours of 'free-will'!

(xiii) *John 3.1ff.: the case of Nicodemus* (778-779)

Now let us hear of a case of 'free-will'. Nicodemus is surely a man in whom you can find no lack of anything for which 'free-will' avails. What in the way of effort and endeavour does he leave undone? He confesses Christ to be true, and to have come

---

[1] *licet non de condigno, sed de congruo.*

from God, he refers to his signs, he comes by night to hear and discuss further. Does he not seem to have sought by the power of 'free-will' all that pertains to godliness and salvation? But see what shipwreck he makes. When he hears Christ teach the true way of salvation, by new birth, does he acknowledge it and confess that in time past he sought it? No; he starts back, and is confounded; and not only says that he does not understand it, but turns from it as an impossibility. 'How can these things be?' he says (John 3.9). And no wonder; for who ever heard that man must be 'born again of water and of the Spirit' to be saved (vv. 3, 5)? Who ever thought that the Son of God must be 'lifted up, that whosoever believeth in Him should not perish, but have eternal life' (vv. 14-15)? Did the best and acutest philosophers ever mention it? Did the princes or this world ever acquire this knowledge? Did any man's 'free-will' ever endeavour after it? Does not Paul acknowledge it to be wisdom hidden in a mystery, foretold indeed by the prophets but revealed only by the gospel, so that it was from eternity secret and unknown to the world (cf. 1 Cor. 2.7)? What need I say? Let us ask experience: the whole world, human reason, yes, 'free-will', are forced to confess that they had not known nor heard of Christ before the gospel entered the world. And if they did not know Him, much less did they, or could they, seek Him, or make endeavours after Him. But Christ is the way, the truth, the life, and salvation (ch. John 14.6). 'Free-will' is therefore confessing, willy-nilly, that by its own strength it neither knew nor could seek those things that belong to the way, the truth and salvation. And yet, in the teeth of this very confession of our own experience, we madly argue with empty words that a great power remains within us, which can know and apply itself to the things that belong to salvation! This is just to say that Christ, the Son of God, was lifted up for us, which is something that none has ever known or could conceive of; but that this very ignorance is not ignorance, but knowledge of Christ, that is, of the things that belong to salvation! Do you not yet see the palpable truth that those who assert 'free-will' are plainly crazed, calling that knowledge which they themselves admit to be ignorance? Is not this what in Isa. 5 is described as 'calling darkness light' (v. 20)? Thus mightily has

God stopped the mouth of 'free-will' by its own confession and experience; yet not even so can it keep quiet and give glory to God!

(xiv) *John 14.6, 3.18, 36, 27, 31, 8.23: salvation is by Christ alone* (779-781)

Moreover, since Christ is said to be 'the way, the truth, and the life' (John 14.6), and that categorically, so that whatever is not Christ is not the way, but error, not truth, but untruth, not life, but death, it follows of necessity that 'free-will', inasmuch as it neither is Christ, nor is in Christ, is fast bound in error, and untruth, and death. Where and whence, then, comes your intermediate, neutral entity (I mean, the power of 'free-will') which, though it is not Christ (that is, the way, the truth and the life), should not be error, or untruth, or death? If all the things that are said of Christ and of grace were not said categorically, so that they may be contrasted with their opposites, like this: out of Christ there is nothing but Satan, out of grace nothing but wrath, out of light nothing but darkness, out of the way nothing but error, out of truth nothing but a lie, out of life nothing but death—were these things not so, what, I ask you, would be the use of all the apostolic discourses and, indeed, of the entire Scriptures? They would all be written in vain, for they would not compel the admission that men need Christ (which is their main burden), and that for the following reason: something intermediate would be found which, of itself, would be neither evil nor good, neither Christ's nor Satan's, neither true nor false, neither alive nor dead, neither something nor nothing (perhaps), and its name would be called 'the most excellent and exalted thing in the whole human race'! Now, choose which you will have. If you grant that the Scriptures speak categorically, you can say nothing of 'free-will' but that which is the opposite of Christ: that is, that error, death, Satan and all evils reign in it. If you do not grant that the Scriptures speak categorically, you so weaken them, that they establish nothing and fail to prove that men need Christ; and thus, in setting up 'free-will', you set aside Christ, and make havoc of the entire Scripture. Though with your lips you pretend to confess Christ, you really deny Him in your heart. For if the power of 'free-will' is not wholly and damnably astray, but sees and wills what is good and upright and pertains to salvation, then it is in sound health, it does not need Christ the physician, nor did Christ redeem that part of man; for what need is there of light and life, where light and life exist already? And if that power is not redeemed by Christ, then the best part in man is not redeemed, but is of itself good and sound. And then God is unjust if He damns any man, for He damns that in man which is very good and sound; that is, innocent! No man is without 'free-will'; and though the bad man abuses it, yet according to your teaching the power itself is not destroyed, but can and does still endeavour towards good. And if it does, it is undoubtedly good, holy and just; wherefore, it should not be damned, but separated from the man who is to be damned. But that cannot be done; and if it could, man would then be without 'free-will', and would not be man at all; he would have neither merit nor demerit, nor could he be saved, but he would be simply a brute beast, and no longer immortal. It remains therefore, that God is unjust to damn this good, righteous, holy power in man, which even in a bad man does not need Christ!

Let us proceed with John. 'He that believeth on him' he says, 'is not judged; but he that believeth not is judged already, because he hath not believed on the name of the only begotten Son of God' (3.18). Tell me: is 'free-will' among the number of them that believe, or not? If so, then again it has no need of grace, for of itself it believes on Christ (Whom of itself it neither knows nor conceives of!). If not, then it is judged already; and what does that mean, but that in God's sight it is damned? But God damns only the ungodly. So it is ungodly. And what godliness can that which is ungodly endeavour after? Nor do I think that the power of 'free-will' can be excepted from this condemnation, for John speaks of the whole man as being condemned.

Moreover, unbelief is not a 'gross affection', but is the supreme affection, seated and ruling on the throne of will and reason, just like its opposite, faith. Now, to be unbelieving is to deny God and make him a liar, as it says in the first chapter of I John: 'If we believe not, we make God a liar' (5.10). How then can this power, which is opposed to God and makes Him a liar, endeavour after good? If this power were not unbelieving and ungodly, John ought not to say of the whole man that he is judged already, but to say this: 'Man is judged already in respect of his gross affections; but he is not judged in respect of his best and most excellent part, for that endeavours after faith, or, rather, already believes!' So, when Scripture so often says: 'All men are liars', we should say, on the authority of 'free-will': 'On the contrary; it is rather Scripture that lies; for man is not a liar in his best part (that is, his reason and will), but in his flesh only (that is, his blood and bones); so that the totality from which man gets his name (that is, his reason and will) is healthy and holy.' And the Baptist's statement, 'He that believeth on the Son hath everlasting life; but he that believeth not the Son shall not see life, but the wrath of God abideth on him' (John 3.36), must be understood like this: 'upon him', that is, upon man's gross affections, abides the wrath of God; but upon the power of 'free-will', that is, of will and reason, abides grace, and life everlasting! In order to keep 'free-will' standing, you must invoke a *synechdoche*, to wrest all that is said in the Scriptures against ungodly men and limit it to man's brutal part only, so that his rational and truly human part may be preserved. In that case, thanks to the assertors of 'free-will', I may sin without qualms, secure in the knowledge that my reason and will (my 'free-will', that is) cannot be damned, because it is never destroyed, but for ever remains sound, righteous and holy. And as long as my will and my reason are blessed, I shall be glad for my filthy animal flesh to be taken away and damned; so far am I from wanting Christ to be its Redeemer! Do you see where the doctrine of 'free-will' brings us? It denies all things, divine and human, temporal and eternal, and derides itself by such a series of enormities!

Again, the Baptist says: 'A man can receive nothing, except it were given him from above' (3.27). Here the Diatribe may desist from showing off its wealth of words by enumerating all the things that we have from heaven. We are discussing, not nature, but grace; we ask, not what we are on earth, but what we are in heaven before God. We know that man was made lord over things below him, and that he has a right and a free will with respect to them, that they should obey him and do as he wills and thinks. But our question is this: whether he has 'free-will' God-ward, that God should obey man and do what man wills, or whether God has not rather a free will with respect to man, that man should will and do what God wills, and be able to do nothing but what He wills and does. The Baptist here says that man 'can receive nothing, except it be given him from above'. Which means that 'free-will' must be nothing!

Again: 'He that is of the earth is earthly and speaketh of the earth; he that cometh from heaven is above all' (v. 31). Here again, John makes all those that are not Christ's earthly, says that they savour and speak of earthly things; and he leaves none in an intermediate position. But 'free-will' is certainly not 'he that cometh from heaven'. So it must necessarily be of the earth, and savour and speak of the earth. If there were a power in any man which at any time, in any place, or by any work did not savour of earthly things, the Baptist ought to have made an exception of that man, and not said generally of all that are outside Christ, that they are of the earth and speak of the earth.

Later, in the eighth chapter, Christ also says: 'Ye are of the world, I am not of the world. Ye are from beneath, I am from above' (v. 23). Those to whom he spoke had 'free-will', that is, reason and will; yet He says that they are 'of the world'. What news would he have brought, had He merely meant that they were 'of the world' with respect to their flesh and gross affections? Did not all the world know that before? And what need was there for Him to say that they were 'of the world' with respect to that part of them which they had in common with the brutes? For in that sense beasts are 'of the world' also.

(xv) *John 6.44: the inability of man to believe the gospel* (781-782)

Next: when Christ says in John 6: 'No man can come to me, except My Father which hath sent me draw him' (v. 44), what does he leave to 'free-will'? He says man needs to hear and learn of the Father Himself, and that all must be taught of God. Here, indeed, he declares, not only that the works and efforts of 'free-will' are unavailing, but that even the very word of the gospel (of which He is here speaking) is heard in vain, unless the Father Himself speaks within, and teaches, and draws. 'No man, no man can come,' he says, and what he is talking about is your 'power whereby man can make some endeavour towards Christ'. In things that pertain to salvation, He asserts that power to be null.

'Free-will' is not helped by what the Diatribe quotes from Augustine in an attempt to discredit this plain and powerful Scripture: that is, the statement that 'God draws us as we draw sheep, by holding out a branch to them' (cf. Augustine, *Tract. in Joannis ev.*, 26.5). From this simile the Diatribe would have it inferred that there is in us a power to follow the drawing of God. But the simile does not hold in this passage. For God displays, not just one, but all His good gifts, even His own Son, Christ, and yet, unless He inwardly displays something more and draws in another manner, no man follows Him; indeed, the whole world persecutes the Son whom He displays! The simile well fits the experience of the godly, who are already 'sheep' and know God as their Shepherd; living in, and moved by, the Spirit, they follow wherever God wills, and whatever He shows them. But the ungodly does not 'come', even when he hears the word, unless the Father draws and teaches him inwardly; which He does by shedding abroad His Spirit. When that happens, there follows a 'drawing' other than that which is outward; Christ is then displayed by the enlightening of the Spirit, and by it man is rapt to Christ with the sweetest rapture, he being passive while God speaks, teaches and draws, rather than seeking or running himself.

(xvi) *John 16.9: the natural prevalence of unbelief* (782-783)

Let me adduce one more passage from John. In the sixteenth chapter, he says: 'The Spirit shall reprove the world of sin, because they believe not in me' (v. 9). Here you see that it is sin not to believe on Christ. And this sin is seated, not in the skin or in the hair, but in the reason and the will. Since he makes the whole world guilty of this sin, and since it is notorious from experience that the world is as ignorant of this sin as it is of Christ, so that it has to be revealed by the Spirit's reproof, it is apparent that 'free-will', along with the will and reason, is adjudged in the sight of God to be led captive by this sin, and so to stand condemned. Hence, so long as it is ignorant of Christ and does not believe on Him, it can will and attempt no good thing, but necessarily serves that sin of which it is ignorant.

To sum up: Since Scripture everywhere proclaims Christ categorically and antithetically, as I said, and thereby subjects all that is without the Spirit of Christ to Satan, ungodliness, error, darkness, sin, death and the wrath of God, every statement concerning Christ is a direct testimony against 'free-will'. And such statements are innumerable; indeed, they constitute the whole of Scripture. If, therefore, we conduct our argument with Scripture as judge, the victory in every respect belongs to me; for there is not one jot or tittle of Scripture left that does not condemn the doctrine of 'free-will'!

Though the great theologians who guard 'free-will' may not know, or pretend not to know, that Scripture proclaims Christ categorically and antithetically, all Christians know it, and commonly confess it. They know that there are in the world two kingdoms at war with each other. In the one, Satan reigns (which is why Christ calls him 'the prince of this world' (John 12.31), and Paul 'the god of this world' (2 Cor. 4.4)). He, so Paul again tells us, holds captive at his will all that are not wrested from him by the Spirit of Christ; nor does he allow them to be plucked away by any other power but the Spirit of God, as Christ tells us in the parable of the strong man armed keeping his palace in peace. In the other kingdom, Christ reigns. His kingdom continually resists and wars against that of Satan; and we are translated into His kingdom, not by our own power, but by the grace of God, which delivers us from this present evil world and tears us away from the power of darkness. The knowledge and confession of these two kingdoms, ever warring against each other with all their might and power, would suffice by itself to confute the doctrine of 'free-will', seeing that we are compelled to serve in Satan's kingdom if we are not plucked from it by Divine power. The common man, I repeat, knows this, and confesses it plainly enough by his proverbs, prayers, efforts and entire life.

(xvii) *Rom. 7; Gal. 5: the power of the 'flesh' in the saints disproves 'free-will'* (783)

I forbear to insist on the Achilles of my arguments, which the Diatribe proudly passes by without notice—I mean, Paul's teaching in Rom. 7 and Gal. 5, that there is in the saints and the godly such a mighty warfare between the Spirit and the flesh that they cannot do what they would. From this I would argue as follows: If human nature is so bad that in those who are born again of the Spirit it not only fails to endeavour after good, but actually fights against and opposes good, how could it endeavour after good in those who are not yet born again of the Spirit, but serve under Satan in the old man? And Paul is not here speaking of gross affections only (which is the universal expedient by which the Diatribe regularly parries the thrust of every Scripture); but he lists among the works of the flesh heresy, idolatry, contentions, divisions, etc., which reign in what you call the most exalted faculties, that is, reason and will. If, now, the flesh with these affections wars against the Spirit in the saints, much more will it war against God in the ungodly and in their 'free-will'! Hence in Rom. 8 he calls it 'enmity against God' (v. 7). May I say that I should be interested to see *this* argument punctured, and 'free-will' safeguarded from its attack!

(xviii) *Of the comfort of knowing that salvation does not depend on 'free-will'* (783)

I frankly confess that, for myself, even if it could be, I should not want 'free-will' to be given me, nor anything to be left in my own hands to enable me to endeavour after salvation; not merely because in face of so many dangers, and adversities, and assaults of devils, I could not stand my ground and hold fast my 'free-will' (for one devil is stronger than all men, and on these terms no man could be saved); but because, even were there no dangers, adversities, or devils, I should still be forced to labour with no guarantee of success, and to beat my fists at the air. If I lived and worked to all eternity, my conscience would never reach comfortable certainty as to how much it must do to satisfy God. Whatever work I had done, there would still be a nagging doubt[1] as to whether it pleased God, or whether He required something more. The experience of all who seek righteousness by works proves that; and I learned it well enough myself over a period of many years, to my own great hurt. But now that God has taken my salvation out of the control of my own will, and put it under the control of His, and promised to save me, not according to my working or running, but according to His own grace and mercy, I have the comfortable certainty that He is faithful and will not lie to me, and that He is also great and powerful, so that no devils or opposition can break Him or pluck me from Him. 'No one,' He says, 'shall pluck them out of my hand, because my Father which gave them me is greater than all' (John 10.28-29). Thus it is that, if not all, yet some, indeed many, are saved; whereas, by the power of 'free-will' none at all could be saved, but every one of us would perish.

Furthermore, I have the comfortable certainty that I please God, not by reason of the merit of my works, but by reason of His merciful favour promised to me; so that, if I work too little, or badly, He does not impute it to me, but with fatherly compassion pardons me and makes me better. This is the glorying of all the saints in their God.

(xix) *Of faith in the justice of God in His dealings with men* (784-786)

You may be worried that it is hard to defend the mercy and equity of God in damning the undeserving, that is, ungodly persons, who, being born in ungodliness, can by no means avoid being ungodly, and staying so, and being damned, but are compelled by natural necessity to sin and perish; as Paul says: 'We were all the children of wrath, even as others' (Eph. 2.3), created such by God Himself from a seed that had been corrupted by the sin of the one man, Adam. But here God must be reverenced and held in awe, as being most merciful to those whom He justifies and saves in their own utter unworthiness; and we must show some measure of deference to His Divine wisdom by believing Him just when to us He seems unjust. If His justice were such as could be adjudged just by human

---

[1] *scrupulus.*

reckoning, it clearly would not be Divine; it would in no way differ from human justice. But inasmuch as He is the one true God, wholly incomprehensible and inaccessible to man's understanding, it is reasonable, indeed inevitable, that His justice also should be incomprehensible; as Paul cries, saying: 'O the depth of the riches both of the wisdom and knowledge of God! How unsearchable are His judgments, and His ways past finding out!' (Rom. 11.33). They would not, however, be 'unsearchable' if we could at every point grasp the grounds on which they are just. What is man compared with God? How much can our power achieve compared with His power? What is our strength compared with His strength? What is our knowledge compared with His wisdom? What is our substance compared with His substance? In a word, what is all that we are compared with all that He is? If, now, even nature teaches us to acknowledge that human power, strength, wisdom, knowledge and substance, and all that is ours, is as nothing compared with the Divine power, strength, wisdom, knowledge and substance, what perversity is it on our part to worry at the justice and the judgment of the only God, and to arrogate so much to our own judgment as to presume to comprehend, judge and evaluate God's judgment! Why do we not in like manner say at this point: 'Our judgment is nothing compared with God's judgment'? Ask reason whether force of conviction does not compel her to acknowledge herself foolish and rash for not allowing God's judgment to be incomprehensible, when she confesses that all the other things of God are incomprehensible! In everything else, we allow God His Divine Majesty; in the single case of His judgment, we are ready to deny it! To think that we cannot for a little while *believe* that He is just, when He has actually promised us that when He reveals His glory we shall all clearly *see* that He both was and is just!

I will give a parallel case, in order to strengthen our faith in God's justice, and to reassure that 'evil eye' which holds Him under suspicion of injustice. Behold! God governs the external affairs of the world in such a way that, if you regard and follow the judgment of human reason, you are forced to say, either that there is no God, or that God is unjust; as the poet said: 'I am often tempted to think there are no gods.' See the great prosperity of the wicked, and by contrast the great adversity of the good. Proverbs, and experience, the parent of proverbs, bear record that the more abandoned men are, the more successful they are. 'The tabernacle of robbers prosper,' says Job (12.6), and Ps. 72 complains that sinners in the world are full of riches (Ps. 73.12). Is it not, pray, universally held to be most unjust that bad men should prosper, and good men be afflicted? Yet that is the way of the world. Hereupon some of the greatest minds have fallen into denying the existence of God, and imagining that Chance governs all things at random. Such were the Epicureans, and Pliny. And Aristotle, wishing to set his 'prime Being' free from misery, holds that he sees nothing but himself; for Aristotle supposes that it would be very irksome to such a Being to behold so many evils and injustices! And the Prophets, who believed in God's existence, were still more tempted concerning the injustice of God. Jeremiah, Job, David, Asaph and others are cases in point. What do you suppose Demosthenes and Cicero thought, when, having done all they could, they received as their reward an unhappy death? Yet all this, which looks so much like injustice in God, and is traduced as such by arguments which no reason or light of nature can resist, is most easily cleared up by the light of the gospel and the knowledge of grace, which teaches us that though the wicked flourish in their bodies, yet they perish in their souls. And a summary explanation of this whole inexplicable problem is found in a single little word: *There is a life after this life; and all that is not punished and repaid here will be punished and repaid there; for this life is nothing more than a precursor, or, rather, a beginning, of the life that is to come.*

If, now, this problem, which was debated in every age but never solved, is swept away and settled so easily by the light of the gospel, which shines only in the Word and to faith, how do you think it will be when the light of the Word and faith shall cease, and the real facts, and the Majesty of God, shall be revealed as they are? Do you not think that the light of glory will be able with the greatest ease to solve problems that are insoluble in the light of the word and grace, now that the light of grace has so easily solved this problem, which that was insoluble by the light of nature?

Keep in view three lights: the light of nature, the light of grace, and the light of glory (this is a common and a good distinction). By the light of nature, it is inexplicable that it should be just for the good to be afflicted and the bad to prosper; but the light of grace explains it. By the light of grace, it is inexplicable how God can damn him who by his own strength can do nothing but sin and become guilty. Both the light of nature and the light of grace here insist that the fault lies not in the wretchedness of man, but in the injustice of God; nor can they judge otherwise of a God who crowns the ungodly freely, without merit, and does not crown, but damns another, who is perhaps less, and certainly not more, ungodly. But the light of glory insists otherwise, and will one day reveal God, to whom alone belongs a judgment whose justice is incomprehensible, as a God Whose justice is most righteous and evident—provided only that in the meanwhile we *believe* it, as we are instructed and encouraged to do by the example of the light of grace explaining what was a puzzle of the same order to the light of nature.

I shall here end this book, ready though I am to pursue the matter further, if need be; but I think that abundant satisfaction has here been afforded for the godly man who is willing to yield to truth without stubborn resistance. For if we believe it to be true that God foreknows and foreordains all things; that He cannot be deceived or obstructed in His foreknowledge and predestination; and that nothing happens but at His will (which reason itself is compelled to grant); then, on reason's own testimony, there can be no 'free-will' in man, or angel, or in any creature.

So, if we believe that Satan is the prince of this world, ever ensnaring and opposing the kingdom of Christ with all his strength, and that he does not let his prisoners go unless he is driven out by the power of the Divine Spirit, it is again apparent that there can be no 'free-will'.

So, if we believe that original sin has ruined us to such an extent that even in the godly, who are led by the Spirit, it causes abundance of trouble by striving against good, it is clear that in a man who lacks the Spirit nothing is left that can turn itself to good, but only to evil.

Again, if the Jews, who followed after righteousness with all their powers, fell into unrighteousness instead, while the Gentiles, who followed after unrighteousness, attained to an un-hoped-for righteousness, by God's free gift, it is equally apparent from their very works and experience that man without grace can will nothing but evil.

And, finally, if we believe that Christ redeemed men by His blood, we are forced to confess that all of man was lost; otherwise, we make Christ either wholly superfluous, or else the redeemer of the least valuable part of man only; which is blasphemy, and sacrilege.

VIII

CONCLUSION (*W.A.* 786-787)

Now, my good Erasmus, I entreat you for Christ's sake to keep
your promise at last. You promised that you would yield to him
who taught better than yourself. Lay aside respect of persons!
I acknowledge that you are a great man, adorned with many of
God's noblest gifts—wit, learning and an almost miraculous
eloquence, to say nothing of the rest; whereas I have and am
nothing, save that I would glory in being a Christian. Moreover, I give you hearty praise and commendation on this
further account—that you alone, in contrast with all others,
have attacked the real thing, that is, the essential issue. You
have not wearied me with those extraneous[1] issues about the
Papacy, purgatory, indulgences and such like—trifles, rather
than issues—in respect of which almost all to date have sought
my blood (though without success); you, and you alone, have
seen the hinge on which all turns, and aimed for the vital spot.[2]
For that I heartily thank you; for it is more gratifying to me to
deal with this issue, insofar as time and leisure permit me to do
so. If those who have attacked me in the past had done as you
have done, and if those who now boast of new spirits and
revelations would do the same also, we should have less sedition
and sects and more peace and concord. But thus it is that God,
through Satan, has punished our unthankfulness.

However, if you cannot treat of this issue in a different way
from your treatment of it in this Diatribe, it is my earnest wish
that you would remain content with your own gift, and confine
yourself to pursuing, adorning and promoting the study of
literature and languages; as hitherto you have done, to great
advantage and with much credit. By your studies you have
rendered me also some service, and I confess myself much
indebted to you; certainly, in that regard, I unfeignedly honour
and sincerely respect you. But God has not yet willed nor

[1] *alienis.*   [2] *ipsum iugulum petisti.*

granted that you should be equal to the subject of our present debate. Please do not think that any arrogance lies behind my words when I say that I pray that the Lord will speedily make you as much my superior in this as you already are in all other respects. It is no new thing for God to instruct a Moses by a Jethro, or to teach a Paul by an Ananias. You say that *'you have wandered far from the mark, if you are ignorant of Christ.'*[1] I think that you yourself see how the matter stands. But not all will go astray if you or I go astray. God is One Who is proclaimed as wonderful among His saints, so that we may regard as saints persons that are very far from sanctity. Nor is it hard to believe that you, as being a man, should fail to understand aright, and to note with sufficient care, the Scriptures, or the sayings of the fathers, under whose guidance you think that you are holding to the mark. That you have thus failed is clear enough from your saying that *you assert nothing, but have 'made comparisons'.*[2] He who sees to the heart of the matter and properly understands it does not write like that. Now I, in this book of mine, HAVE NOT 'MADE COMPARISONS', BUT HAVE ASSERTED, AND DO ASSERT; and I do not want judgment to rest with anyone,[3] but I urge all men to submit! May the Lord, whose cause this is, enlighten you and make you a vessel to honour and glory. *Amen.*

---

[1] *'I know well enough that I shall be told: Let Erasmus learn Christ and bid farewell to human sagacity: no man understands these things but he that has the Spirit of God. If I do not yet understand what Christ is, then, of course, I have hitherto wandered far from the mark.'*

[2] *contulisse.*   [3] *'I have made comparisons: let judgment rest with others.'*

INDEX OF SCRIPTURE REFERENCES

Heavy type indicates references which occur in sub-headings in the text